The
LAST
STAND
of the
PACK

Timberline Books

STEPHEN J. LEONARD AND THOMAS J. NOEL, EDITORS

The Beast
BENJAMIN BARR LINDSEY WITH HARVEY J. O'HIGGINS

Colorado's Japanese Americans
BILL HOSOKAWA

Colorado Women: A History
GAIL M. BEATON

Denver: An Archaeological History
SARAH M. NELSON, K. LYNN BERRY, RICHARD F. CARRILLO,
BONNIE L. CLARK, LORI E. RHODES, AND DEAN SAITTA

Denver's Lakeside Amusement Park: From the White City Beautiful to a Century of Fun
DAVID FORSYTH

Denver Landmarks and Historic Districts: Second Edition
THOMAS J. NOEL AND NICHOLAS J. WHARTON

Dr. Charles David Spivak: A Jewish Immigrant and the American Tuberculosis Movement
JEANNE E. ABRAMS

Enduring Legacies: Ethnic Histories and Cultures of Colorado
EDITED BY ARTURO J. ALDAMA, ELISA FACIO,
DARYL MAEDA, AND REILAND RABAKA

Frank Mechau: Artist of Colorado, Second Edition
CILE M. BACH

The Gospel of Progressivism: Moral Reform and Labor War in Colorado, 1900–1930
R. TODD LAUGEN

Helen Ring Robinson: Colorado Senator and Suffragist
PAT PASCOE

The History of the Death Penalty in Colorado
MICHAEL L. RADELET

Ores to Metals: The Rocky Mountain Smelting Industry
JAMES E. FELL, JR.

Season of Terror: The Espinosas in Central Colorado, March–October 1863
CHARLES F. PRICE

A Tenderfoot in Colorado
R. B. TOWNSHEND

The Trail of Gold and Silver: Mining in Colorado, 1859–2009
DUANE A. SMITH

The

LAST
STAND
of the
PACK

Critical Edition

by **Arthur H. Carhart**
in collaboration with **Stanley P. Young**

Reprint edited by
Andrew Gulliford and Tom Wolf

UNIVERSITY PRESS OF COLORADO
Boulder

© 2017 by University Press of Colorado

Published by University Press of Colorado
5589 Arapahoe Avenue, Suite 206C
Boulder, Colorado 80303

 The University Press of Colorado is a proud member of the Association of American University Presses.

The University Press of Colorado is a cooperative publishing enterprise supported, in part, by Adams State University, Colorado State University, Fort Lewis College, Metropolitan State University of Denver, Regis University, University of Colorado, University of Northern Colorado, Utah State University, and Western State Colorado University.

∞ This paper meets the requirements of the ANSI/NISO Z39.48-1992 (Permanence of Paper).

ISBN: 978-1-60732-692-2 (pbk.)
ISBN: 978-1-60732-693-9 (ebook)
https://doi.org/10.5876/9781607326939

Library of Congress Cataloging-in-Publication Data

Names: Young, Stanley Paul, 1889–1969, author. | Gulliford, Andrew, editor. | Wolf, Tom, 1945– editor. | Carhart, Arthur Hawthorne, 1892– Last stand of the pack.
Title: The last stand of the pack / by Arthur H. Carhart ; in collaboration with Stanley P. Young ; reprint edited by Andrew Gulliford & Tom Wolf.
Other titles: Timberline books.
Description: Critical edition. | Boulder : University Press of Colorado, [2017] | Series: Timberline series | Includes bibliographical references and index.
Identifiers: LCCN 2017018051| ISBN 9781607326922 (pbk.) | ISBN 9781607326939 (ebook)
Subjects: LCSH: Wolves—Control—Colorado—History. | Wolves—Reintroduction—Colorado. | Carhart, Arthur Hawthorne, 1892–
Classification: LCC SF810.7.W65 L37 2017 | DDC 636.08/3909788—dc23
LC record available at https://lccn.loc.gov/2017018051

Artist Becky Hoyle Lukow from Fruitland, New Mexico, has chosen to donate the artwork for this book cover because she believes in wolf recovery in the southern Rockies. See her other wildlife work at www.lifeimagesbybecky.com or contact her at 505-598-6978.

Contents

Foreword

STEVE LEONARD

Like a well-made sandwich, Andrew Gulliford and Tom Wolf's reprint of Arthur H. Carhart and Stanley P. Young's *The Last Stand of the Pack* satisfies because of its main ingredient—Carhart's 1929 defense of wolves—and because of its other meaty components, including Wolf's introduction; Gulliford's substantial epilogue, "The Past and Future of Wolves in Colorado"; and contributions from Tom Compton, Bonnie Brown, Mike Phillips, Norm Bishop, and Cheney Gardner. With the exceptions of Compton, a rancher with a PhD in zoology, and Brown, who views wolves from the perspective of the Colorado Wool Growers Association, the contributors look forward to the day when gray wolves return to Colorado.

That so many articulate voices have come to the defense of the wolf is heartening, at least to wolves, because until recently the hairy, powerful, cunning animals with big teeth—"the better to eat you with"—have had few advocates. Eight centuries ago, St. Francis of Assisi arranged a détente between the hungry wolf of Gubbio and the townsfolk. They agreed to feed the wolf and the wolf promised not to eat them. A similar, less perfect compromise has been worked out in zoos and animal sanctuaries where wolves are confined, fed, and viewed. Remembering *Little Red Riding Hood* and Walt Disney's *Three Little Pigs* (1933), with its hit song, "Who's Afraid of the Big Bad Wolf?," many—perhaps most—Americans prefer that wolves be imprisoned behind stout fences.

Carhart and his friends may not change the minds of those strongly opposed to wolf reintroduction. Still, this republication of the original work along with contemporary comments may facilitate the reappearance and protection of the splendid carnivores in the state. At the very least, it will trigger debate. That makes it a welcome addition to the University Press of Colorado's Timberline Series, which aims to showcase important and sometimes provocative books on Colorado.

The
LAST
STAND
of the
PACK

Wolves mentioned in *"The Last Stand of the Pack"*

Nickname	Place of death
❶ Unaweep Wolf	Unaweep Canyon, Uncompahgre Plateau
❷ Rags the Digger	Cathedral Bluffs, Rio Blanco County
❸ Phantom Wolf	Ruby Canyon cowcamp and Big Salt Wash north of Fruita
❹ Bigfoot	North of De Beque
❺ Lefty & Gray Terror	Burns Hole, Eagle County
❻ Greenhorn	Greenhorn Mountain, between Pueblo and Huerfano counties
❼ Whitey	Apishapa River, Huerfano and Las Animas counties
❽ Three Toes	Apishapa River, Huerfano and Las Animas counties

Wolf pelts in Colorado Museums

✖ New Castle Historical Society ▼ White River Museum, Meeker
✪ Denver Museum of Nature & Science

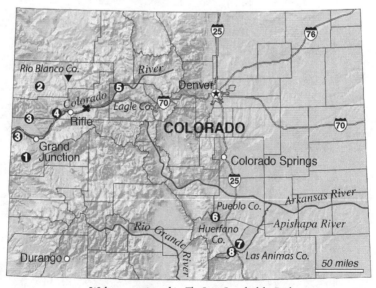

Wolves mentioned in *The Last Stand of the Pack.*

Introduction

TOM WOLF

Trappers Lake, at the headwaters of the White River, echoed in August of 2014 to the sounds of wilderness lovers celebrating the fiftieth anniversary of the Wilderness Act. Missing in action, however, was wilderness itself. And in the pandemonium we all knew it: missing in action was the wolf in Colorado.

And yet the wind, blowing up canyon, seemed to bear a still, small voice. The same up-canyon wind that had recently spread a disastrous, watershed-wide wildfire also carried, perhaps, a light, silent sound: a wolf—the howling of a lone and lonely wolf—slipping by the ranchers' rifles, sliding down from Wyoming, searching for a mate. Or was it just the wind?

This same wolf-scented wind blew through a young landscape architect, Arthur Carhart, in the fall of 1919, as he ascended to Trappers Lake through the White River National Forest in northwest Colorado. His assignment from the US Forest Service: destroy Trappers Lake. But then something else happened, something miraculous. Carhart knew that Trappers Lake was (and is) sacred to the Ute Indians. But how did he get from that knowledge to the wisdom of wilderness? Paradoxically, the absence of the wolf at Trappers Lake was as crucial as its presence.

However unlikely a candidate for divining wilderness wisdom, plain-vanilla Carhart was the chosen one, the prophet who heard that ineffable, mysterious, ultimately ungraspable

DOI: 10.5876/9781607326939.c000

voice at Trappers Lake. Like Elijah on the mountain in the Book of I Kings, he was commanded to return to his Forest Service bosses in Denver with the most subversive message of all: let it be. Here is the map of Trappers Lake that you ordered me to make, Carhart said, together with all the roads and building sites you wanted. I have done my duty, but now I call us all to a higher duty: let it be. Let Trappers Lake be!

Carhart's superiors in the Forest Service, including Aldo Leopold, knew instantly that this upstart was on to something grander and more glorious than any of them could imagine—something uniquely American, something that could mark America as the Chosen Land, as God's own country.

Such patriotic talk is unfashionable today, uncool. Even less cool is the concept that America's public lands exist in part to make us better Americans—a people with the courage and grace to live with wolves and manage wolf-filled wilderness guided by the best science.

Carhart succeeded in protecting Trappers Lake. Or did he? Just as Carhart and the Forest Service agreed to set Trappers Lake aside, both were enthusiastic participants in a systematic federal program designed to slaughter every last wolf everywhere in America. Given the wisdom of hindsight, how can we today reconcile the seeming contradictions of our past? How can we learn once again to live with the wolf?

Part of being an American is believing that we are always blessed with another chance—another opportunity to listen to the prophetic voice of Arthur Carhart. If there is hope for us, it lies in understanding and resolving the bloody conflicts, the civil wars, of our past. If there is hope for us, it lies in learning to live with the wild, with the wolf.

That is why we return to *The Last Stand of the Pack*.

Ardent Arthur Carhart quit the Forest Service in 1922, soon after deciding that federal bureaucracies were as much the problem as the solution for Americans who love the wild. Free at last, he decided to write the book that became *The Last Stand of the Pack*. Cold-blooded Stanley P. Young, Carhart's coauthor, provided the science for their book, while the enthusiastic Carhart provided the saga. Together, they produced a true thriller—if you recall that *thrill* means "pierce" and *enthusiastic* means "pierced or seized by the divine."

The Last Stand of the Pack was good, but its most important reader thought it was not good enough. After its publication in 1929, Carhart spent the rest of his long life trying to put wolfless wilderness into words. By that measure, he failed. But by 1950, this cheerful curmudgeon had become America's most popular and widely read conservationist.

It took the great female writer Mary Austin to prod Carhart and alert him to his prophetic potential. As a child, she also had experienced a mystical union with nature. As a friend and neighbor in Santa Fe of the great wildlife biographer Ernest Thompson Seton, she knew that Indian ways with wolves might guide Carhart to fulfilling his prophetic role. Soon after the publication of *The Last Stand of the Pack*, she wrote to Carhart,

> *I thought your wolf book might have been truly great if, after mastering all the government reports, you had thrown them in the fire, called on whatever gods you worship and written the story without a thought of its possible audience.*

Carhart promised Austin he would try to write a second wolf book. He never succeeded. Let us hope that someone young is out there, someone young enough to write the imaginative book that will reunite Americans behind a true wilderness—a wilderness with wolves.

Who was Arthur Carhart? It is not enough to remind readers that he was more than a lifelong Christian and Republican. Like the wolf in the wilderness, he remains elusive. True prophets are never appreciated in their own lifetime—or in their own country. Carhart lived from 1892 to 1978. Growing up in East Denver, I knew him as both a neighbor and a magnificent storyteller. Maybe someday some imaginative kid will wander into another of Carhart's creations, the Conservation Collection at the Denver Public Library. And maybe that kid will grow up to write the wolf book we need.

In the meantime, *The Last Stand of the Pack* will have to remain literally true for Colorado's children. They will have no wolves in Colorado until we learn to say to hell with our differences and reunite behind our true heritage as Americans: a wild wilderness.

The Last Stand of the Pack

by Arthur H. Carhart

in collaboration with Stanley P. Young

DOI: 10.5876/9781607326939.c001

A Dedication

They are the heirs of the Mountain Men. They are the followers of the last frontiers. They are the friends of all animals; the compassionate, regretful executioners of animal renegades when such outlaws must die that other wildlings may live.

On far trails, wind swept, snow blanketed, hail pelted, on trails where frost bites or sun bakes, on trails where danger stalks with them as a close companion, these determined men carry on the tradition of the organization to which they belong. They get their wolf!

They have made these true stories with their own acts. It has been our privilege to record them. To these men who live these stories day by day, the predatory animal hunters of the U. S. Biological Survey, this book is dedicated.

ARTHUR HAWTHORNE CARHART
STANLEY PAUL YOUNG.

Foreword
The Day Wanes

There was plenty of food for the gray wolves before the white men came. The great armies of shaggy bison that moved northward with the summer or sought some sheltered spot during the days of winter cold, were a constant source of meat for the wolves that followed them like gray shadowy death.

Calves, old bulls that were too weak to keep up with the stream of their fellows or were driven away from the herd by stronger bulls, and weakened cows, fell to the lot of the big gray lobos. Indians killed bison, to be sure. But the red men left little of the meat for the wolf packs to snarl and fight over. The red brother killed only for necessities; for meat, robes that were needed by that individual hunter and his family, and not for so-called sport which was actually slaughter.

For centuries those great masses of bison were a never failing supply of sustenance for the wolf packs. Pronghorns too, in plenty, populated the plains. Fleet they were, bounding away with their white-flagged rumps showing as a snowy spot when they ran from danger. But there were cripples among these, too; old worn-out bucks and does. Little fawns, foolish, inquisitive, helpless, made wolf meat when the stalking killers came across these baby antelope when mothers were absent or frightened away.

When winter's robes swirled over the open plains and frayed out in long streamers from the mountain ridges, the hunting was poorer for the wolves. They would sometimes come close to humans then, prowling around the winter lodges of Crow, Pawnee, Comanche and Cheyennes. The Indians did not make a business of hunting the gray wolf. To some men of the wolf clans, the big gray was a brother, a fetish not to be harmed. To others he occasionally gave his skin for their usual adornment or clothing.

There were some natural enemies of the wolf. But few there were that could stand before the rush of the little packs that formed where there was good hunting. Occasionally fighting in the pack itself, between dog wolf leaders, would eliminate some old lobo too slow with his flashing, slashing teeth, or one who was not springy in aged muscles that once had carried him to leadership.

Famine took its toll too. The law of the wilderness was inscribed by fang and tooth; kill or be killed. With most foes the wolves could hold their own. Famine, when it stalked, was one enemy that the gray wolf could not conquer.

Men in shining armor came one day from the southwest. Pigmy thunder, carrying death, belched from sticks they carried. Gunpowder and ball came into the life of the gray wolves of the great plains. It was the beginning of the invasion of white men and with it came the first step toward the doom of the great gray killers.

Other expeditions with gay banners and with brown-cloaked friars riding beside the adventurers followed those first men that were seeking the mythical treasure cities. They trailed in winding, sinuous lines over the grassy plains working their way along the foothills, or following the streams that flowed to the eastward, until they came almost to where the Missouri bends toward sunrise seeking the great Father of Waters as it swirls to its union with the great gulf.

These men were seen by the wolves. But to the ancestors of Lefty, Unaweep, Rags, Whitey, Three Toes and the rest of the renegade leaders of the last days, this coming of the men of whiter skin meant nothing. Occasionally these invaders shot a wolf with a blunderbuss. More often they killed deer, pronghorns or bison, cut the choice meats from the loin and left the carcass for the wolves to gorge on and then later be a place where coyotes congregated around weathered white bones.

Coyotes followed the gray killers of the plains. Sometimes they were camp followers of an individual wolf or a pack, picking the scraps after the wolves had finished in their blood and meat fests. With all the great hordes of wolves that traveled the unmarked highways of the prairies and the countless coyote scavengers that followed them, there was no mixture of these species. Wolf stood distinct and coyote remained coyote throughout these years. They were sometimes at war, the wolf driving the coyote away when he felt so disposed, sometimes undoubtedly killing the tawny skulker-scavenger. Never has there been half-breed wolf and coyote.

A man pushing up the Arkansas and leading a band of half-starved soldiers from the United States was a vital event for western wild life. Winter gripped the little command when they reached the sandy bars where the Fontaine qui Bouille, the creek of the Boiling Spring and the Arkansas River come together. To-day there are steel plants on that site, busy with clanking machinery and sweaty, working men and the railway station with its many tracks carries the sign "Pueblo." Perhaps not even a sagacious scholar of the man tribe could have foreseen that a century and a quarter after Pike and his men camped at the site of Pueblo there would be a city there at the streams' junction.

Pike, leader of that ragged band of western heroes, built a tiny earthwork fort. He had been following the homeward trail of Melgares, Spaniard, who had penetrated earlier in the year far into the Pawnee Republic, and now that Pike was near territory claimed by Spain, the American must needs be cautious.

This little fort, huddled in the sandy river bottom, was a landmark in the conquest that finally made life a gamble with death for the last of the gray wolves. But such a state of affairs did not come to the wolf legions at first. Rather there followed days when food was easy, could be had for the taking without stalking, and the wolves became fat, sleek followers of the mountain men that rode fearlessly on dangerous trails some of which were not even blazed by daring explorers.

Long haired, these mountain men were, sometimes boisterous, sometimes quiet. They lived in a hostile land by virtue of the trueness of their aim and their readiness to kill. During the fur season they combed the streams of the mountain lands for the prime pelts of beaver that were, in those days, the equivalent of treasure. As summer opened the ice-bound streams and the fur bearers lost the silky thickness of their coats, these men in worn, fringed buckskin found their way to Taos and bartered, drank and made love to the dark-eyed Spanish girls or fought with hot-tempered sons of Dons.

A little mud fort and trading post sprang up where Pueblo now stands. Another was at a point on Grenaros Creek which flows from the mountain called Greenhorn, or in Spanish, Cuerno Verde; some say named for a Pawnee Chieftain known as Cuerno Verde and others say because the mountain is green and in the shape of a horn when outlined by a map. Another important trading point was Bents Fort near where La Junta now stands.

These were bonanza days when wolves glutted themselves for buffalo robes were in demand. Every home must have its shaggy robe from the bison of the plains. Every dandy must have his buffalo skin coat.

Butchery followed. Some men killed thousands in a season. Buffalo robes were selling in the middle west at the startling figure of $5.00 to $10.00. A good coat made from the hide of a bison could be bought for some $20.00 or $30.00. Slaughter surged over the plains. Carcasses were left to rot. Only the hides were of value. Sometimes only the loin or liver was taken by the hunters for the meal of the day. Most of the time they would not touch the meat.

Raw hides were selling at 11c apiece over the counter at the trading post at Pueblo!

At that time a good hunter would make himself right good wages for the bison were inexhaustible! They were everywhere on the plains; these buffalo were even a detriment to the first railways for they often streamed across the tracks in their migrations and delayed the anxious passengers in the gorgeous little day coaches that to-day would seem so stuffy, small, and uncomfortable.

This killing of bison brought days of plenty for the wolves and their ilk. They did not even have to down the game. It was there ready for them to tear and chew and gobble. The hunter was their friend. He reached out with his long-barreled rifle, brought down the bison, skinned it even, and left the carcass for a feast for the carnivores. Rarely did hunters kill wolves or coyotes. They were handy in cleaning meat from the carcass and preventing the great stench that might otherwise arise from skinned buffalo bodies.

But lean days came. The "inexhaustible" supply of bison dwindled. Prong-horns were next. And later the market hunters began the senseless slaughter of the deer which has resulted in depleted game ranges of the west where there should to-day be the best hunting in the country. Wolf meat was becoming hard to get; the packs became gaunt and ready to kill anything that promised a good meal.

Then came men with trundling wagons over which billowed the grayish white of canvas tops. Settlers were only a few years behind the traders and trappers. The frontiers were beginning to crash and fall before the men that were following the trail of Pike and his band of fearless soldiers.

With these homesteaders came horses, sheep and cattle. It was a new supply of food for the wolves. Between the remnants of game and the domestic stock, the wolves got along. Settlers grumbled but steers were not worth much on the hoof so far from markets and when meat was wanted there were still deer or elk to be killed and hung up in the log buildings to chill and freeze.

Wire fences appeared. Open range passed. The great trail herds that formerly wound their way from the plains of Texas into the wide meadowy stretches of Wyoming and Colorado, ceased to come north under the care of the happy-go-lucky, hard riding, hard fighting cow hands from the Panhandle. Domestic stock increased. With the increase the wolves got more of a food supply than they had had for some years. Still domestic stock was not so valuable but that some tribute could be given to the killers of the plains by ranchers.

Stockmen invaded the hills. Cattle herds increased. Wolves followed the mountain migration. Range was cropped until it lost its character and new forage was not there the following spring. The Forest Service was created and the great National Forests established. Grazing regulations came. Brisk demands arose for this public range at nominal fees. Every good grazing unit was taken over by some rancher and grazed as much as it would carry under the regulations.

The wild things that lived on the range were crowded out. Food for them was taken by domestic stock. Poaching, too, helped to hasten the process; for a certain class of settlers even to-day do not hesitate to "get a little venison" in defiance of the protective laws. But the most powerful factor in almost smashing the deer, elk and antelope herds has been the over appropriation of their hereditary food supply by the dogies of the ranchers, often under the direction of agencies of the State.

The old world of the wolves now was falling about their heads. There began to be bounties on them. Even in the then remote sections such as the place where Caywood settled near Meeker, the cattlemen had begun to pay bounties for the scalps of the gray wolf slaughterers. With a very nominal bounty on wolves, Caywood soon after he took his homestead, in less than a month killed enough of these "varmints" to buy a new wagon, new harness for his team, outfit his family with some new clothes and lay in the seasons provisions from bounty money. What Caywood did near Rio Blanco, others did in other sections of the hills and on the plains. Hunters picked up many dollars from stockmen and Government agencies.

The gray wolf is no fool. He rapidly became educated. He had to learn or lose his life. Some failed. But others gained knowledge of men. Campaigns against them became more keen. Greater bounty was offered. Stock was no longer cheap and one critter lost made an appreciable dent in the yearly returns.

White faces crowded out the old long horns. Pure bred bulls took the place of scrubs. Beef went soaring with the demand for meat to feed armies that battled in the fields of France.

Bounties went up again to unheard of amounts. Men made it a business to try to get certain notorious wolves. They trapped, poisoned, hunted, and always those wolves that were able to survive by the aid of sharpened wits, became more canny, more elusive, wiser in the ways of predatory man. They eluded these independent hunters and kept on with their killing.

Finally the U. S. Biological Survey and its Predatory Animal Control work stepped in where the bounty hunters had failed. Men were put on the trail of stock-killing wolves. These hunters were on salary. They had only one general instruction. It was "get your wolf."

War to the death had been declared when Hegewa came into Burns Hole looking for Lefty, the killer.

Many wolves fell into their hands through ordinary methods. Some of the younger, less experienced, were taken by the poison route. Others were trapped.

But there were certain pack leaders, renegades, that had become wise beyond all other wolves, in keeping out of the snares of the hunters, that stood head and shoulders above the common run. They were past graduates at avoiding traps, knew poison and the methods man practiced in giving it to them, knew when a man was armed with a gun and when he was weaponless.

Nine of them were thus outstanding. Nine of them were wolves of super training, almost unbelievable intelligence. With the old world of their kind gone forever, they made last defiant stands against man and his death machines. They tested the cunning of the best wolfers that the Biological Survey ever employed.

The buffalo are gone. The pronghorns, the antelope, are barely holding their own on isolated ranges, often able to live only through the constant friendly care of the ranchers who have come to realize that earlier action of settlers has made an almost gameless country, where once good hunting prevailed. With the old food supply gone, the wolves had turned almost wholly to the domestic stock. And from that time they were fated to fall before man.

These last nine renegades in Colorado and the killer packs they led marked the passing of a typical figure of the old west; the big buffalo or gray wolf; sometimes called lobo wolf. Never did more intelligent wolf live than some of those nine. Never were more dramatic hunts for man or beast planned and carried out than those campaigns planned by some of the hunters that trailed these renegades, stock-killers.

That the old gray wolf should pass without some record of his exit on the western stage being written seemed likely. He would simply cease to be and his final dramatic defeat would remain unregistered. Buried in dusty files of the Biological Survey were the terse official reports of the hunters. Locked in their minds were the many little incidents, the side lights that are so important as incidents of those dogged hunts.

But a happy combination of events made it possible to get from these records the facts. Additional information was gleaned from the field men. All possible data was gathered, sifted, and the truth retained. Every possible quirk of the mind and actions of the renegade, remnants of the once numerous buffalo wolf, has been put into this record. All vital incidents of each hunt are true. All wolf lore is positively fact. Those who have worked on this record have tried to make this a book so full of wolf lore that nothing that is true of these old gray, heady, cruel killers was left out.

Man has won. The wilderness killers have lost. They have written their own death warrants in killing, torture, blood lust, almost fiendish cruelty. Civilization of the white man has almost covered the west. And with that nearly accomplished, there was no place left for the gray killers, the renegades of the range lands.

They were great leaders, superb outlaws, these last nine renegades. They deserved and received the profound respect of those men who finally conquered them. Defiant, they were striking back at man, playing a grim losing game but never acknowledging defeat until fate had called the last play.

Old Lefty of Burns Hole

Soft sounds filled the night. Murmuring winds, the yip-yap of far-distant coyote, the mellow hooting of an owl—and the soft pad of wolf feet.

The four-year-old led. He had mastered the fighting gray demon that for years had headed the pack. The old leader now ranged alone. He had been one of the greatest fighters on the range. But his teeth were worn down. He had become what the wolfers call a gummer. This new wolf surpassed the old leader. Never in all the upper valley of the Colorado had there been such a strong back, rangy body, deep chest in a wolf.

They traveled quietly. Occasionally a whimper or a snarl came from the pack. They foraged beside the trail as a matter of habit, but the leader stuck to the runway. They were crossing a ridge between cattle feeding grounds.

Faint man taint came on the breeze. The leader stopped, stood motionless. His mane bristled. His lips came back from his teeth in a silent snarl. The others fidgeted. The leader's delicate nostrils moved, sniffing. He started forward cautiously.

One instant there was quiet. The next, raucous turmoil!

From the path there leaped a thing which clenched the left forefoot of the four-year-old. Steel jaws set on the sinews and bone, just below the dewclaw.

The sagebrush swayed as the pack fled scurrying. The leader leaped, fell, turned, bit snarling at the thing that held his paw.

He plunged. Again he was thrown, savagely. He attempted to sink his teeth into this unknown torture that had so suddenly leaped out of the solid earth.

But the trap chain was solidly wired to a rock. There was no give to it, no swivel permitting it to turn. There were not even offsets in the jaws. They cut in. Already the flesh was torn by the wolf's first instinctive hurtling leap.

The wolf lunged back toward the trail along which a moment before he had trodden in safety. He circled, tugging, thrashing through the low scrub brush within the radius of the chain.

He stopped, panting. Then another wild dive. Sinews and flesh tore. The big wolf sickened.

He lay down a moment, ill and dizzy. The circulation was cut off. The paw was numbing. The pain eased.

Slowly, cautiously, the wolf wavered to his feet, tried to sneak away from the trap. So long as he was quiet the trap was quiet. When he moved, it moved. It hurt him with every motion.

Rage—animal rage—unreasoning, fierce, without check, surged through his wolf soul. He dived, stumbled, fought the trap, slammed it against the rocks near the trail, gnashed at it with slavering mouth, cut his lips, left blood-flecked foam on the cruel biting metal jaws. The trap held. His fighting madness continued.

Long he fought the trap in blind fury. It was dive, twist, plunge, stumble, shake the imprisoned foot, turn and snarl, bite, kick out with his other legs, lay panting for a moment and then up in a wild scramble in an effort to escape the thing that held him.

The bewildered pack came back. They whined, came in to help, but were turned on and snapped at by the frantic leader. They slunk through the brush only to return, fascinated by the spectacle.

Dawn paled the eastern horizon. It limned the castellated peak to the south-eastward across the wide river. Still the fight raged intermittently. There was not the crazed plunging of the first hour. Instead, there was dogged persistent tugging, turning, twisting. This continued perhaps for hours. The leg was numb. Occasionally the wolf stopped to lick where sinew still held him. The bones had been broken in that first wild, hurtling scramble ending with the taut jerk of the chain. The sinew was not so brittle, would not break. Nor would it cut like the flesh and skin.

Twisted many times, frayed a little, cut a bit by the sharp edges of the trap, the tendons still refused to give release. Instinct alone prompted him to twist and turn.

Clear dawn climbed up from beyond the ridge. The red flame of the sun ball mounted over the Gore mountains. Day life of the range started. A rabbit came loping down the trail, stopped, leaped in frenzied fear as he sighted the bedraggled, gaunt form in the trap, kicked his stout hind legs in fright, and sped away like a ghost thing through the sage. Magpies came to bicker and curse, waiting for the wolf to die. They would be there before the trapper. At least the wolf's eyes would be a feast for the magpies if they did not peck through the protecting hide and rip at the flesh. Meanwhile they flapped and cawed and screamed and said vile things to each other in the manner of magpies.

The pack was gone. With morning it had sought safety in the higher slopes.

Morning and afternoon both came and waned. But the stout heart of the wolf would not permit surrender. Rests were more frequent. The fight continued fiercely, even though subdued. The trap cut more deeply. The twisted chain was knotted. The strong body got more purchase with its lunges even though they were more feeble.

Evening was near. It brought no truce. Occasionally the tired wolf would lie and pant, with lolling tongue. Then the struggle would start again.

Evening cool came into the shadows. The sun set. New vigor and just a little new courage came to the wolf. He spun, plunged, bit at the leg, leaped groggily, tugged—

He stumbled forward and lay panting as the last shred of frayed tendon fiber cut through.

He was free. But in the trap was that big, well-formed wolf foot.

He struggled up, limped a few feet, looked back through the deepening dusk at that bloody stump in the trap. Then he lifted his blood-stained head and whined. It was a new sharp note. Hate, the vicious hate of man and his chattels, had seared into the soul of that wolf.

He had escaped. But he was a sick wolf. He stumbled, hobbled, stopped for breath, licked his poor maimed stump where blood oozed from the end around the broken bone. After each stop he struggled up and on. The will of a leader, a conqueror, drove him ahead. That power did not lie in his brawn alone. There was some of it lodged in his stout wolf heart.

He reached half shelter beside the clear stream in the next ravine. Here he lay for many moments resting and lapping up the cold water that helped to allay the fever that had started to flow through his veins. The left stump was tongue-licked, once, twice, hundreds of times, in an effort to allay the pain. Repeated licking kept it clean, finally started it toward healing.

His mate came. She whined, ran away, then returned, trotted anxiously beside him as he limped toward secure higher country. Painfully, he forced his way through the brush away from trails. He distrusted trails, distrusted everything. The second dawn came. He slept in the sun by an oak thicket. His mate nervously scouted the near country. Sun was fading when she returned with the partial remnants of a rabbit she had just killed. Fever gripped him now. He raised his heavy head, his eyes wide with pain. He growled menacingly. The mate slunk away. He slept. He awakened and hobbled to a spring, drank gulps of the pure, cleansing water, then slept again.

The next morning the fever was passing. In a few days it was gone. The stump healed a little. Infection had not entered the wound, the fever being body reaction. More days passed. The last scab dropped from the red, scarred stump and it became black, calloused. The wolf started again to follow the trails. The pack came back to this part of their range. With it came a new challenge of leadership. But the wolf with the stump avoided his kind. In his heart grew greater hatred of man and traps. For without his four feet he might not dare to fight again for kingship, and leader was the only place that this wolf would accept in any pack.

Rutting season came. When the pack came back again the four-year-old, the stump entirely healed, returned to the pack. He stalked through their midst on three legs, holding the stub carefully from the ground. A young wolf made a lunge at him. The leader leaped, threw his ponderous weight back of the blow, sunk his curved, scimitar teeth. The youngster twisted, cried in pain, scrambled away. The leader turned, his fangs bared, stalked to the center of the circle, looked at each of the possible dog wolf leaders, slowly walked up to them in majestic movements marred by the curious hitching walk, sniffed at them, growled, bristled.

In all the circle none protested his return to command.

A leader had returned in Burns Hole, a king of the wolves had asserted his right to rule.

That night he led the pack in their raid on a pasture within rifle shot of the Benton ranch.

New cunning was in this wolf. There was a vicious, cruel, wanton lust of murder in his heart. Man had maimed him. He retaliated. Steers bellowed and ran frantically from that leaping gray death that hurled itself at their heels. Fat heifers, snorting and bawling, plunged through the night to fall before vicious onslaught, or ran blindly into the tearing barbs of fences where they floundered while blood-smeared wolf teeth ripped them to pieces before their last gurgling breath came gustily through slit windpipes.

Nor did one killing of one night, one week or one month quiet the thirst of this super killer, the wolf with the left foot missing. No stockman in northern Eagle County was immune from the raids of his band of slaughterers. No part of the range but heard the bellowing call of the crippled leader, the excited howls of the pack as it coursed at the heels of a doomed cow critter.

Years rolled along. Poison, traps, rifles took their toll from the coyote packs, cut into the other wolf packs, finally eliminated all wolves but those that ranged fearlessly and unhurt under the direction of the three-footed renegade that greedily slaughtered stock and game for the pure lust of killing.

By sheer power he held sway over the killers that came under his dominance. Weighing nearly a hundred and twenty pounds, with teeth that were capable of clipping through bone in one snap, with cunning brain, he became the terror of the wild that lies in tumbled slopes around Castle Peak near Burns Hole, Colorado.

Thus emerged the renegade. Thus was the hate of man and traps founded with him. Thus did Old Lefty of Burns Hole, the wolf with "left front foot missing," come to be the scourge of all living things in the wide sweep of wild range in which he and his murderous pack made their kills.

II: STRANGE SCENT

Eight years had passed since Lefty had lost his foot. Each had added its wisdom of man, traps, poison. Lefty had seen magpies spotted over the flats where a dead carcass had been ringed around with poison pellets. Some of the young wolves swallowed these tempting morsels of beef flank and pork tenderloin fats. One had died. The others had tasted the bitterness of straight strychnine in time and had disgorged the death-dealing drug. Many times he had seen coyotes shiver in death as poison ate out their life.

Mating season was on. Lefty ran at the head of the pack. No other wolves had been in this section of the country for years. In all of Colorado, only the renegade killer wolves were left. Ordinary traps and ordinary hunting would never stop them in their depredations. Old Lefty was one of the wisest of the surviving leaders.

He had greater bulk. He topped all other wolves of the pack by a full inch in stature. Fifteen pounds of fighting fiber he had in excess of the greatest dog wolf that ran with him. Barring the invasion of a wolf such as no one had ever known, with teeth sharper, with muscles more springy, with greater alertness, or the coming of a man versed in wolf lore greater than that possessed by this wolf himself, Lefty would for years lead his marauders over the slopes of Castle Peak.

Recently there had been new man scent on the range. He could not tell why it made him uneasy. This stranger had been there but a few days. Lefty had not seen him in all their early forenoon and late evening scouting. But the tracks of this man on long wooden feet had been left in the snow in many of their runways. Lefty bristled whenever he saw these tracks.

Now the gray-coated leader hobbled ahead, leading his band along an established runway between hunting grounds. The crispy crackle of the snow under their feet made faint music. The light breeze whipped loose snow along the drifted crust. It hissed lightly in passing.

It was another killing time for the wolf pack. In this season they ran together. Later they would separate and find their dens. In a few months there would be woolly, soft, whimpering whelps nuzzling their mother's breasts. That would be spring. But now in mid-January there was no softness in the wind. It was full of nip and bite. It was the time of wolf raids on the stockmen, the setting traps, the spreading of poison.

Suddenly Lefty stopped, froze in his tracks.

New scent! New wolf scent filled his nostrils!

Deep, rumbling, in his throat came the challenge, boiling up from the rage that surged within him. Mincingly he strutted around that foreign wolf smell. It was on a scent post of Lefty's. It was the wordless challenge of an invader to combat!

No wolf could stay on Lefty's range without Lefty's permission, and then that permission had to be battled for!

The pack shied out of the trail. Lefty sniffed, advanced, stopped, growled, then bared his teeth and snarled. Vicious hate filled his heart.

For with that wolf taint there came the slightest taint of that foreign man!

Lefty edged around that scent post. Something told him it was not safe. Instinct came to back up that uncanny reasoning which warned him that strange wolf scent and strange man scent together at one of their own scent posts was not a normal combination of odors.

The other dog wolves growled, strutted, nosed out toward that challenging scent. They too would fight the intruder until he found his proper place in the pack or was killed in the ordeal of adoption! The females sniffed, whined. The coming of a stranger twitted their curiosity, inveigled their feminine fancy to see this wayfarer that dared challenge the pack by leaving his scent on their range.

Lefty growled, snarled, lunged at the closest female, driving her back. The thought of the strange wolf faded. In its place was the unknown fear caused by this new combination of scents.

Cautiously, Lefty started around that place. Normally, he would have rushed heedlessly at the scent post, sniffed, howled, challenged the invader, hunted him until it was decided who was master of the range.

But now, cautious wolf mind warning of danger, he led the pack out of the old trail.

Then there was the quick, leaping snap of a trap. It was a futile snap. For a young female wolf had yielded to the instinct aroused by that strange dog scent. She had rolled on the ground near the scent post. And in rolling had tripped the pan of the trap set.

For a moment the wolf pack stopped, looked back. The incautious young female had left a jaw full of hair in the steel lips of the trap. But it had not even nipped the hide in its quick clutch at the wolf.

With a sharp whine, Lefty started off, away from the trail, climbing over little windfalls, using his round stump to lift him over tiny obstructions. Unhurried was the flight. There was no racing away from some dread thing. But rather, they sensed danger, and following the heady old leader, they put snow-covered distance between them and that danger at the rate of an easy fast trot.

The next night Lefty returned to sniff the scent post. That strange wolf scent made his hair bristle on his broad gray back. He lifted his head and howled, challenged that intruder. But along with the wolf scent he got man scent; and that lifted in his wolf mind the picture of the torturing hours in that old trap eight years before.

In wide circles, he traveled from this scent, then came back. Each time he bristled, growled, sent out his bellowing challenge over the snow-covered mountain side. Enemies only could leave that scent on Lefty's range, and he challenged them both, man and wolf.

But although he hunted and howled his dare to battle, he could not find the antagonists. The pack moved on to a new kill, then back over the ridge south of Castle, and started recircling their run that led near Bull Gulch. Lefty was in the lead. It was night and they foraged as they traveled.

Ahead there came a cry. Lefty stopped, listened, sniffed. The coyote that had sent out that shrill screech was not hunting, had not made a kill, was not calling his mates to a feast of carrion meat. Something had struck, struck mortally at the coyote. It was there in the cry.

Some new challenger was on the range, perhaps that new wolf; some enemy hinted at in that new man scent. Lefty leaped ahead. He raced the trail with the pack following. But there was caution in his movements. His sensitive nose was stretched wide at the nostrils to catch the faintest scent; his ears alert to detect the first sound.

Into an open space bordered by oak thickets they ran, swerved, stopped. For there, thrashing in a steel trap, was the luckless coyote that had blundered into a set placed for Lefty himself. Lefty hesitated, swung out of the trail, sniffed, and then went on. But there was blood lust in his wolf heart. The deep-toned growl that rumbled in his throat poured forth maledictions on the man that was back of that trap set and the strange wolf scent that had no wolf tracks, no trail with it.

Some instinct, some deep-seated animal sense, warned Lefty that all this meant new war for the wolves; meant trouble, that loomed as a dark, indistinct horror in this land of winter, where the wolf ruled the animal world by the law of fang.

A blood feast, filled with vicious, slashing, cutting slaughter of a two-year-old at the John Welch ranch was Lefty's concrete answer to that specter the strange scent and the trapped coyote aroused in his killer-wolf mind.

III: HUNTER HEGEWA

Burns Hole is the solidified aftermath of a volcanic blowout. Lava beds, pot holes, tangled masses of rock roll and tumble, mounting in choppy sequence to the crest of Castle Peak where, perched on the topmost turret of the rocky battlements and pillared ramparts which give the peak its name, is the Holy Cross National Forest fire lookout.

The land drops away from every side of the peak. To the north and westward the twisty ravines and cañons worm their way down to join the unhurried Colorado as it winds around sweeping bends or riffles over rock ledges. South and eastward the drainage from Castle seeks the Eagle, a branch of the Colorado.

Because it is so rough it has been exempt from homesteading except where there are little green valleys among the dryer slopes of the peaks and ridges. But it is good cow range.

Piñon pine and western cedar clothe the slopes of Castle and carry their green banners down the edge of the streams, where western cottonwood flaunts its lance-shaped leaves. Giant sagebrush sometimes reaching seven feet in height inhabits the flats, while mountain mahogany, thimbleberry, western wild currant, and in the wet spots, dwarf willows, form the shrub colonies that fill in between the spaces preëmpted by the more imposing cedars and pines.

The Bull Gulch cow camp squats below Castle Peak in a grassy park surrounded with a mixed stand of lodgepole pine, yellow pine, and aspen. It is a single-room shack typical of mountain cow country. Across the park is a little corral and a shed for saddle stock. In midwinter snow, pitted by bright sun, spreads a mottled white blanket over the open ground of the park, which in several places is trodden down into paths by men living at the shack.

Inside the cabin there is one good-sized room. It is low-ceiled, with unfinished boards forming the roof, over which patent roofing is nailed. Nail points on which sway tenuous cobwebs protrude through the boards in many places. The walls are logs from which the bark peels in scrofulous flakes. In the corner a sheet-iron camp cookstove often blushes with cherry-red fervor from the spitting piñon pine fire it holds in its roaring paunch. Bolted to the wall near the stove is a tin-lined cupboard. The whole front lets down on hinges. A swinging hinged leg supports it when lowered to make a table for the men at the camp. In the corner are rumpled bedrolls.

Two men faced each other across the table. It was breakfast time. Outside the cabin January morning sun was flooding the chilly, snowy woods.

"I hate to tell yuh 'I told yuh so,'" drawled the big, lanky cow hand who sat with tin cup held in both hands, sipping noisily at the hot coffee. "But yuh've got this to console yuh, Hegewa, this ain't no common wolf you've missed takin'. This old he-wolf with his left front foot missin' is the smartest lobo in the Rockies."

The man addressed as Hegewa was thirty-odd years, medium in height, with premature crow's-feet lacing out from the corners of his blue eyes—wrinkles brought there by days in the open, facing winds and sunshine. A tousled crop of tawny hair tending toward curliness formed a mop on his head. The lower part of his face was clothed with a wind-seared pointed beard. In spite of his thatch and beard, Hegewa appeared extremely clean and well-kept for a man living in the open, bedding and boarding wherever chance might take him. He was clothed in red and black checked woods shirt over a white, soft-collared dress shirt, and heavy corduroy breeches. On the back of his homemade board chair hung a cartridge belt filled with high-power ammunition. A thirty-thirty rifle such as is usually carried by a government hunter leaned against the wall. He had been sent in to Burns Hole two weeks previous, with instructions to get Lefty and his gang before he came out. No other answer would terminate his present mission. Only the death of Lefty and his pack would be acceptable in a report to the Biological Survey office of Colorado, located at Denver.

Hegewa glanced up, his merry blue eyes squinting a little as he looked at the big, good-natured, sun-tanned cow-puncher.

"You don't need to tell me, Tex, that this ain't no common wolf. I know now."

"Well, yuh had a darned good try at it," declared Tex, soothingly.

"Had? Just what do you mean?"

"Well, yuh don't expect to keep on tryin' fo' him after missin' all the chances yuh have had, do yuh?"

Hegewa was quiet a moment. When he spoke it was in a low, even tone, his words clean-clipped.

"You don't seem to get me, Tex. I came in here to get that wolf, Lefty. I'll stay here until I do. It's get the wolf or have my own official hide hung up to dry. Lefty's hide'll be dryin' days before mine will."

Tex grunted, reached for the sirup can, poured himself a generous portion of black sorghum and handed the can across the table to Hegewa.

"Hev some o' this lick?" he suggested.

Breakfast dishes washed, Hegewa strapped on skis and slid away from the cabin to inspect traps. Yellow lamplight cheerily lit the one square window of the cabin when he came back, tired, cross, empty-handed. Tex did not ask questions until after the meal. Then rolling his cigarette dessert and applying a match, he ventured the question, "What luck?"

"No luck," replied the hunter, "or damned rotten luck, whichever you want to make it. The pack came along over the trap set last night. They found the foreign wolf scent I had put there. Mating season still on and one of the females rolling in the snow where that scent was placed touched off the trap. It clipped a handful of hair out of her, but that was all. I'm darned lucky if it doesn't scare them out of the country. 'Though it appears that it didn't scare them much."

"No use, old timer. Yuh kain't land that pack. Yuh mought as well pull right now. I tell yuh, they ain't to be catched. Fo' eight year they've tried it around heah and the best wolfers on the range ain't got hide nor hair on 'em."

"Say, will you cut out that calamity howlin'," snapped Hegewa, testily. It was all he had heard since he came to McCoy. Everyone had repeated it to him, this assurance that there was no use in trying to trap Lefty. Only fate, said the natives, could bring that wolf to his death.

"Well, no offense," suggested Tex, drawling. "But one of the Benton boys rode by to-day and says that they are bettin' five to one in the valley that yuh'll not get Lefty in the fust six months. And I'm just givin' yuh friendly wahnin' that it will be wahm spring afore you'll get any of the pack and yuh won't get Lefty nohow, even—"

"I will get Lefty! Can't I drive that into your head?" exploded Hegewa. "He's a wolf. Haven't I got more sense than a wolf? I've caught more than a dozen in the past year—cleaned out a whole pack near Pagosa Springs just last month for good measure."

"But they ain't Lefty," declared the cowboy, dolefully.

Hegewa smoked in silence, but a scowl had settled on his face, and for several days the gangling cowboy found him not over-sociable. The hunter was away in the mornings soon after it was light enough to travel. Night came before he got back. Then came a morning on which the clouds banked high on the crest of Castle and the sky seemed over-freighted with snow.

"You're not goin' out to-day!" exclaimed Tex, as the hunter prepared to leave the cabin.

"You bet I am."

"Don't be a dahned fool, Hegewa," exploded Tex. "They's the all-firedest blizzard hangin' up there on the top of Castle that's brewed over this heah country this wintah. And by afternoon they'll be snow siftin' down so thick you'll not be able to see ten rod. Besides, one day don't make no difference. Yuh goin' to be chasin' this wolf gang for quite a while yet, acco'din' to my reckonin'. Goin' out aftah him to-day may get yuh own pelt instead of his'n."

Hegewa turned fiercely on his cabin mate.

"Didn't I tell you to quit that calamity howlin'? Can't I make you understand that all your yappin' about my not gettin' Lefty is all wrong? I'm goin' to get him, goin' to nail him, I tell you, Tex! Do you understand? That wolf may be canny, he may be nigh human. I know he is. But he's sentenced to death by the U. S. Government and I'm his executioner. And by God! I'll kill him and wipe out his pack if it's the last job I do, so help me!"

Hegewa stood a moment above Tex, his eyes blazing, his jaw clamped tight, hands clenching and unclenching. Then he pivoted, picked up his rifle, jerked his cap down a little tighter, buttoned his heavy wool-lined corduroy coat, and slammed out the door.

"Damned stubborn jackass," murmured Tex, as he flipped his cigarette into the open front of the stove. "I suppose I'll be goin' out and haulin' him in, stiff and cold, to-morrow, so the magpies'll not be disfigurin' him. And all because he thinks he's a better man than that Lefty wolf."

But no thought of death troubled Hegewa as he climbed the slopes below Castle Peak. Instead, his mind was filled with the persistent suggestion that perhaps Lefty was more than his match. Each recurrence of the thought, as had each similar observation by ranchmen, made Hegewa more determined to kill Lefty and triumphantly smash the pack.

Weak, chilly sunlight seeped through a dull leaden arch of snow-filled clouds. Hegewa, protected by the heavy coat, responded to the wild storm mood cooking and stewing over Castle Peak. Born in the southwest, raised on the open range, he had followed the call of his pioneer blood. Almost by instinct he had fallen into this work of the Biological Survey.

The snow hissed under the ski runners. The gusty wind made a chant of the wilds. There was trumpeting wind thunder high on Castle. It came booming softly to him as he climbed ridge or raced down slope. Wilderness, stark, challenging, man trying, encompassed him. He gloried in his ability to face it, master it.

Hegewa shot down an open slope, swerved by a tree, pitched down another slope, and then straightened out for the easy sweeping run over a slightly inclined mesa. It was life to get out into unsullied country such as this. He kicked down on the skis exuberantly, his sinewy body swaying. Old Lefty was ahead. Wilderness was around him. Blizzard Gods were preparing to charge from the high country, dashing in leaping wind charges over the country below and scattering harried snow dropping from overladen clouds.

A snowshoe rabbit leaped from cover, kicked soft snow, dashed in zigzag flight, dived behind scrub cedar tree, froze. His white winter blended with the clean snow. Only big eyes and narrow black ear edgings stood out against the colorless background.

"Better hide, Bigfoot," called Hegewa as he slipped by. "Lefty'll get you if you don't."

At noon the wind was higher. Wilderness song hummed in the trees, came softly chorusing from the place where clouds boiled on Castle or ran as an undertone to the sound of racing snow particles that scuttered along the crust.

Tireless, Hegewa kept heading away from the cow camp. Below on the ravines there were cow ranches. Only a few of them were inhabited during winter. The hunter was practically alone, except for the wildlings and nature spirits.

Afternoon came. It was time to head back to the cabin. He must try another day to find wolf tracks which would tell him quickly where the pack was running. He should know all their runways and habits before he set another trap. Too little of this knowledge had caused failure of his earlier trap sets. In the face of almost antagonistic scoffing of Tex, he must be certain when he struck again.

The trail flattened out in a swale where meadow grass, rank and dry, protruded above the low drifts. Except for the few patches of this sear grass sticking up, the snow was unbroken. Hegewa slid along, reaching the lowest point in the plain.

He stopped. His eyes fastened on a faint sign in the snow crust. Other faint tracks led on. He stooped, peering, straightened as though released by a trigger, and started rapidly following this trail of the pack.

Up the draw, over a low ridge, through a thicket of mountain mahogany, it threaded. Then out in the open again, faint but certain.

The trail entered the shelter of a thick stand of young yellow pine. Here the tracks were clear and unblurred by wind. Hegewa stopped short. His heart thumped a little faster than from mere exertion. For there was a distinctive, unusual mark in that snow.

It was the fresh peg-leg track of Old Lefty!

From these tracks of the leader Hegewa conjured up the picture of the rangy, strong dog-wolf that was Lefty—cruel, merciless, fearless, filled with all wilderness cunning, taught in the graduate school by the steel trap where he left his foot, and the eight years he had been sought after by local hunters. Hegewa clicked his tongue softly as he visualized Lefty.

Evening threatened. The blizzard growled. But the wolf pack had passed by less than an hour before. These were the first fresh tracks he had sighted for days. He shifted his light pack.

"Follow it," he decided. "Only chance I've had. Maybe no other for weeks. Keep at it until nightfall, then back to the cabin. I can make that by midnight."

With new zest he set out. He noted that Lefty traveled on three legs except when leaping some obstruction. When a barrier was met, the stump, a round pad, would make its imprint in the snow.

An hour's climbing brought Hegewa up near the breaks where timber became scraggy. A few hundred feet higher superhardy, deformed stragglers crept up to timber line, the frontier of the forest.

The wolf pack skirted the high sides of the timber, avoiding the ridgy topography below, swinging around the side of the Castle to the slopes that dropped into the Eagle. The wolf trail led steadily away from the cow camp.

He kept plugging on stubbornly. The sun was blotted out. A spiritless dusk settled. The tracks became indistinct. Chill wilderness spirits seemed to reach out hands to grip the hunter. He shivered, looked up to where the blizzard was poised in one last tremendous uppiling of clouds, ready to launch its ice-infused hurricane down over Castle.

For the first time Hegewa doubted. There was death in that boiling zero-touched mass. He stopped. New wailing came to the wind. A puffy gust zipped by. It pried beneath his warm coat. The hunter looked ahead through the fast-dying light filled with swirling snow eddies. It was hard to give up this fresh trail. When a renegade like Lefty is hunted, no slightest chance leading to possible capture can be passed by. But the wind decided it. With a howl it ripped through frantic pine boughs, racing in cloudy snow swirls that spouted up in the timber like smoke columns. It held chilling, gloating storm power. Hegewa felt a creepy feeling along his spine. Something hinted at fear of the wilderness, a new, a very new, sensation to him.

"Maybe Tex was right," he half murmured. He turned back toward the cow camp. "Maybe it *is* my pelt instead of Lefty's."

Now the blizzard was ready to play with any victim caught in its icy talons. It leaped, howled, gleefully threw rifts of stinging snow through the trees that shivered and shook like things whipped by barbed lashes. The turmoil was bewildering, grand, awing, numbing in its intensity.

Hegewa could see but a few feet. He brushed the snow from his eyes, tugged at his mittens to make their fur-lined warmth fit closer to his numbing hands. He ran headlong into a thicket of lodgepole. He fought out to open space. His next slide nearly dashed him over a hidden cliff where the long tongues of snow curled and lapped.

A new idea flashed into his mind. To get at Lefty he had to survive the blizzard!

With new fierceness, he fought on. He *would* get that wolf!

The stunted types of timber line had passed. Hegewa was now in the taller trees which are found at elevations a full two thousand feet below timber line. Up higher no living thing could stand unsheltered before the blizzard and survive. It was less frightful in this forested section of lower elevation. Even here it seemed impossible to spend the night in the open and live through the ordeal.

Another tree barrier got in his way. A big uncrusted drift caught the end of his ski, dumped him. He lost his pack sack, dug in the snow for it, found it, got up, hurried along.

Darkness came. Night conspired with the storm to blind him. He felt tired, sleepy. He worked laboriously ahead through the thick timber impeding progress. Wilderness forces, usually friendly, lashed and battered at him, blocking his way. Still lurked that new fear, the haunting thought that it might be his pelt instead of Lefty's.

Then in the snow cloud, as though in a vision, there came a mental picture of himself muzzling the captured Lefty as the wolf lay helpless in the trap. He could almost feel the wolf's head under his hands.

Clean cut, the mental image stayed a moment, then vanished.

Hegewa stopped, shook himself, laughed a strong, unafraid laugh. He dashed the snow from his beard and eyebrows. He *knew* he would live to get his wolf.

→❦

New sun shone through the snow-scoured air the next morning. Tex had sat up far into night, waiting for the shout of Hegewa. But no call had come. Tex had gone to bed. His nightcap cigarette was half burned when he suddenly spoke to himself in the darkness of the room.

"The danged fool," he said with admiration creeping into his tone. "The danged fool, I believe he knew just how much of a storm would break and took the risk anyway, just hopin' to meet up with that wolf."

But now Tex anxiously looked out over the clean white snow that billowed away under the trees in soft curves. He poured himself a cup of strong coffee. He rolled another cigarette. He scowled at the graying ash. There was work ahead. Hegewa could not weather this storm. Tex felt he must find the hunter and get the stiff body to some ranch or town before the magpies or coyotes would make it nothing but a rack of bones. This thought of the stark wilderness tragedy hiding in the forested slopes above made the usually happy Tex shiver.

A shout came from the woods. Tex snapped erect, plunged for the door. He peered wonderingly at the figure on skis that came swooping into the yard. It was Hegewa, snow-covered, with icicles on his beard and frost on his eyebrows, but alive and almost uninjured.

Tex stood staring.

"Fo' the love of John," he exploded. "What ranch did yuh stay at?"

"No ranch. Under a spruce."

"Quit yo' joshin', Hegewa, no one could live outdoor last night. Sleepin' under a spruce in a blizzard! Oh, hell, tell us somethin' easy!"

"It's a fact," declared Hegewa. But no argument would convince Tex.

"Sure thought yuh was a goner," he remarked later, after a frost bite on Hegewa's finger had been treated with snow.

Breakfast over, Hegewa insisted on going out again. Late in the afternoon he came in excited.

"The game's up," he declared with conviction. "I've got them located. I know their main runway around Castle Peak. They've been over it early this morning since the blizzard let up. I picked up the track from what I found before the blizzard last night. I'm goin' to hook the old leader tonight!"

Tex grinned indulgently. Hegewa was boisterously happy.

The following morning he did not wait for breakfast, but gulped hot coffee as he dressed. Hurriedly he snatched a bacon sandwich as he left.

Tex watched his form disappear in the morning-tinted woods and then began dishwashing. It was before noon when Hegewa came back carrying the pelt of a coyote. Dark disappointment sat heavily on his features.

"You may be right now, Tex," he growled, after he had ripped off his coat and thrown it in the corner. "I may not get Lefty after all."

"Jest beginnin' to realize it?"

"It's my own luck—or his! I had this trap that caught the coyote set in the runway. Lefty fooled me before because of one unusual thing. It's that three-legged gait of his'n. He hobbles along different than other wolves. But last night I set this trap in such a way that he'd have to put down that stump of a leg and throw his weight on another. Set the trap to catch that other leg as he hobbled forward.

"The idea was perfect. Lefty did come along. He did set his foot down according to Hoyle. But not on the trap. This coyote had got there first. The twigs in the trail I had laid there to guide Lefty into the trap as he led the pack forced this coyote to blunder plumb into the set ahead of Lefty.

"The whole wolf pack shied around this trap. They swung off through the brush, fifty feet off their regular run. Lefty set his peg foot down every time he came to a limb in the trail just as I figured he would.

"But they're trap-wise, those wolves. And they've seen this coyote in the trap. They'll never go over that run again, or if they do they'll shy so far—

"By gosh, there's a last try. They'll shy, Tex! They'll start a new runway around that old trap set. That's it! That's the dope! Why in the world didn't I think of it. If they're not scared out of the country that new trail is the very ticket. They'll shy! Over that new trail. I've still got a fighting chance!"

Hegewa was pulling on his coat as he talked, hurrying to tumble out of the cabin and speed to the place where the blundering coyote the night before had ruined his best chance of snaring the wise old leader of the Burns Hole killer wolves.

IV: NO QUARTER

New killing lust filled the heart of Lefty the renegade as he traveled the snowy trail over the divide between Posey and Cottonwood creeks. The last kill had been two nights before. The pack had swung up on the slopes of Castle to sleep off the blood drunk they had enjoyed.

Man hate gnawed at Lefty's wolf heart. At several points he had found that wolf scent mixed with the faintest man scent which had shied the pack out of the runway the night before, around the stricken coyote. Lefty's coarse mane bristled as there flashed through his mind the recollection of that hated wolf-man odor. He growled intermittently in his great throat as he trotted along.

They approached the place where they had detoured around that struggling coyote. Lefty slowed his gait. Repressed growls seemed to be boiling within him. He stopped dead in the trail as they came to the brush-bordered opening. The pack moved uneasily. The sprung trap was still in the old runway, the snow was still torn up. The coyote was gone.

Lefty swung his head from side to side. His muscles bunched, his hair raised menacingly. He stepped from the trail, moved a few feet, looked back at the trap set where the coyote had cried in terror. He started to back track, then turned and followed the new detour. A stick got in his way. He set down his peg leg, lurched forward to get his footing.

Out of the snow leaped a trap!

With a bellow, Lefty plunged away as the thing closed on his paw. The pack fled through the sagelike demons in a fright. Lefty leaped, thrashed, threw down his stub to protect himself in his lurching, floundered in the snow, and then a second set of steel jaws gripped swift as lightning.

After years of trap-wariness, after evading the best wolfers in Colorado, the un-believable had again happened. Lefty was in a trap; not one trap only, but two!

But Lefty had cheated traps before. All the old rage at the man-made thing seethed as threw the sinew of his body into breaking the grip of the steel vise. He floundered ahead. No stake held him this time. On the end of the chain was a drag with twisted prongs. It caught and held, broke loose, caught again, leaving a trail that anyone could follow. Nor did Lefty care in his wild plunging to escape this dragging horror whether he covered his trail or left a broad mark.

Down gully, half smothered in snow, bellowing his rage, challenging the Thing that had hold of him to come out to fight, lunged Lefty. No fear, no cring-ing, only mad hate, the spirit of the renegade, mastered him.

The 180-degree half circle of one of the prongs on the drag hook caught in the base of a scrub oak. Lefty threw his weight against the obstruction, was jerked back viciously. His foot hurt. There was no numbing in these traps. Circulation continued to the end of his leg. Offsets in the trap provided for that. But even the sharp pain of the wrenched paw did not stop the killer. Again came the throw of his massive body. Powerful bone and wolf muscle bent the curved hook that no man could bend even with the help of simple tools. It released. The hook was a hook no longer as it let go of the oak.

Then through a nightmare of fighting, panting, lunging effort stumbled the leader of the killers of Burns Hole. Hours passed and still he snarled, bit at the trap, voiced his hatred while timid woods dwellers cringed in their coverts at that fighting, blood-lusting cry.

⇥⇤

Hegewa had not waited for breakfast. He had left Tex mixing batter for flapjacks after having gulped a cup of strong, burning hot coffee. Tex had eaten leisurely, smoked his usual several cigarettes, and after lazily shuffling his way through stable routine, had returned to the house to attack the pile of breakfast dishes. He had soused hot water in the battered dish pan, had draped the grayish dish towel over a handy chair back and, rolling up his sleeves, was about to ease his hands into the soapy water when the excited cry of Hegewa came clearly from the timbered slope above the cow camp.

"Tex, oh, Tex!"

There was triumph in his shout.

Swooping in graceful lines, Hegewa seemed to glide up to the door on wings rather than the wood of skis.

"I've got him; I've got the old scoundrel! He's up there somewhere with the drag and two traps on his feet! Come on. I've got to have help. He's fighting mad! No one man can stand up to him even if he is messed up in two traps. Get your things on and get your lariat. Hurry!"

Not waiting for Tex, Hegewa stomped into the cabin. He grabbed a couple of cold flapjacks, devoured them, poured coffee from the blackened pot, gulped it, and then reaching into the supply cupboard, slipped a can of baked beans into his jacket pocket for emergency lunch. From there he went to the place where a light hunting ax was hanging on the wall, and lifting it from the hook, attached the ring in its leather scabbard to his belt.

Tex scrambled into his Mackinaw. With the water still steaming in the battered old dishpan, the two men slid away on skis from the cabin, over the snow trail that led to the captured Lefty.

Up the snowy slopes that break away from Castle, then through little open parks, across sagy flats where four-foot sagebrush stood only a foot above the white of the winter blanket, they labored. Hegewa, hardened to the travel, impatiently hurried forward, intent on the final capture of the murderer that lay at the end of that trap-gouged snow trail. He incessantly urged the puffing Tex to greater efforts, talking as he went.

"See how the old cuss fought here!" he exclaimed. "Just look at the way that drag has ripped up the country. Trail like a bull was on the end of that chain instead of a wolf. Here he stopped and rested. See his great form in the snow. Gosh, Tex, that old duffer is the biggest wolf— Say, man, look at that sage rooted up. Looks like a locomotive had been through here."

In a thicket of sage and oak, his fur roughened by the struggle of the night and morning, at the end of the trail, Lefty stood, defiant. The men eased across the open space in front of him. The wolf's mane bristled.

There came again, clear now, that hated man scent, the scent of Hegewa!

With a roar Lefty plunged. His jaws snapped!

"Get him, Tex!" cried Hegewa excitedly. "Get a noose under them legs."

Tex, riding skis with awkwardness, straddled after the wolf.

"Swing the loop under the legs that ain't caught in the trap. Then we can jerk them out from under him. Jerk the minute you start to tighten. He can snap through that lariat rope like thread."

"He'll break his teeth if he bites this rope."

"Don't fool about it," ordered Hegewa, maneuvering to head Lefty back where the toggle would catch in the brush again. "He can bite through five folds of that if he has to. Yank them legs the minute you get them snared."

The wolf floundered through the snow. His baleful eyes, reddened at the rims and wide with the effort that had sapped his strength, glared at the two pursuers.

The rope swung through the air. It fell short. The wolf plunged after it, snapping. Hatred for man things welled up in a blind, ferocious rush at the snaky snare.

"Now!" yelled Hegewa as the toggle caught. "Now get him!"

Tex threw again with a hastily made loop. It caught. Lefty plunged. But the cow-puncher, accustomed to the quickness of calf or yearling, caught up the slack and the furry wolf squirmed in convulsive twistings as he tripped.

"Hold him, old-timer! Don't let an inch of slack get in that rope."

The wolf was strung out between the drag caught in a big sage and the taut rope that hummed as he struggled. Tex grunted as the burly wolf battled.

Hegewa raced to a small aspen growing in a thicket. With quick, slicing strokes of the camp ax, he felled the tree. A pole four inches thick and six feet long was lopped out of the lower part of the tree. He came back toward the snarling, challenging wolf that was testing the strength of the big Texan.

"Hold her tight. I'm going to get this down on his neck."

Lefty stopped, panting. In a moment Hegewa had the pole lying down in the hollow of his neck.

But the touch of it sent madness rushing in Lefty's veins again. He leaped free of the ground, threw the pole off like it was a bit of a stick, jerked Tex forward as the rope tugged from the hurling strength of his body. The sage that held the other end of the trap chain cracked.

"Don't give him slack," yelled Hegewa.

"Who in hell's givin' him slack," puffed Tex as he set back again to jerk the wolf out taut between trap and lariat.

The pole dropped into place again. Lefty lay panting, stretched on the snow. Small sage was beaten down around him on all sides.

The wolf looked up to glare at that man figure that moved cautiously along the pole, a noose of stout cord in his hand. From the deep vital core of the wolf killer there rumbled threats, animal curses, defiance to the last drop of wolf blood in his veins.

Slowly, Hegewa put more weight on the pole. Lefty's neck sagged in the snow. He started to struggle. Tex pulled on the lariat. Hegewa put more pressure on the pole.

After a moment of easing along the pole, the hunter was out near the neck. Almost below his hands the red-edged mouth of Lefty lay, a threat to life and limb if those bone-shearing teeth could only come into play. It is a ticklish moment in wolf trapping, this moving out on a pole to where the hunter can straddle the neck of the killer and truss up his mouth with baling wire or cord. Below Hegewa lay one of the greatest killer beasts of the West.

Slowly, ever so slowly, Hegewa eased one knee down on the panting wolf. The other slid over his neck. There would be a struggle if Lefty started an attack. There was no getting away now by a quick dive for safety. It would be man strength against wolf strength if Lefty fought.

Warily, the hunter eased down that noose over the cruel jaws that had ripped the life from many throats of livestock. The noose dropped. With a quick deft move it clamped those deathly jaws shut. Another quick turn caught the muzzling cord back of the wolf head.

Lefty had quit!

Hate still filled his heart. But there had come fear, the knowledge that he had at last met his master. The wolf killers of Burns Hole faced obliteration, for the keen wolf mind of Lefty the man hater, the killer renegade, would no longer guide them from pitfalls or lead them in their joyous carnival of slaughter on the ranches in the valley. A moment after he was muzzled, Hegewa had Lefty hog tied, trussed up until he could barely move.

"I can't see the idee of takin' him alive," declared Tex as he stood over Hegewa, watching the hunter work with a stout collar, fitting it around the neck of the glaring Lefty.

"I'll get some of his buddies. They'll come back lookin' for their leader. I'll get 'em when they do. Lefty with a collar, tied out with a light chain, will just naturally be too much for 'em to pass up. And when they get nosin' around they'll fall into traps."

Three nights and three dead wolves proved that Hegewa was right. Then the others of the pack scattered. Finally Hegewa brought in a bottle of Lefty's scent and the green hide of the old leader, while magpies pecked at his freezing carcass.

"I suppose you'll quit now and get out of here," observed Tex just a little wistfully as they sat smoking after the supper dishes were washed. "Reckon you'll keep yore job now that Lefty is dead."

"I couldn't have kept it if he'd stayed alive. But you know, I feel sorry trappin' those renegades, Tex. Gosh, they're brainy old devils. But they bring their own sentence on themselves. Nope, I'll not be gettin' out right away. There are still four wolves left. I'll not get out of here before the last one is trapped. That's the orders. I stay until I carry 'em out."

"I reckon that won't be long," drawled Tex as he looked at the gray hide that Hegewa was working over. "Lefty was their king. And he's dead."

"He was some old renegade!"

Whitey of Bear Springs Mesa

Brilliant February sunshine spread over southeastern Colorado as the mud-spattered automobile driven by Stanley Young plowed up to the gateway of the Shaw ranch.

Clear skies had followed the snowstorm of the day before. Conditions of the roads were terrible. Young had driven his car through storm and mud from Denver because of the urgent call of stockmen near Thatcher, Colorado, who had been losing stock to a wolf pack headed by a fierce old killer, Whitey.

The car slewed up to the gateway. Young brought the car to a stop near the ranch house, and climbed out. He was dressed in faded Stetson, Mackinaw, blue shirt, riding breeches, puttees, and army shoes, all of which had seen considerable wear.

This was to be his base of operations against the gray raiders of Bear Springs Mesa.

Jim Shaw, owner of the ranch, old-time cattleman, came to the door.

Shaw was short and wiry—an old-timer who had been on many of the long drives of the old trail herds from Texas to the ranges of Montana. He had been crippled in his youth while following the trade of cow-puncher and buster, by bad horses that fought and maimed. He was not bowlegged from years in the saddle, but he carried the unmistakable stamp of the western horseman. His hair was white, and his mustache, which spread amply above a broad, thin-lipped mouth, made a white band across his weathered countenance.

"Come in," welcomed Shaw, as he extended his knotted hand to Young. "Come right in and make yourself to home. We're mighty pleased to have you come. Mighty glad!"

"I came near not getting here," remarked Young, as he threw his bag on the little porch.

"How's that?" asked Shaw.

"Big fight on in the legislature back in Denver," said Young. "Senator Callen and Senator Tobin along with Claude Rees, Gotthelf and Headlee, have been trying to pound through a bill to appropriate funds for coöperation between the state and the Biological Survey. We haven't enough money to send out the hunters we should really get to lick these old renegades. Lack of men is the reason I am down here personally."

"There shouldn't be much trouble in passing that sort of a bill in the Colorado legislature," remarked Shaw.

"Oh yes, there is," replied Young, straightening up. "There is a tough fight on. There is a bunch in this state that have been making money from trapping predatory animals for bounty, and they are bringing all the pressure they can to defeat that bill. If we clean out the animal killers, there'll not be any bounty left for them."

"And they're fighting?" asked Jim Shaw.

"Tooth and toenail," replied Young.

"Well, I'll be darned," Shaw exclaimed. Then, after a pause, "I suppose there are such people. Fact is, I guess there's some of them around here."

"Really promised those men I would go back to Denver when that bill comes up. I'll get a great kick, too, from licking those bounty advocates—anywhere I meet one."

Young paused a moment before entering the house and glanced over the widespread landscape.

The Shaw ranch was situated on a shoulder of Bear Springs Mesa. Rolling grass lands stretched away to the northwest toward the Apishapa and Huerfano Rivers. Westward over the rising billows that had been thus wrinkled when the Rocky Mountains, sprouted or spurted up, the view was a vast plain. Beyond were the ragged pinnacles of the distant Sangre de Cristo Mountains, the twin cones of the Spanish Peaks, and the blunt nose of old Greenhorn Peak, where its smooth, rounded, treeless snout lifts into the blue.

Southwesterly from the ranch breaks and promontories fringing Bear Springs Mesa rose in disheveled slopes patched with piñon and cedar. The broad table-land of the Mesa was lifted in that same earth writhing which shoved up the mountains to the west, but the Mesa had been pushed up in an almost level form, like a blocky island in the sea of the plains—an island of limestone and sandstone arising from the sedimentary earth crust; a badly disintegrated, gigantic, dominating cubicle.

On top of the Mesa are little hollows, grassy draws and jutting little cliffs, under the edges of which chipmunks, lizards, snakes and coyotes find refuge. At the edge of the table-land weather and wind have worn arroyos—gulleys slashed into the limestone side of the Mesa.

In this vast sweep of open country, treeless in the plains, covered with the low-growing piñon on the slopes of the Mesa, the two-story adobe ranch house of Shaw's seemed tiny. The exterior had been whipped often by the hurrying wind of the Huerfano, which carries sand that cuts any surface except the most adamant. These mud walls had been baked and rebaked by the hot mid-July sun that pours out layer after layer of heat over the open plains of southeastern Colorado. They had been pounded and bombarded by the snows that swoop down from where they gather and hang for hours on the rounded nose of old Greenhorn. The shingle roof had aged along with the adobe walls and blended into the gray and brown tints of the landscape until the whole house seemed a part of the earth upon which it stood.

To one side was a corral of piñon and cedar poles, grayed, weathered, hung together at some points with hay wire, and at others spiked to the posts. At one side of the corral was a 'dobe barn. It was little more than a wickie-up in which grain was stored and in which meager shelter for stock was found when the storm demons leaped in ghoulish carnival over the shoulder of the Mesa.

Everything here was tempered, softened and worn by the elements. To establish such a ranch, to hold it against the battering forces of the frontier, to maintain a foothold and make a living is no soft task. It requires all of the fight that men have everywhere to keep body and soul together, spirits from drooping and an unsoured soul, and in addition the will and determination to win through that frontiersmen must possess.

Young sensed some of this struggle that had carved this ranch out of the open range. He turned toward Jim Shaw with the realization that here was another man who, like himself, was instinctively a follower of the frontier.

"I reckon you and I are going to have a chance of being partners," said Young, smiling.

Shaw looked up, his deep-set blue eyes twinkling. "I guess you're right," he said.

From this base and with Jim Shaw and his neighbors, Stanley Young started his campaign against the killer wolves of Bear Springs Mesa.

II: GHOST SCENT

Jim Shaw and Young sat beside the big kitchen range. They were lounging easily with chairs tilted, smoking comfortably, talking lazily, intermittently. There was neither the hard, driving pressure of a business conference in the talk, nor was it without purpose. It was that leisurely conversation which men of the outdoors engage in and through which they learn much and reach understanding.

"You may have some trouble here, before you get through," observed Shaw.

Young turned his probing blue eyes on the rancher. "Not from the wolf."

"No, not from Whitey necessarily, but maybe from some of the local bounty trappers. Some of these half-starved dryland farmers. Strang, for instance; maybe Calcott or Roberts. Their kind just resent any Federal man coming into this section. But you say you've bumped into this afore, even in the legislature."

"Yes," replied Young with a slight sigh, "we have."

Silence fell for a few moments as the two men smoked.

"You'll have trouble with Whitey, too," said Shaw, after a moment. "He's a crafty old cuss. I've seen lots of wolves, but he's the headiest. If you catch a glimpse of the old rascal you'll recognize him. Whitest pelt on a wolf I've ever seen. He's an old one; gray from years of bleaching in sun and rain."

"There are eight others with him, you say?"

"Yeh, but Whitey is the brains of the outfit."

Young puffed at his pipe.

"Guess we'll start after him in earnest to-morrow," he mused. "The last week of riding I've got about all the dope I need to start operations. How big do you reckon Whitey's run is, Jim?"

"Oh, about a hundred miles around. You're a better man than we've had here before if you can set a trap with a pan about two inches across and catch him, in all that range."

"I'll set about twenty-five."

"But at that, all those trap pans together would not be as big as two dinner plates," replied Shaw. "And that isn't a very big spot in big country like the Mesa."

"I've got something else that will bring old Whitey around."

"What?"

Young arose, went into his room, and returned with a bottle of amber fluid. He held it up to the lamp light.

"Scent," remarked Young. "Ghost scent from a dead wolf. Hegewa, one of our hunters, took that from Old Lefty over in Burns Hole, before he killed Lefty. Lefty is dead, but his scent will make Whitey wild."

Shaw looked at the bottle with interest, asked questions, then conversation again lagged.

For a time they smoked in silence, then Young got up and stretched.

"Guess we'll get an early start to-morrow and string out a few traps."

Young turned to Shaw as he was about to step from the room.

"You don't think there's going to be big trouble with these nesters, do you, Jim?" Hostile humans can make a trap and poison campaign against wolves far more difficult than if they coöperate or are neutral.

The old man was silent for a moment.

"No," he said slowly, "I guess not really big trouble. But if it comes to a show-down on anything you can count on me and the McDaniels boys. If you can hang up the hide of that old devil Whitey, there ain't nothin' that I'll not do, even to thrashing some of those darn fool homesteaders."

"Don't want to get you in bad with your neighbors."

Shaw snorted. "Hell with 'em. I got you in here and I'm goin' to see you ain't bothered even if it comes to gun play. You just go ahead and figure if anything breaks loose, Jim Shaw'll be with you when it does."

"Maybe I better take you back to the legislature with me," laughed Young. "I can use a few more good fighters there, too!"

As Stanley Young dropped to sleep that evening, he realized that Jim Shaw never would have mentioned any opposition unless it was serious. This warning meant real trouble ahead.

Young, Shaw and Guy McDaniels rode the trail next morning. The sun was bright, but the wind still carried winter nip. Green seemed to be creeping into the plains country, but the gray brown of winter cloaked the Mesa.

For a time they rode in silence. McDaniels rolled a cigarette and lit a match with a flick of his thumb nail. He was a long, weather-bitten man, a cow-puncher who had ridden on the big cow ranges of Tom Pollock and Al Sanford near Seligman, Arizona. With his brother, Dawson McDaniels, he had come to homestead in the Thatcher section near Shaw's ranch.

Guy McDaniels was dressed in the regular winter outfit of the genuine Colorado cow-puncher. This uniform of service is worn riding boots, leather chaps, nicked and scarred from riding through brush. Under the chaps are copper-riveted overalls. Guy wore a Mackinaw and a worn, wide-brimmed Stetson.

The trail offered a slippery surface where adobe mud gave greasy footing for the tough cow horses. On the pommel of Young's saddle there were strung eight number fourteen wolf traps. They rattled as the horse stumbled and slipped in the trail.

"Steady, boy," cautioned Young. Then to his companions, "Good thing this horse is not spooky. If he was he might spread me around in the mud some. I've carried traps on horses that objected with all four feet."

Guy McDaniels grinned. "Looks to me you're mighty modest in the number of traps you're settin'. I'd of brung a whole pack animal loaded if I was out for Whitey."

Young eased himself in his saddle and faced his two companions.

"I'll tell you boys what I'll do. You both seem skeptical. You show me a right fresh wolf track, and if I don't get a wolf in twenty-four hours, I'll buy you the best dinner I can get at the hotel El Capitan in Rocky Ford. If I do get the wolf, you buy it. Is that a go?"

Shaw smiled.

Guy McDaniels laughed shortly, then grinned hugely at the cocksure challenge.

"I reckon," said Shaw.

"All right, you show me that track."

A mile passed. The three horsemen reached a sheltered road oozy with mud. They traveled for a few hundred yards over the slippery trail, each peering for signs. Suddenly Shaw reined in.

"There's a fresh track, Young," he said, pointing.

A few hundred yards along the trail Young stopped.

"Here's a set," he declared. "See where the old dog wolves have been scratching the ground. It's a regular scent post. Probably that little bunch of grama grass. We'll drop a couple of traps here anyway."

Carefully Young made the trap sets. Excess earth was carried away in a square of descented canvas. The trap pan was covered with a piece of canvas so sticks would not block the jaws when the trap was sprung. Trap and cloths had been cleared of man scent by being buried in a manure pile for several days. Keen wolf noses can detect the faintest man scent, and they will dart from trail, avoiding cleverly placed traps, avoiding even their own scent posts if some man is scented.

Young finished the set by putting a few twigs in the trail. This is a trick of the best wolfers to direct the steps of their victims into the dead center of the pan.

"Now for the medicine that will make Whitey lose his head," said Young.

He took the bottle out of his pocket and shook a few drops of the scent of dead Lefty on the little tuft of grama grass.

Further riding, bacon sandwiches for cold lunch, mud that tired the horses and made the riders feel none too secure in the saddle whenever a pony slipped, all marked the passage of the day. The sun crept down toward the Spanish Peaks. All traps set, the three riders turned homeward.

"They'll come along that runway to-night," declared Young, as Guy McDaniels stopped at his own ranch. "I'll have a wolf to-morrow."

"More power to you," laughed McDaniels, a little derisively.

The sun had not reached its noon point the next day when Stanley Young rode his sweaty horse into the ranch yard at the McDaniels' place.

"I've got a dinner coming at Rocky Ford," he cried, as he jumped from the saddle. "Caught a she-wolf last night. Want you fellows to help me hog tie and muzzle her."

With many cheery exclamations about luck, the McDaniels saddled their horses and were soon following Young back over the trail to where the gray female tugged at the trap.

"I'll say that's worth a dinner," remarked Dawson as they finished trussing the wolf. "I'll sure give more than that to get rid of that old Whitey. Too bad it wasn't him."

"I'll get Whitey," declared Young. "He's mad crazy about that new wolf he thinks is on the range. Just runnin' circles, lost his head completely. He thinks Old Lefty is on his range lookin' for a fight. When a wolf gets that way you can get him to blunder into a trap."

News of the capture of the first wolf spread over the countryside. A few days later a new, sinister factor entered the campaign against Whitey and his pack. "Two-legged wolves," as Jim Shaw characterized them, started stealing traps.

"The rotten thief," exclaimed Jim Shaw when the first trap was stolen. "Why, the darn scalawag. I know who it is, Young. I can reach out and put my hands on him in an hour's ride. Can't we hang it on him hard?"

"Wish we could," exclaimed Young disgustedly, kicking at a chip in the ranch yard. "This trap stolen was on a good scent post set where I had hopes of snagging Whitey. That set is spoiled now. I hate that worse than the loss of the trap, but you just watch my smoke if I catch any of these wise hombres around here. Prison for him."

"I'm plumb darned tired of this myself," declared Shaw, his old blue eyes snapping.

A few days later Young reported two more trap sets raided and the chance for catching any more wolves at these points ruined for the season.

"Hell's fire!" exploded Guy McDaniels. "I'm getting fed up. I'm for making some red hot calls on a few measly skunks around here and warnin' 'em proper. What you say, Jim?"

"I feel like you, Guy," replied the old-timer, his eyes squinting. "But Young says it's worse to start anything and not finish it than if you let things ride. For if you don't prove nothin', then they feel safer than ever in their stealin'. We can't have that. Just the same, I'm gettin' mad enough to do something."

"We've had all I care to take," growled McDaniels.

"The time's comin', boys," counseled Young. "Give 'em rope and they'll trip at their own game."

Several days of inaction only served to raise the ire of the cattlemen.

"Dang those nesters," exploded Jim Shaw, when Young reported several more trap sets ruined. "I'd like to lay my hands on them for a little while. Just say the word and the boys and me will make up a little posse and call on a few of those thievin' hombres."

"Wait. We'll get a crack at them and when we do—"

"I'll be there with bells on," finished Shaw, his eyes snapping, his jaw muscles tensing. "But don't wait too long!"

The next day Shaw and Young hurried away from the ranch to ride the trap line. Young had made a trap set near a new scent post. They left the house in a great rush without washing dishes.

"We'll sure snag him to-day," said Young, as they trotted their horses away from the ranch.

He was still buttoning his coat. He had communicated some of his excitement to Jim Shaw. They rode at a fast trot directly to this new scent post set. Although Whitey had passed that way the night before, no trap at that set had been sprung. For half an hour they rode along the trail of the wolves. Topping the ridge, Shaw reined in his horse abruptly.

"Looks like a dead steer down there," he said.

"May be a wolf kill," remarked Young. "Let's go see."

At the carcass of the dead steer, they found in the signs in the trail the story of the murderous attack by the wolves. Young touched the carcass.

"Not cold. Can't possibly have happened more than three hours ago," he said, looking up. "Look at this."

He pointed to the track of a great dog wolf in the sandy soil.

"Old Whitey!" said Jim Shaw.

Young straightened from his stooping position suddenly.

"Jim, my prediction will come true after all, sure as shootin'. You and I will have that old fellow before the day is over. Wolves fill up on meat until they are happy drunk from blood. Then go off to some place under a sheltered tree where they can stretch out in the sun and sleep off the drunk. That's what Whitey's done. Come on, let's get on this trail."

They rode for ten minutes along the sandy trail and then topped a little saddle. The trail swung around a thick, high stand of piñon trees. Suddenly a little valley flashed into view and both men reined abruptly. The soft earth under the feet of the horses had muffled any sound. For a moment both peered in silence at the landscape before them.

"Good Lord, look!" exclaimed Young in a low, excited voice. "He's over by that low piñon. Look quick!"

Instinctively Young's hand dropped, grabbing for the stock of the rifle he had carried continuously since he came to Bear Springs Mesa. His eyes were on the form of Old Whitey as the wolf stood the piñon, his head nodding in drowsiness. Young's hand came away empty. He reached down again, glancing quickly at the holster.

"Oh, hell," exclaimed Young.

"What?" asked Jim Shaw.

"I left the rifle at the ranch."

For a moment they stared at each other dumfounded.

"I'd give a hundred bucks for a shooting iron," "Just a hundred cold ones!"

"I'd raise you another hundred," agreed Jim Shaw mournfully.

They looked back toward the wolf. Almost as though their voices had carried, they saw Whitey snap alert. His head dropped. His nose stuck out to catch the scent. Then with a whirl he was away through the sage and back of a clump of piñon. Almost as though he had been a ghost picture, he disappeared from their view.

Fervently, feelingly, with admirable thoroughness, Young sent a string of selected profanity after Whitey.

"Amen," said Jim Shaw when he stopped for breath. Both turned their horses and headed back slowly over the trail they had come over so enthusiastically but a few moments earlier.

Lucky chance had again saved Whitey from death. Every other time he rode the trails of the Mesa Young had carried the rifle. Eagerness and the hurry to get away from the ranch had served the big wolf well.

Some days later, Young and Shaw sat after supper in their usual places by the kitchen range. More stolen traps, no more catches, an increasing hostility in the neighborhood—all had slowed the campaign against Whitey.

"I started setting more blind sets without scent to-day, Jim. I've got one big trap set with four number fourteens up in a little open park on a saddle. Whitey seems to follow that old road that leads over there quite consistently. Another set of traps I've put down in a little arroyo. No more scent post sets."

"I thought maybe you'd snag him with that scent," observed Shaw glumly. "But now we're back to just settin' traps like most of us has around here in the past five years. It don't look very good to me."

"Well, I'm betting on a couple of those trap sets. They're in regular runs, and— Listen!"

Weirdly, high-pitched at first, piercing the little night noises and the soft roar of the kitchen range, there came a cry, chilling, blood-curdling, the call of the wolf leader to the pack. Both men hurried out of doors.

Star-shine illumined a few of the near-by objects. The first velvety darkness gradually became less dense. A moment passed. Again in great sliding pitch from high yowl to trumpeting bellow came that howl which sends involuntary shivers up and down human spines and makes animal life cringe. Although a mile away, it broke through the night and came clearly, menacingly to the ears of the two listeners.

"He's hunting that trapped female," declared Young, in a low, awed tone. "He's looking for the lost member of the pack. Wolf leaders come back time after time to where they last saw their running mate. They always give that call for the pack when they do."

For a moment the two stood listening. Again came that summons of the wolf king to his subjects. Then came faintly the beat of horses' hoofs. A rider stopped at the gate. It was Guy McDaniels. He greeted Shaw and Young as he came forward.

"Been to town to-day. Here's a bunch of mail for you, Jim. And here's a couple of letters for Young. And a telegram, too."

"Guess this means I go back to Denver pronto," said Young, as he took the telegram, ripped it open, and held it in the light from the open door. "Yes, that's what it is. Our Predatory Animal Coöperation Bill is coming up. I'll have to leave."

He flipped it over to Shaw.

"Hell!" exploded McDaniels, "I thought you were going to stay on the trail of Whitey until you got him."

"I'll be back," declared Young. "I've got to go to Denver now. I promised Tobin and Rees and some of the other men I'd come when they sent for me. This wire is from the secretary of the Colorado Stockgrower's Association. Tomorrow I'll take up all the traps but those in the blind sets and then beat it."

"Guess your job here will be waiting for you when you get back," said Jim Shaw gloomily.

Young, too, was reluctant to give up the hunt for the big white animal criminal even for a few days. Almost as though in defiance, Whitey had struck a killing streak since Young had started his campaign. Between February ninth and March twenty-eighth he had led the pack in killing nine long yearlings outright. A tenth had been literally eaten alive. The inside of the rump of this steer had been ripped out, great chunks of flesh torn from the living animal, until its viscera had sagged out through the rip in its abdomen. In agony the torn cow critter had staggered to the water hole near the MacDaniels ranch and there, driven by the maddening thirst of fever, had gulped water until it could hold no more. Hideous, torturing death that had crept through its poor torn body was cheated by a bullet from Young's rifle when he found this victim of Whitey's murderous band, still gasping and struggling at the water hole.

As the Survey man prepared to leave he promised himself that only unforeseen emergencies would prevent him from coming back to the Mesa to put a stop to Whitey's orgy of slaughter.

Justice to the other inhabitants of the range demanded Whitey's death!

III: THE WOLF KING

The peace and contentment which had been Whitey's was shattered. Some sinister thing had come to the Mesa. It had taken one of the pack. Instinct warned the wolf leader that an unsensed danger threatened all his followers and himself.

Before this had happened, everything had been as tranquil as is possible in the lives of killers that are hunted. Three-Toes, his mate, had whelped in a den at the head of an arroyo. For several years he had run with this she-wolf that had lost, in a trap, two toes from her left front foot. Their yearlings of the previous season were now in the pack, following Whitey's leadership. They were capable of hunting by themselves. Soon Whitey should leave them to train the whining cubs that tumbled in the smelly room at the end of the den tunnel. But now, with the unknown death threatening, he was needed at the head of this pack of yearlings.

Sunny days of late winter and first spring had passed in contentment until this trouble had loomed. A hated, foreign wolf scent had appeared on the Mesa. It had maddened Whitey, made him recklessly angry.

He charged along wolf runways, strutted around scent posts, scratched and pawed the ground, howled defiance, and then, circling, tried in vain to find this foreign wolf.

Then he had come to a scent, a trap set where a nester had stolen a bobcat from Government traps. Whitey knew the kill had not been made by predatory animals. It was man killing. From this time on he started following no trails, dodging familiar lines of travel, avoiding ranches.

During the day he would lounge on a little rocky cliff above the den in which rolled his puppies. Uneasily he would drop down and stick his nose into the den. He would be greeted by the gutteral "ge-e-er-whoof," of his mate, that told all was well in the den. Sensitive to his new wariness, the pack became hard to handle.

The old wolf was caught in a dilemma. On one hand he must lead his pack safely over dangerous trails, by snares, traps, pitfalls. Otherwise they might blunder into ambush. On the other hand, if he did not stay at the den lookout someone might find it, block its entrance, and then dig out the fuzzy whelps.

For several days indecision whisked through the wolf leader. Then one evening, leaving Three-Toes and the whelps safe in the den, he trotted across the valley of the Apishapa, up on the Mesa, and out on a promontory above the Shaw ranch. He lifted his head, threw back his ears, and from his throat sent forth the call to the pack.

Like ghosts the yearlings slipped out from sheltering piñon and sage. They trotted toward their leader, ran off for a few hundred feet, then came back nervously, scurrying. With a short, sharp, gruff bark Whitey mustered his following and started on a trail heading south.

By shadowy cliffs, through patches of piñon where dark shadows were piled up beneath the somber night, across sagebrush flats, he led his band. They reached a crossroad. Whitey turned off their old runway. The pack hesitated, milled, then strung out behind the leader. Southward they loped steadily away from the Mesa and their old familiar runways.

Morning found them down where the imaginary line between New Mexico and Colorado is obliterated in the vast expanse of cedar brakes, sagebrush and limestone-bordered arroyos.

Here the wolves scattered and slept. Noon had not come when Whitey aroused himself and started along a trail. He gave no notice of his going. His course continued southeastward. He reached a small dry creek. This he followed for several miles downstream, then turned sharply back on an angle, and disregarding trails, made his course a direct line for the Apishapa. He had laid his trail southward at first to throw the yearlings off the track. They would be confused by his actions; probably after several days of hunting him they would give it up. They would follow the leadership of some of their own number for a time at least, and he would be rid of the responsibility of leading them and also protecting the whelps and his mate. The pack would be safe so long as it stayed away from the Mesa. Now Three-Toes and Whitey could give undivided attention to teaching the whelps how to kill, how to avoid dangers.

Afternoon came. Whitey rested. Recollections of the soft baby wolves, of Three-Toes in the dark den came. Again he started along the trail in the easy trot of the traveling wolf.

After dusk he deserted the trail, made a quick raid on a ranch, killed a nesting hen turkey. He reached the south edge of the Mesa, threading his way up a cow trail in an arroyo. He reached the top of the table-land, deserted the trail, crossed a sagy flat, edged by a grove of piñon that seemed to spill over the side of an old rock limestone cliff. Here he was forced back into one of the old trails. Every moment there grew that desire to get back to the den and see if anything had befallen his family during his short absence.

He dropped down to an old woods road. His feet were tender from the long run. He sought trail that would not torture his tender foot pads. The old road led up to rising ground, over a saddle from where in the daytime he might see far across the valley of the Apishapa almost to where the den was hidden under the limey cliff.

Piling up in an appeal that would not be denied there came a yearning to be across that valley, to nose into the den, to hear the welcoming gruff growl of his mate, to sniff at his babies.

Caution was discarded. Yearning and anxiety mastered him. He whipped into a faster gait, a long, rangy, speedy lope. The soft brown woods road raced under him. Above, the white stars twinkled from the blue-black ceiling of the earth. A powerful mixture of joy and fear drove Whitey heedlessly forward. Ahead, enframed by the piñon, he could see the outline of the saddle. He stopped, sniffed, turned sharply, hesitated, whined. Some instinct seemed to reach out and stay his running journey.

Then the desire to be with Three-Toes and the babies mastered him. With a quick, sharp whine filled with anxiety, he raced forward, toward the den where Three-Toes and the puppies awaited his return.

First dawn lighted the eastern horizon when Three-Toes returned from a lonely, unsuccessful hunt. She sniffed at the mouth of the den, then tested the morning breeze with her nose. Inside of the den she was greeted by the whines of her whelps. Night had passed. Whitey had not come to the den.

A dread, a fear hitherto unknown to Three-Toes, flashed through her. Acceding to the demands of the whelps she huddled down in the den and surrendered her breasts to the babies. But even the mauling of the pups did not erase that instinctive fear that had leaped into her mind when she found that Whitey had not returned to the den.

IV: THE BLIND SET

Early April had driven greenery up into the floor of the plains, and sand lilies were spreading their tiny white stars when Young returned. It was April eleventh. A few days before the legislature had passed the Coöperative Predatory Animal Bill after a sharp clash over the comparative merits of the Survey with its salaried hunters and the old bounty system.

Guy McDaniels greeted the Survey man heartily. "We're glad you're back, Young," he declared. "Have you heard the news? Strang got old Whitey in a trap back of his ranch. I've paid my bounty on him—twenty-five bucks. Willingly, too. Strang sure was lucky."

"Yes, he wrote me about it," replied Young. "Said he had caught Whitey in one of his coyote traps. Did you see Whitey's carcass, Guy?"

"Sure did."

"Was it Whitey?"

"Not a question."

"I sure would like to have nabbed him myself," declared Young, a bit wistfully. "Wish I had been the man to stop his raiding."

"Pshaw now," consoled McDaniels. "Luck was with Strang."

"It must have been," declared Young. "If Strang caught the wolf in that small trap, luck was sure with him. I can hardly believe that a big he-wolf like Whitey would have stayed in any homesteader's coyote trap!"

"Well, he sure got him," affirmed Guy McDaniels.

"Yeh, I saw his skull and hide at Jonas Brothers," supplemented Young. "I guess it was Whitey, all right. Strang wanted me to buy his hide and skull, but as long as I didn't catch him myself, I don't know as I would want it. It would always remind me of the fact that the Survey had one whale of a try in catching this old fellow and then had a rank amateur come right in after our campaign and catch him in a dinky little trap."

Guy McDaniels was no ordinary cook. The first meal was a celebration of Young's return and the subduing of Whitey. Even the festivities did not blot out Young's wonderment at Strang, with his poor trap outfit and limited wolf lore, catching the canny old leader of the Bear Springs pack.

The spring sun was warm as three horsemen rode away from the McDaniels ranch next morning. They were Young, Jim Shaw, and Guy McDaniels. The whole range of the wolves was to be reconnoitered. The remainder of the pack must be obliterated. That would not be hard, now that the old leader was dead.

Through the breaks, by the little limy cliffs where cedars clung with their roots dug deep for moisture, where the wind flowers lifted their pale lavender bells, where green grasses showed lush and inviting under protecting shelter, they rode. It was a happy day. Winds seemed to spring out of little cañons, rush by with boisterous shouts. Then in an instant stop in dead silence. These mischievous gusts were like the romping rush of a child who hides behind a door, dashes forth, cries "boo," and then immediately becomes quiet and serious. Nature was alive, fresh, inviting. The three men rode in easy, partial silence, occasionally joking, now and then pointing out some sign bearing on the quest. They were a part of the day and the place.

Noon with its cold lunch, the resting horses, the warming, caressing sun came and passed. They tightened cinches and again started along the rough road, seeking the tell-tale prints of wolf feet. The horses, knowing that midday had passed, began nosing around toward their home corral.

"Say, would you fellows ride over to that little park on the next ridge?" asked Young. "I left some blind sets there, and I'd like to check up on them so long as we are this close."

"Sure," agreed both cowmen.

They rode in single file, then double, then single file again, Young leading. They were not fifty yards from the trap set when Young reined in his horse abruptly, excitedly.

"Say, something's happened," he almost shouted. "Look."

The ground had been ripped up, was torn and scarred. In the span of a moment they were all three scrambling off their horses.

"Where are your traps?" asked Shaw.

"There where you see that depression. But they're gone."

"They sure are—sure are."

All three were scanning the ground. Each was an experienced trailer. The action of days before began to unfold as their eyes quickly caught the significance of the scarred ground.

"Here's the mark of a drag hook plain as day," cried Young, starting off in the direction of the tiny furrow which had been gouged by the trailing hundred and eighty degree half circle hook.

Almost at a trot the three began following the mark. They reached a thicket of piñon.

"For the love of Mike, look at that," cried McDaniels, pointing to the tufts of hair that were strewn on the ground.

"White," shouted Young. "White as sure as shooting. The old fellow was caught here, not near Strang's!"

"Sure it's Whitey?"

"Look at that track. I'll bet on it—bet my last dollar," cried Shaw excitedly. "No other wolf in this section has a paw like that old cuss has."

"That hair is enough for me. Old fellow shedding. He dragged the trap and chain here, got hung up and thrashed around something awful."

"Then Strang didn't catch him?"

"You damn betcha he didn't," declared Young. "And we'll prove it pronto. We're going to interview this Strang and his buddy Calcott, who caught a hundred-pound wolf in a No. 3 coyote trap!"

"The skunk, the dirty thief," cried McDaniels. The thought of the reward he had paid the homesteader flashed into his mind.

"Let's go," suggested Young. "Jim Shaw is a marshal. We're armed. There may be big trouble, but if there is all I ask of you, Jim, is that you let us be your deputies. I'm just fed up on this sneak-thievin' on the trap line. Here is where one hungry homesteader finds that it's bad medicine to fool with Government property."

They hurried to their horses. Shaw mounted. Young was ready to lift his foot to the stirrup. Then McDaniels pointed to some fresh digging fifteen feet eastward of some old trap set.

"What do you suppose that is?" he asked, pointing.

Young hurried with him to the place where the ground was disturbed. They poked a stick in the dust and loose earth. With a quick, vicious snap there leaped out of the ground the powerful steel jaws of a wolf trap.

"I thought so," growled the Survey man. "Pretty crude, pretty damned crude. He's brought these back here and reset them, I'd think nothing happened. 'Fraid to keep Government traps in his possession. This stunt comes mighty near insulting my intelligence."

He yanked out the four big wolf traps, chained in double tandem and equipped with a half circle drag hook, sprung each and slung them over his saddle.

"Let's get moving," he said. "I think there's a man named Strang headed for Leavenworth. He don't know it yet. I'll tell him the news. We've got the goods on one of those bounty thieves and I'm going to put on the screws so every bounty hound in the state will know about it. That letter he wrote will convict him if nothing else will."

Plain as a wide road to practiced eye was the trail of Whitey. Scattered fur from the shedding hair was everywhere. The hook had caught, released, caught again and gouged into the earth. At times the riders traveled at a slow trot, at others they walked their horses. Through thickets, down little cliffs, on through the brush Whitey had fought with two traps on his feet. The track led to a tangle of cedar and piñon where there had been a terrific struggle. Here it stopped. For a moment all three looked at the trail sign without speaking. They turned and started down the trail. Young glanced at Guy McDaniels. A dark scowl was spread over the face of the cowman. Young looked at Jim Shaw. Grim lines had settled about the old man's mouth. He was looking neither to the right nor left, but peering ahead with squinted eyes. Anything might happen when they reached Strang!

"Confound that whelp," broke out Guy McDaniels. "Do we have to wait for law to take its course? If we do he may squeal out of it."

"He'll have a hard time doing that," declared Young.

"By gosh, this law can do what it wants to," said McDaniels. "I know what I'm going to do!"

"I know what I'd like to do," said Jim Shaw sharply, turning to gaze at McDaniels. "Maybe it ain't according to Hoyle, but it's awful darned effective."

"Now look here," argued Young. "We've got a fur thief with all the stuff necessary to send him over the road. Don't go and spoil it by takin' it out on his measly hide."

"Oh, the law can have its hand," declared McDaniels, "but I've got a personal grudge against this hombre for taking that reward money away from me. If there's anything left when I get through, you can have it!"

For a moment they rode in silence. Then Young reined in his horse. "Now listen, boys," he said. "This is really my party after all. You stand by and see what comes up. If anything pops loose, you can use your own judgment, but let me have a try in handling it my way first."

Guy McDaniels continued to scowl. Jim Shaw looked away across the landscape. Young knew that there never had been the most cordial feeling between these ranchers and the dryland homesteaders. Nesters had taken up their range in homesteads that were not capable of supporting a home, had broken through fences and run stock on Shaw's and McDaniels' pastures and had otherwise helped to build unneighborly feeling.

"I don't know whether or not I'll agree to that," said Guy McDaniels slowly. "It all depends on how Strang acts. I'll give you first crack at him, Young, if that's all you want. But if anything breaks, then I'm goin' to get action."

"Is that agreeable, Jim?" asked Young, turning to Shaw.

"Yes, I reckon," replied the old cattleman. "But I'm hot under the collar and don't you fergit it! But I'll give you first say."

"All right, Strang's ranch the next stop," directed Young. "And Jim, remember, if there's any trouble, Guy and I are deputies. There may be a real hot time. I'm going to knock a full confession out of this fellow if I have to wring his neck. If he gets nasty there may be some real hell a-poppin'."

"You know there will!" said Guy McDaniels feelingly.

"Let's hurry up," said Jim Shaw, the lines on his usually happy face deepening.

Strang's ranch was like many that have sprung up like short-lived weeds in the dry country section of the West. They usually stand for several years and then are deserted after the homesteader realizes that there is no more real homestead land in the West. Finally they go to pieces. Mud house with dirt roof, a half-wrecked barn, a few rickety old corrals and some scrawny livestock often represent the zenith of wealth for a drylander. Like any human, when poverty driven, they will become lawbreakers for another sack of flour.

A businesslike trot brought the three grim riders to the ranch yard. Strang himself was coming from the corral carrying an ax and a pail.

"Guilty. Guilty as hell," breathed Jim Shaw, as Strang seemed to hang his head and avoid their gaze.

Guy McDaniels leaped from his horse and started to stride forward scowling. Young sprang to his side.

"Easy, boys, remember I get first chance. He's my meat. It's the Federal law that can hang it on him hardest. If there's a scrap you tie in, but I've got first right to talk to him."

Young stepped forward to meet the ragged, disreputable homesteader.

"Strang, I want to talk to you about your catching Whitey in a No. 3 coyote trap."

The nester shifted uneasily, his eyes whipped from side to side, then came back to rest on the toes of Young's boots. He set down the pail and shifted the ax to his right hand.

Young caught the wary glance Strang gave that ax.

"Well, what of it?" he growled.

"We just run on to something that looks might funny."

Calcott, another man of the stamp of Strang, came gangling out of the cabin. He sauntered uneasily up to Guy McDaniels.

"Come over here to one side," he said. "I've got something to tell you."

McDaniels dropped the' reins of his horse and followed Calcott toward the pile of bleached cedar and piñon, where a sawbuck and bucksaw were weathering in sun and rain.

Jim Shaw hitched at his belt, loosened his big six-shooter. His old blue eyes were squinting, glinting. He leaned lightly against his horse, watching the two pairs of men, ready for the first possible break.

"Strang, you stole that wolf out of a Government trap." Young snapped the accusation at the nester.

Strang jerked a little about his arms; his eyes shifted rapidly. The fingers of his left hand closed and unclosed.

"You can't prove it," he snarled. "You can't prove that, damn you!"

"I can. I've got the men right here to do it, too. We found the old trap set, where Whitey thrashed through the woods, and where he hung up beyond the ridges back of your ranch. Jim Shaw and Guy Daniels will swear to what they've seen to-day. If you think that the testimony of three men against you can't prove you're a bounty thief, then you go to it. See if you can squirm out."

"That all the evidence you've got? What'll the court think if I tell that McDaniels and Shaw have been trying to pry me out of this homestead and get the range, and that this is a frame up? You know very well the Colorado courts favor a homesteader."

"You're not up against any State court; you've tampered with Federal property. You'll face a Federal court. I mean to see that you land in Leavenworth just to show other trap thieves that they can't get away with this rough stuff they've been pulling."

"Leavenworth! Not the Federal prison?"

"You know it; the Federal prison and about ten or twelve months and five thousand dollars maximum fine. How do you like that, you trap thief!"

"I'll not go."

"How can you help it?"

"I'll not, I tell you," stubbornly protested Strang. "You'll have a hell of a time sending me there."

Jim Shaw moved easily away from his horse. His hand hung loosely from his belt, hooked there by his crooked thumb.

"Will you go peaceably," demanded Young, "or will we have to arrest you?"

"Arrest. Who in hell has the authority to arrest me, and what for? I'll have to see a warrant first!"

"Jim, come over here," requested Young. "I want this fellow pulled for stealing Government property. I'll swear out the information and the Government will handle the case and him."

"Strang, you seem to have gotten into a mess," remarked Jim Shaw, as he came sauntering toward Young and the nester. "I guess I'll have to take you in."

The nester turned fiercely on his neighbor. His eyes glistened with mingled fright and hate. At the moment, like a cornered animal, he seemed about to fight.

Shaw's hand strayed carelessly to the butt of the old revolver.

"Better come peaceable, Strang. You'll make it worse if you scrap."

"I'll not go! You can't take me! You've got nothing on me! It's a frame up! I tell you, I'll not go!"

In front of the vision of the homesteader there had loomed the horror of the gray walls of the Federal prison. Slowly, ever so slowly, Strang's body tensed. His muscles tightened, his hands gripped convulsively at the ax handle. The ax started to move stealthily.

Jim Shaw's gnarled hand closed with finality on the old gun!

A door slammed. A child squalled petulantly. A woman's voice, tired, querulous, called from the open cabin door.

"Nate, oh, Nate, bring me some wood, can't you?"

Strang glanced toward the little cabin. A child in a soiled dress came trotting out of the door, bareheaded, unkempt, a little gangling and undernourished.

"Mamma wants wood, Pop," piped the little voice.

Strang reached down his dirty, unlovely hands and patted the little girl's head with rough caress.

"Got to help the old woman," he mumbled, turning abruptly from Shaw and Young.

For a moment the two men stood looking after the shambling figure of the homesteader and the sad-looking child.

"How many kids?" asked Young.

"Three. One's near a babe."

"All scrawny?"

"Nigh half starved, most of the time, I guess," replied Shaw.

There was a catch in the old man's voice. A long pause.

"What are you going to do, Young? It seems sort of—"

Jim Shaw's voice trailed.

"Don't know now what to do."

Guy McDaniels came striding up with Calcott, the latter slouching along shame-facedly, his hands seeking his frayed overall pockets, his face plainly stamped with sheepish embarrassment.

"Calcott owned up," said McDaniels, "and returned his half of the reward I paid."

"I told Strang he was doin' wrong," protested Calcott. "I knew sure that we'd have trouble over this because it was monkeyin' with the Gov'ment."

From the house there came the high-pitched voice of a woman, scolding, whining, nagging. Strang's snapping, snarling reply was lost in the renewed squalling of the baby.

"What do you want to do about Strang?" asked Young of McDaniels.

Silence dropped on the group. Calcott shifted uneasily.

The cabin door opened, slammed shut as Strang came slowly back to the group near the corral.

"I've owned up, Nate," said Calcott. "No use to buck the Gov'ment."

"No, I guess not," murmured Strang. "My woman has been sayin' the same. I was drove to it. I'm ready to go along with you, Shaw, or whatever you say to clear up this mess. Though God knows what'll happen to the kids if I land in Leavenworth."

His voice caught in spite of the brave show he tried to make.

"I'll tell you what I'll do," snapped Young. "You pay back McDaniels' money. Then you go into the house and write Dr. Nelson of the Survey a letter telling all about your taking Whitey out of that trap, with Calcott helping you muzzle him. Then you write a letter to Jonas Brothers in Denver and tell them to turn the hide and skull over to me pronto. If you'll do that, I'll not press the matter."

"I've had enough of this sort of thing around here," flared McDaniels. "I don't agree with you, Young. We've got the goods on these two. Let's show these thieves around Bear Springs Mesa just how unhealthy it is to keep up this stealing!"

"No. No, it's not Strang nor Calcott that have changed my mind, Guy. It's those kids and that woman in there. They have had enough grief without our piling it on. It's for their sake that I'll not make charges against Strang."

"Well, maybe that's right," agreed McDaniels slowly. "The kids would suffer."

"How about it, Strang?" asked Young.

"I'll do what you say," grumbled the nester.

"All right, come into the house and write those letters right now.

"But just let me warn you, both of you, right here; I'm going to stay here and clear out the rest of that pack of wolves and if I find any of you two-legged coyotes sneakin' around any of my trap sets, I'll shoot you through to the Federal prison so fast it will make your head dizzy, kids or no kids. Savvy? And tell that to your buddies. It ain't healthy to fool with Survey traps nor animals caught in them. Get me?"

Rags, the Digger

Jo Neal, weather-tanned, dressed in well-fitting business suit, but unmistakably a Colorado cattleman, drew out from the wall the chair offered him by Stanley Young, until he could tilt back comfortably. He proffered a cigar to the Government man, bit the end off of its mate, licked it, and then lighted it. The same match started the glow on the cigar Young smoked. Aroma of good tobacco filled the high-ceilinged office of the Biological Survey.

For a few moments the two talked of Neal's trip to Denver, stock markets, mutual friends. Then Neal, puffing out a great plume of bluish smoke, broached the principal reason for his call at the Survey office.

"When can Caywood get on the trail of that wolf, Rags," he asked.

"Don't know," replied Young. "He's still in the hospital."

"Heard he was. How did Bill hurt himself?"

"He was packin' in to Lord's ranch last fall, early. Planning on a campaign against the coyotes there. Pack horse started to crash by Bill in a break to get out to a pasture. Bill's horse whirled like any good cow pony, trying to head off the pack horse, slipped in the mud, fell, and broke Bill's leg just above the ankle. It's taking a long time to heal. He's more than fifty, you know, and bones don't knit so rapidly after a fellow is about so old. But Caywood's up on crutches now and probably will be able to do something this spring."

"Not before that?" asked Neal.

"'Fraid not."

"That's tough. I had hoped he could go in to the Cathedral Bluff section right away. I've boasted that whenever we've asked for help from this office, within forty-eight hours there would be a Survey hunter on the trail of any killer wolf. Guess this is the exception that makes the rule."

"I can send in one of the other boys. Start him right off. I can send in Hegewa, the fellow that's just cleaned up on Old Lefty of Burns Hole."

"No use. Caywood's the man. He knows more about wolves than they know about themselves. He thinks like a wolf, only more so. Don't think that there is any use sending in any fellow except Bill."

"Well, Hegewa did a pretty good job on the Burns Hole pack. See, here is Lefty's skull, and there is his hide in the rough."

Young reached over on his desk, took the machine of bone which had housed that crafty brain of Lefty the killer and laid it on the desk before Neal. The great dry hide of Lefty he laid on the floor.

"Whopper," remarked Neal. "Caywood's the only fellow to catch that Rags wolf, though. It isn't hearsay that I base that on, either. I've known Bill for years. Rags, too, for that matter. Remember that big white wolf hide that is in the home ranch house? Well, that fellow Bill took when we were paying bounties out of the funds of the stock associations. Caught him right in sight of my ranch.

"Suppose you know that Caywood made a living for himself and family out of bounties stockmen paid him. He knows wolves from hell to breakfast, backwards and forwards. But you know that."

"Yes. That's why we got him in the Survey. I'll write Bill to come in there just as soon as he is able, but I don't want him to get on his feet before he should. He's too good a man to cripple."

"Well, put him in there as soon as you can. If we don't get this killer, Rags, he'll get us."

Welcoming April sun heated Bill Caywood's back as he rode along the Piceance Creek trail. The pack horse ambled ahead, stopping to swing his nose down to nip a tuft of grass that had sprouted temptingly in some sunny, protected nook. It was good country, a great day even for Colorado, and ahead there was a game—a real man's game—the capture of Rags, murderer wolf, dead or alive.

Bill Caywood grinned a little, whistled without making much sound, decided to let the horses peg along without whistling, hauled out a plug of tobacco and sunk his ragged teeth into the sweet-bitter block of well-cured leaves.

Caywood on the horse did not give a sense of his bigness. For the horse was large, and being in scale with the man, the proportions of the man seemed ordinary.

Big-shouldered, slightly stooped, not quite bow-legged but evidently a rider of cowland trails, Caywood represents the type of frontiersman that put much of the work into the winning of the western wildernesses. Dogged in a hunt, untiring in upbuilding of communities, quiet, high-powered, these men have been the bulwark of western progress.

Caywood's face was smooth-shaven, or had been a couple of days previous. His grayish locks curled slightly at the ends peeping out from under his weather-buffeted Stetson. Sun had caressed his cheek or seared it with rays that had turned his skin to the tone of brown old leather. Weeks in the hospital had brought the pallor of indoors to lighten this outdoor tan. Winter frost had bitten and nipped at his cheek and brow, while whimsical laugh wrinkles had vied with weather in lacing his face with the unnumbered furrows which come to the visage of men who ride the open trails.

He was back at work. Caywood was glad. He was not able to hike. But there was the big, powerful bay that rolled along the trail so easily underneath him. The pack horse ahead had more sense than some cow waddies, and most dudes, making the third member of a party which could go out into any country and make a go of it. Besides the satisfaction of getting back in the work there was need of it. Hospital bills and living costs mean money out whether one wants them to or not.

The pitch of the trail, the rattle of the rocks beneath the horses' feet, the new apple green of budding oak leaves, the soft, clean, cool green of the aspen and the purple-gray softness of the aspen catkins all cried out for notice. The sun threw shadows under the shady side of the piñons, heated their needles, steeped out their resinous spice until the air was fragrant with the freshness and tanginess of the clean-air country of Colorado.

Magpies flopped away from the trail, cawing. Chipmunks went bouncing away, galloping as though the chipmunk devil was in hot pursuit. Near a safe cranny where they could dive out of harm's way, they would sit and chatter at

Caywood as the cavalcade followed the trail. A piñon jay screeched from a tree, darted like a blue bolt out from the shadow, bored his way through the air to the next piñon, was lost in the swaying branches of the pine. A cottontail caught in the act of sampling a bit of green spring salad composed of fresh bunch grass leaped away, dived through the aisles of the scrub oak, stopped beside a stone, froze to immobility except for his twitching nose, then when Caywood came too close, again scurried through the rustling carpet of last year's oak leaves until the white bobbing flag of his cottony tail was lost to view beyond the red stems of a wild rose thicket.

The sun sloped down. Shadows came to spread out over the eastern sides of the hills. Camping time was not far ahead. In a bend of Piceance Creek he stopped. The pack horse had preceded him, had in fact almost instinctively picked the place his master would camp, and was now eating grass in the little meadow which lay between the creek and the limestone cliffs.

"There, boy," said Bill as he slapped the horse "wrangling" off the pack. "Go on and fill your belly with real range grass. Feels good, don't it? this gettin' out on the trail again."

The horse tossed his head, walked lazily a few steps, munched grass, the chomping of his grinders audible above the little wind whispers in the aspens, then lay down in a dusty patch of old gopher diggings and rolled, grunting luxuriously in the pleasure of stretching work-tired muscles.

Camp soon arose out of the pack. A six by eight light canvas pyramidal tent was slung between two poles and pegged down, around the floor. Blackened cooking utensils were strung out around a fireplace made of two flat stones, the long way of the fire pot being parallel to the direction of the cañon so it would catch the up and down cañon winds. Water from Piceance Creek was soon simmering over the fire, coffee was added, and a couple of hunks of ham sputtered in the skillet. Supper over, the last of the camp fire glowing between the stones, night wind beginning to sigh in the aspen thicket, Bill Caywood threw down his bedroll on the canvas floor of his tent and crawled in between the blankets for a peaceful night of rest.

A coyote howled over the ridge, chattered, was joined by others, yapped again, quieted. Wind surged by or a light breeze stopped to rest among the aspens and then hurried on down cañon. The transparent blackness of clear mountain night filtered through the cloth of the tent.

Freedom of the trail was ahead of Caywood. He was glad, at peace. Cities cramped, were constricted with walls. The confines of the hospital room had irked the hunter more than the itching pain in his leg. But here was God's big open country with clean air, clear waters, nights packed full of well-earned, healthful rest, and a game ahead—a game desperate, unrelenting, gripping.

For Old Rags of Cathedral Bluffs had been sentenced to die, and Bill Caywood was the executioner. He would "get his wolf."

II: NO SIGN

April showers spit on the trail of sun-warmed earth, plants and animals as Caywood in the days following rode the trails looking, always looking, for the track of the big he-wolf.

"You're up against a devil, Caywood," Bob Coats, stockman, had declared when Caywood had first stopped at his ranch soon after the camp had been established on Piceance Creek. "Rags is a spooky old cuss. One time he's here. Then he ain't. Maybe show up twice in one week, then not again in a month."

"I haven't seen his track," replied the hunter. "Only coyotes so far."

"There are wolves here, though. The worst is Rags," declared Coats pessimistically. "I know something about those hombres, Bill. I've tried every set I know on Rags. I've give up. I've caught over forty-five wolves in this section since I came here years ago. I know a common wolf as well as I know you. But Rags is spooky, just too clever. He travels alone sometimes; sometimes with two other wolves. I've heard of him as far west as Willow Creek over in Utah. That's around a hundred and fifty mile away. He ranges a stretch about fifty mile wide and nigh a couple hundred long. Somewhere in that stretch is Rags. It's up to you, Bill."

Caywood spat a long string of brown juice at a beetle that was trying to climb over a chip in front of the ranch house porch and looked up to the greening hills speculatively. Then he said, "Guess I'll go up toward the Roan Cliffs to-morrow. Want to go along?"

Caywood and Coats rode the trail the next morning, keen-eyed, alert, looking for that telltale track which would advertise the fact that the killer was again on the range. The Roan Cliffs lifted their colorful, ragged sides to the southward, and far in the distance eastward there stood the blocky headlands of the White River Plateau. They rode silently most of the way.

"Looks like a good stock year so far as feed is concerned," observed Caywood.

"Market is not so good yet," replied Coats. "Cattle sure to come back, though, if we can weather through this depression."

More sounds of the trail. Wind in the oaks, rustled through leaves of aspen, swished down in a swoop over the ground and made the new grass growth shiver in the gust. Rocks in the trail rattled under the horses' feet. One of the horses sneezed gustily.

"Funny you ain't picked up track of Rags," remarked Coats a little later. "Can't miss it. It's different than any other wolf."

"How?" asked Caywood.

"Back feet bigger than his front feet."

Caywood whistled a little under his breath.

Wolves universally have larger front feet than rear feet. A track made by a wolf with feet larger behind would be easily recognized.

"That seems the way with all renegades," served Caywood. "They're usually crippled some way, and then go bad."

"Don't think that Rags has been nipped that way. His hind feet are just naturally larger. Then there's that ragged look of his coat. He's an individual, all right. Just a wise old lone lobo that is head and shoulders above the rest when it comes to thinkin'."

Noon came. They stopped by a clear little stream. Bacon sandwiches, some cheese, cold biscuit—frugal lunch, but plenty for outdoors men—was eaten. Caywood, for dessert, bit off a gigantic chew of plug tobacco, passing the brown square to Coats. For a moment they lolled on the hot ground comfortably stretching their muscles. The horses fed near by. Sagy tang mixed with spicy pine scent was in the air.

"I've often wondered, Bill, why you stay with this game as you do," remarked Coats. "Ever since I can remember you've been around here wagin' war on the wolves. What you goin' to do when they are all gone?"

"Don't know," replied the Government hunter. "Guess I'll dry up and blow away like a tumble weed. I couldn't no more go into town and live, settle down in some store or something like that than I could fly on horseback. Guess it's in my blood, this outdoors. My daddy and mother started me out on this career. They came across the plains in an ox-drawn prairie schooner when I was only three years old. I've lived in the outdoors, near the ragged edge of what we call civilization, ever since. It's meat and drink to me. No chance for me reformin' and settlin' down so long as I can navigate on horseback."

Silence between the men for a moment. Coats whittled a sliver from a bit of pine and picked his teeth more from habit than from the need of the operation.

"Where you goin' to hit for next, Bill?" he asked. "You've covered this range pretty well without seein' Rags."

"I'm waitin'," replied the wolfer. "Rags'll show up. This is his range. You know enough about wolves to know they keep travelin' the same old lines for all their lives. Only somethin' upsettin' as all git out will turn them from their paths. You've even killed Rags' mate a couple of times yourself and he's never left the range. Just comes back, driftin' through, killin', gorgin' himself, sleepin' off his blood jag and then out for more killin'. So I'll wait for him."

"Do you get a kick out of capturing a wolf anymore?"

"Oh, yes—and no," replied Caywood thoughtfully. "I've just got a lot of love and respect for the gray wolf. He's a real fellow, the big gray is. Lots of brains. I feel sorry for him. It's his way of livin'. He don't know better. And I feel sorry every time I see one of those big fellows thrashin' around in a trap bellowin' bloody murder."

Again a pause.

"Guess I'm too much a part of this outdoors to hold any grudge against animals," continued Caywood. "It's part the way that wolves go after poor defenseless steers, murder does and fawns and drag down bucks that helps me go out and bring them in."

"Well, you've never been on the trail of a worse killer than this Rags," observed Coats. "He's a murderer—straight out animal murderer. I believe he'd tackle a man if he got the chance, I really do."

"He might," replied Caywood. "Usually, though, they get licked when you come up to them in traps. They give up. Rags is probably no different than all the others that way."

Coats shook his head as he got to his feet and stretched preparatory to going after his horse. "Rags is no common wolf. I've had the chance to watch his work, tried to catch him, for fourteen years. I know enough about that hombre to make me respect him powerful. I'm not sayin' what he would do if he got a man cornered. But I'd rather have it the other man than myself if he ever did decide to eat human meat!"

The day was as sterile of results as those that had preceded it. The sun shone, the trees nodded gayly in the winds, grasshoppers were beginning to buzz in the hot dusty stretches of trails, penstemons were lifting lavender or blood-red flowers on sunny slopes, but nowhere had they seen wolf sign.

Three days later Bill Caywood sauntered into the office of Jo Neal in Meeker.

"Hello, Bill!" greeted the cowman as the bronzed hunter poked his head inside the door. "Come in, you old scoundrel. Come in here."

Caywood's deep-set pale blue eyes twinkled under their shaggy brows. His mouth whipped into a grin, his usually thin, set lips wrinkling back good-humoredly from his tobacco-stained teeth. Limping slightly, he entered, stuck out his hand, met the friendly, firm grip of Neal.

"Got Rags?" shot Neal the moment they had seated themselves.

Caywood shook his head. His face became a little stern. He cocked the worn old hat back on his head and reached for the inevitable plug of chewing.

"Here," offered Neal. "Smoke for once." The fat, mellow cigar changed hands and soon was fogging the room with its mate, which was in the hands of Neal.

"What's the matter, Bill?" chided the cowman. "Thought you were such a hell-buster of a wolfer? Can't you land one wolf in three weeks?"

"You know damned well, Jo, that I can. But I ain't even seen hide nor hair of that Rags since I came in here."

"Why, I supposed you'd have him all hung up to dry this time, Bill. Even offered to bet one of them the other day that you would have Rags by the tenth."

"Don't bet," laconically suggested Caywood. "Save your money."

"Rags not gettin' your goat, is he, Bill?" Neal was having a great time jabbing his friend on the thing he prided himself on most—the ability to outguess the best wolf on four feet.

Bill shot a short glance at Neal, squinted, puffed the cigar a couple of times in rapid order, blew out a great cloud of smoke.

"Nope. Ain't got my goat, Jo. Just have to let the old cuss take his time showin' up, that's all. He's been over Utah way, from all I can gather, and it's about time for him to come back. When he comes back I'll be on the job."

Neal was sober in a moment.

"That's what you're in here for, Bill. To get that old brute. He's gettin' the nerve of some of our best ranchers here. Twenty-five head of steers to one wolf in one season is just too much for one man to stand. And that is what Bob Coats lost to him last year."

"Yeh, Bob told me."

"That and the low market is gettin' some stockmen disheartened. Can't let Rags go through another season."

"He won't," replied Bill tersely.

"Well, I know that," replied Neal assuringly. "But whatever you do, Bill, don't let that old devil catch you on foot without a gun. With your leg crippled he'd make mincemeat of you in forty seconds."

"Don't think he'd attack a man in the first place. And in the second, if he does I'll see that he never gets within striking distance. I've seen too many slaughtered steers and cows slashed to shreds by wolf teeth to ever let a real killer get one crack at me. I did have one wolf tackle me one time. He was in a trap and he hit a glancing blow. But he went through two layers of overalls and heavy underwear, deep enough to bring blood. I don't want no more of that."

"Anything I can do for you, Bill?" asked Neal.

"Nope, guess not. Just came in to chew the fat a little. Waitin' for the stage to take me back to Rio Blanco. Thought I'd better drop in and see you."

"Glad you did; come again when you're in town."

III: THE LONE WOLF OF CATHEDRAL BLUFFS

All life was a fight. Every bit of innocent stretch of trail might hold a trap. Each new scent on the range might mean new terror, new danger. Coyotes dropped off, never to appear on the range again. They got caught in traps set under leaves, howled, snarled, and then disappeared.

All life on the range was a battle.

Yet Rags of Cathedral Bluffs was not afraid. He faced his wild life without any fear. There had been a time when each new scent, each unusual thing on his range had driven a shiver of fear through him. Once his heart had known softness, love hunger. But man had killed that. One mate had died in a trap. Another had died in the den defending her whelps. The whelps had been killed too, and the stockmen had paid bounty on them.

Rags once had led a pack that leaped joyously toward the slaughter of bellowing calf or snorting buck deer. But now he ranged alone; or he traveled alone except for those two sneaking wolves that he permitted to follow his trail.

One of these was a smaller male wolf. Rags had whipped him terribly when they had first met on the range above Yellow Creek; had slashed, torn, gouged, scratched until the little dog wolf had cried for mercy and had then come back wagging his tail in submission.

The other wolf was just a hanger on. She mated with this smaller dog wolf that looked upon Rags as his master. Rags would have nothing to do with her except that she was useful sometimes when there was a kill to be made. Often he permitted them to gorge themselves on his fresh kills.

Sometimes they ran three in a pack—a pitifully small pack. And then Rags' instinct to travel alone would blaze up and he would drive the two away. In solitude, feared and hated by everything feathered and furred that lived on the range, Rags, the lone wolf, would pad-pad along beside the trail, alert, watchful, following his creed that it was kill or be killed. He always struck first, without waiting for adversary to attack. It was his religion.

Sheep were coming in from Utah. They streamed along the sheep driveway, blatting, senseless in their continual baaing. But they made good eating. Rags, his coat more shaggy than ever because he was at the end of the spring shedding, became a specter haunting the moving clouds of sheep.

But high country season was coming. It was the part of the year when there was fresh grass, fresh water, on the high range near the White River, on the ridges near Thirteen Mile and Fourteen Mile creeks, back of the Roan Cliffs. Cattle would be out on the range. Nice tender beeves that bawled horribly when the lone wolf struck, slashing tendon, slitting throat. Beef blood, fresh, warm, heady, was tempting to the killer, and his tracks turned back toward Cathedral country.

"Rags is back." The word spread after the first night he appeared on the range. Five head of new stock had been thrown and slaughtered by a lone wolf in a pasture below the Coats ranch. No other wolf would make such a kill in that section without the aid of a pack.

Something different, some new condition was on the range. Rags sensed it as soon as he returned. There was a new wolf scent. Rags bristled at that. But there was also new man scent. And wary, Rags trod beside the trail, not in the regular wild life runways.

He killed again. Gorged. Then slept off the blood drunk under a clump of oak just above a springy hillside. Afternoon sun was setting when he awakened. A noise in the trail below snapped his senses to full alertness.

A man in a weathered hat, in leather coat that was scuffed and torn by riding through brush where there were no trails, was riding a powerful dark bay horse along the forest path. Rags could see the wrinkles of the man's face; the set straight mouth, the high cheek bones, even the little dark of tobacco juice in the corner of Bill Caywood's mouth.

Never before had the wolf experienced the feeling that rushed through his soul as he stood watching the man. Something tugged him toward that man. He growled a little under his breath, trotted a way out of sight, came back to the shelter of a rock, watched Caywood pass again.

Rags sniffed the air. That scent of man, mixed with horse scent, made him uneasy. He wanted to howl; stifled the impulse; started to lope away over a ridge which hid him from the rider. Then he came back to follow through evening dusk the bronzed rider on the dark bay.

New thoughts raced through the mind of Rags, killer. He was getting old. The hardened heart that he had carried for years had suddenly shown a rift in its adamant surface. Rags, lonely, heartsick of the killing, wanted peace, just comfortable old age peace. Seventeen years he had ranged the country around Cathedral. He knew its every twig, every lane, every rock, every spring. All he wanted now was comfort, friendliness, no more hiding, slinking, mad killing. Suddenly he was sick of it. He yearned hungrily for some kindred spirit; longed for companionship until it made something inside hurt.

Somehow the man on horseback, quiet, alert, had touched a chord in the heart of the lonely old wolf that had not been reached even when his last litter of cubs had rolled in the smelly den on Piceance Creek. So Rags followed until evening light went out and the man reached his camp, where a bright little fire sprung up, lighting the pyramid of the little tent.

Then Rags turned and hurried away. Each step he became more impatient. Finally he stretched out in a long lope. New revulsion, new hate had come surging in resistless flood to blot out that one feeble current of friend hunger he had felt.

His hair raised on his back. His muscles rippled under his shaggy hide. Wrath at his momentary weakness came whipping through him. His mouth drooled.

He picked up a cow scent. He followed the trail. It led into the very edge of a ranch. A yearling heifer sprang bawling away from the gray form that raced toward her. Rags, almost blind with anger, in complete reversal of his mood of an hour before, struck, missed in his furious dive.

A door opened. A shotgun barked. Futile shots rattled in the weeds back of Rags. He sped away through the night, off the trail, out of the road. For in trails and roads that were abandoned there had always been traps—man-set traps. Now Rags felt big hate for all men. That quiet man on the horse he recognized as an enemy. One first look at the hunter only had started that fleeting weakness, that letting down of the stern will of the lone wolf. But now his wolf heart beat with the throb of killer hate.

Away through the night, new scent, a steer bawling in agonized futile attempts at escape, blood drunk again, and morning found Rags lolling in the sun below a bunch of oak, licking blood from the shaggy coat on his breast. The day wore on. Below the magpies quarreled over the gruesome thing that Rags had slaughtered.

Evening came. Rags trotted logily along a ridge. The scent of that quiet rider came. His hair bristled. No more of that feeling of friendliness. Hate of the man whipped through him. Rags growled, minced away from a place in the trail where he instinctively knew a trap was set. He stopped, walked back cautiously, sniffed.

Deliberately Rags reached out with his forefoot. Carefully he worked away the first few leaves. Then came loose earth. The edge of the trap appeared. He scratched further, the trap sagged a little. The steel scent made Rags' hair bristle. He growled a little.

Earth flew as he scratched away from the trap set, throwing back the earth he had dug out from around the trap. Then he attacked it from the other side. Every scratch of his paw raked out more earth, more leaves. The trap came into full view. Rags sniffed at it, bristled again. With a final flip the trap came to the surface, stood out in plain sight. On it was the faintest taint of the man who rode.

Again there came something into the thoughts of Rags that was new. The first picture of that man, who was so much a part of the outdoors, came flooding back to his wolf mind. There was something that drew him to that figure. And then again there whipped back the wolf hate of man.

Emotions churning, Rags started away from the trap, stopped, growled, then lifted his head and bellowed forth a great, full-lunged wolf howl that rang back and forth from rock faces in the little cañon below.

With determined movements the big dog wolf started along the ridge. This thing could not keep up. He would not stay here where indecision whipped through him so. Loping, like a shadow of the night, Rags followed ridge and hollow westward. By morning he was far back toward Willow Creek across the Utah border, safe away from that tantalizing man scent of the rider of the dark bay.

IV: RAGS CHALLENGES

"I'm a son of a gun," exclaimed Bill Caywood, the morning after Rags had run away from the dilemma of Cathedral. "I'm a son of a gun! That beats the Dutch!"

Caywood took off his hat, scratched his head speculatively, spat, looked admiringly at the accomplishment of Rags' digging.

The hunter was standing looking down at the trap which the wolf had excavated so neatly the night before. There it lay in all its stark steel ugliness, with the pan right side up, unsprung. Earth was sprayed around over the leaves on every side, where the digger wolf had thrown it in his feverish attack on the hidden trap. But the canniness, the cunning that had been stored away in the brain of that wolf for years had kept his front feet out of that fatal disc which would have snapped the jaws of the trap around his leg.

Never before had Caywood seen a greater manifestation of wolf knowledge. His admiration for Rags mounted in one big leap. A wolf that could spot a trap and edge around it was to be given due credit for his keenness of scent and the brains to keep out of the way of the trap jaws. But a wolf that would spot a trap unerringly, dig from the side, then dig from the other, and finally with a flip lift the unsprung trap out of the set and expose it to greet the hunter on his next trip was in a class by himself.

"You're a smart boy," he said, addressing the wolf tracks that showed plainly in the soft earth. You're a darned crafty old codger, Ragsy. But your uncle'll get you before the summer is over, and he'll get you just because you are so darned smart. You'll start to dig up one of my traps just once too often, old-timer, just once too often."

Bob Coats heard the news of the trap dug up and laughed.

"Didn't I tell you, Bill, that that ain't no common wolf?" he exclaimed. "Rags has more sense than any wolf I ever took and that is quite a number to measure him up by. I've had him dig out three or four traps of mine in a night.

"Mad? Why, man, I just went hog wild tryin' to catch that old duffer after he dug up my first traps. Seemed like he just dared me to set a trap in such a way that he could not throw it up on the ground surface unsprung. And now he's turned the trick on you. Well, that's good!"

"Well, I'll take the dare," said Caywood, his blue eyes flashing. "He's dared me to come at him if ever a wolf dared a man, and I'm on his trail from now on. He killed a steer over beyond that little creek back of the salt cabin night before last. That's how I caught up his track to-day. Led me right to the trap set where he had dug up the trap. He's in this part of the country again for sure. No mistake but that it's Rags. Front feet are smaller than his hind ones. And before he gets out I'm goin' to give him both barrels!"

But Caywood reckoned without measuring his antagonist. There was no way he could tell of that queer reaction, the new surging fear, the curious yearning, that had sent Rags flying back to haunt the sheep flocks and make life one continual nightmare for the Mexican herdsmen. Traps set in the runways caught only coyotes. A lone two-year-old wolf blundered into one trap set. But no sight of Rags or the two wolves that ran with him was found by Caywood, even though he stayed out from early light until dusk blotted out the countryside, making great sooty-black shadows of the piñon pines and ghosts of the white-trunked shivering aspen.

Days passed. No riding of the range could discover sign of Rags if Rags had not been there. Caywood's eyes stung of nights from peering, always peering for that telltale wolf track with the front feet smaller than the hind feet.

"You've met your match," declared Jo Neal one day when Caywood was in the bank at Meeker. "Rags is your equal, Bill. He's the headiest wolf that ever roamed the White River country. He's outguessing you."

"Time will do it," replied Bill quietly, his eyes squinting. "He'll come back some day soon. When he comes I'll still be here. If he gets away the next time, then I'll be waitin' fer him the next trip in. Some day I'll roll his hide up and ship it to the Denver office, and inside of it will be his big old skull. I'm not sayin' when I'll get him, but I will."

More riding. Tireless trailing over the open hills. Coyotes fell almost nightly into the traps set, but still no sight of the lone wolf, Rags.

Then one morning there was a fresh wolf track in the trail. It was not Rags. But it was a wolf. New traps set by Caywood brought results. A wolf, a small one, one of Rags' companions, fell into the set. Caywood was encouraged. Coats declared it was certainly one of Rags' running mates.

A new discovery sent Bill Caywood's spirits bounding. It was that Rags never traveled the trails. For a few feet the big wolf tracks would follow along the beaten path where a wolf would run. Then it would branch off and follow along beside the main runway, a few feet away from where it would seem natural for a wolf to run.

"Here's a surprise for you, old-timer," growled Caywood good-naturedly, as he started work on a trap set along a run where he reckoned Rags would surely come if he was in that part of the country.

"Just try to dig this up and you'll find yourself in a jack pot if ever wolf gets into one of them things." Off the trail, where Rags would likely trot, Caywood set a trap. He did not set it with the usual care. He covered it a bit lightly. The thought of the dug trap was in his mind. If the digger wolf would only stay true to his habit of turning up traps then there was a chance here for Caywood to outwit him.

Back of this one trap Caywood set two others. They were spaced in such a manner that should Rags start digging the decoy trap it was inevitable that his feet would get engaged with the pan of one of the other two traps. They were in the only line of approach.

Carefully Caywood picked up the setting cloth. He dropped the tiniest of twigs in the duff that he had spread over the two traps that were designed to catch the Digger. All depended on that digging habit of Rags whether this new campaign move would be successful. A trap was queer bait, but it might work.

"Now dig that out, darn you," remarked Caywood as he swung into the saddle. "I dare you to!"

V: RAGS RETURNS

Rags, the Digger, had run away from something. It had upset his wolf serenity. First had come that haunting, lonely feeling that had made him follow Bill Caywood to the camp. The reaction had driven him away, loping through the brush when the camp fire had lighted the little tent.

The uneasiness followed him to the Utah ranges where he made destructive forays in the sheep flocks. The herders crossed themselves, murmured prayers or in the same breath cursed, when the big wolf lifted his head and proclaimed to the wild that he was back again in his western range.

He had trotted along the trails in the cedar-fringed draws, slept in the sun, killed fiercely, ravenously glutted his appetite on sheep blood, and then had turned with fiendish delight to harry the blatting woollys, running them hither and thither through the night. It was a great life for a lone wolf killer. The hardness of his heart had returned. Killing, slaughter, blood, warm and steamy with the victim burbling out its dying breath as he ripped at the steaming carcass was his sole end in life.

A new scent had appeared on one of his scent posts. Rags had howled, challenged a great dog wolf, followed by a pack. He had come out of the sage to the westward seeking a fight.

Leaping, diving, slashing with ripping fang, down in the dust, up again, snarling, with the pack nipping at his heels, Rags had thrown his powerful body into the fight with exultant joy. It was his game. Kill or be killed. And the gray wolf, in spite of the help of his pack, had finally broken and run, the wolves scattering before the demon wolf that cried murder with each fresh charge.

The law of the pack had won. Rags had conquered. He was looked on as rightful leader. For when a dog wolf fights and wins there is no appeal. He is the king. All others of the pack recognize him as monarch.

Rags ran with them only two nights. They made devastating raids on a sheep flock. Had then turned their campaign against steers in a pasture near a ranch and sent cold shivers through the fiber of the hardy homesteaders with the gibbering cry of their blood feast. Three yearlings had fallen, making hideous the night with their bellowings of fright.

No truly lone wolf could stay leader of a pack long. They parted. Rags trailed through a country that was filled with choppy, colorful arroyos, where rocks were shaped like men, like phantoms, like demons crouching in the scant tree growth as though ready to leap into life at some magic touch.

Then eastward, eastward and back toward Cathedral his steps turned. He could not fight that pull to go back to the high ranges of the upper White River any more than he could miss his fate that awaited. Under bright stars that flashed in the blue-black vaults of the Colorado sky he followed devious trails. Once he turned southward, raided into the country which lies toward the Colorado River. It was new territory. The novelty of it intrigued him. Something within him urged him to go on southward, not to go back to that country, the old range he had roamed so long, the section near Cathedral Bluffs. But there was something worrying Rags that might have been curiosity, might have been some other fundamental wolf yearning, which kept him headed in a general easterly direction.

So it came that one night, after the pale late moon of the last quarter had dipped down over the La Sals to the westward, Rags stood at the junction of a trail which forked northward and eastward. For a long time he stood to one side of the path, his ears cocked, his nose sniffing the breeze. It was as though he had a tryst here with some wilding. He moved uneasily, whined.

Then out of the night there came a smaller gray form, followed by another. They were the two wolves Rags permitted to associate with him. They touched noses. Rags, still nervous, still upset in his own wolf mind, snarled a little and started northward. But the other wolves did not come. They started down the trail eastward. Rags stopped, stood, whined. Irresolutely he wavered for a moment in indecision. He wanted to go north, but the pull eastward was greater. He turned and swiftly followed the other two toward the higher country near the head of Piceance Creek.

Silently they raced along beside the roadway. Occasionally they would cross. Usually wolves travel in well-beaten paths such as cow trails and old woods trails. But Rags had become thoroughly acquainted with the fact that all wolfers know this and he had thereafter avoided these easier trails and ran beside them.

They came to a scent post. New scent, new wolf scent of a dog wolf, was on it. Rags bristled, stalked around the tuft of grama grass on which the scent was splashed, edged away. The other dog wolf growled and stalked about, his wolf voice rumbling in his chest in deep throaty challenge.

Rags was wary. It did not seem right. There might be a trap there. He could not scent man scent. The wolf scent was without the scent of wolf feet along the trail. That it could come there without a wolf walking the trails about the scent post was curious. Rags could not figure it out, did not try very hard in his wolf mind. Uneasiness came again. And with it came the thought of the bronzed man on horseback.

Rags trotted away. The other two followed. Rags hurried ahead. He had a full meal of sheep inside of him and was not hunting a kill. Rather there seemed something ahead, beckoning to him to follow the trails, to meet with something ahead, some fateful tryst.

The little dog wolf turned back. The she-wolf followed. Rags stopped for a moment and then ran on. He did not care whether the two wolves came with him or not. When he howled for them they would come hurrying to his killing call.

Through the night Rags explored the trails, uneasy, watching through the clear dark brightness of the velvety night. Constantly he sniffed the air for scent which is so quickly caught up by the delicately attuned wolf nose.

Morning came. One of the little wolves came back, nervous, whimpering. Rags gave no notice. His mind was filled with other things. For he had met that man scent which had sent longing, then wild fury boiling through his wolf thoughts. After a time he had quieted, had kept coolly on, seeking, always seeking ahead, following the trail as it called to him.

Day came. Rags slept. The little wolf slunk away through the brush nervously watching from side to side what might be in waiting ready to spring out from behind the bush. For the night before something of steel had sprung out at the other little wolf, had held it captive. That was what had made the wolf that had sought Rags so nervous. Only his frightened follower could not let Rags know what had happened and Rags had seemingly not noticed the extreme nervousness of the smaller wolf.

The sun dropped below the hills westward. Fiery reds in the sky melted into softer oranges, into pinks, into soft gray, dun, brown. Night wind blew down the little cañons. Wild life started to stir. A grouse walked down the pathway not fifty feet from Rags. The wolf stalked, lunged. The grouse whirred to safety in a pine tree above.

Rags started down the trail. He was beginning to be hungry. New beef would satiate him that night and again on the morrow he would stretch out in the sunny places and rest his legs, weary from his hurried trip from the west.

He followed a trail in the dusk. Dropped to a cañon below the ridge on which he had spent the day. Crossed a field of cool, sweet alfalfa. Scouted the possibilities of a pasture near a ranch. Saw a great throbbing thing come up the road with white flashing eyes. Turned tail and scuttled back to the safety of the ridge. Then he came cautiously back toward the ranch, but for an hour could not overcome the scare of that churning metal thing that had now found shelter and quiet in a shed.

Finally Rags turned away, loped across the valley, climbed a ridge, surprised a rabbit that had been busily eating of fresh greens near a springy place, pounced on the bunny, slew it with one quick diving snap, licked the blood from his chops as he gulped bones and all.

Still the restlessness persisted. His return had not solved his problems. He followed a ridge trail, dropped into another cañon, then back toward the highlands. He stopped to rest on Duck Creek, lapped water from its trickle. Morning came, rosy, greeted by the calling of piñon jays. Rags started along a trail that led to the ridge above, between Duck and Dry Corral Gulch. There seemed faint scent here, man scent.

Rags sensed, just as he topped the timber line on the ridge, that he had reached the end of that trail that had lured him back to the Cathedral country. For in the trail ahead, foretold by the faintest of foreign scent, there was a trap set. The wolf stopped, sniffed at the foreign wolf scent, scented that man that rode the big bay horse. He trotted up to the ill-concealed trap, edged around it, growling. Some hate boiled up within him and he bristled. Then in cold calculating, precise movements Rags began to dig, began to uncover the trap which Bill Caywood had so carefully set in a clumsy manner as the curious bait to the other two hidden traps waiting for Rags, the Digger.

VI: MASTER!

Mixed feelings filled the mind of Bill Caywood as he rode out on the trap line. Late June had brought full leafage to the trees, while the grass of the range was showing the effects of grazing. Sheep had been in the Flattop country for many days. It would be but a few weeks until they began to stream out through the Cathedral country, traveling back to the winter ranges in Utah. Summer was passing.

Still Rags ranged free. Bill had increased his efforts to snare the old lobo. But in spite of the tracks Rags left just off trails, never in the run which a wolf would normally take, Caywood had not yet caught a glimpse of the canny old shag-coated wolf. Two nights before he had caught one of Rags' running mates.

The big bay climbed the sloping trail between Dry Corral Gulch and Duck Creek. Bill had a sense of something awaiting him ahead. The bay responded to the thumping of heels against his ribs and was soon snorting from the exertion of the climb.

A ridge was topped. They followed a ridge trail for a way. The trail dipped into a meadowy draw only to climb up over the next timber-garnished rise. Finally Bill could see the little cliff back of the trap set. He glanced down at the trail. With new energy he kicked the ribs of the horse. For there in the dust at the side of the road, faint, yet clearly enough defined to be seen from the horse's back was the telltale track of Rags.

With heart thumping at what he might find, with his keen eyes flashing from sign to sign, he drove the bay forward over the pebbly trail. The cliff seemed to recede. But the final dip to the little depression came suddenly and the next moment Bill Caywood was tumbling from his horse, peering eagerly at the ground torn up around the trap.

"Gosh," exclaimed Bill. "Gosh, I've got him!"

In the duff of the little valley floor there was the mark that makes the wolfer up and away in pursuit. Ahead is the end of his pursuit; is the solution of the peculiar wolf problem each renegade presents. It was the scratch of the drag hook where it twisted and turned as the two slanting, curved tines ripped into the ground.

Up on the bay again, Bill hurried along the trail. Then the scratch quit the trail altogether, crossed over an open meadow, went through a stand of pine. The ground was torn up, scratched, pawed at a place where the drag had caught on a bit of brush. The brush itself was gnawed and there was still just the suggestion of a little fleck of foam from the mouth of the wolf on the branches of shrubs.

A new fear came into the thoughts of Bill Caywood. Suppose he had not caught Rags after all. Suppose that this was some other big dog wolf that was running alone in that part of the country.

But it was a wolf, a big one, that he followed, and he urged his horse ahead.

They came to the edge of a ridge, followed it, then turned, crossing a little open slope and abruptly the horse and man came to a perpendicular drop of more than a hundred feet. Caywood looked to either side to find where the wolf had turned along the crest of the cliff. Either way, there was no sign. He got off, looked at the edge of the cliff. Down over the face of the declivity he saw that mark. No wolf with two traps, six feet of drag chain and a toggle jointed drag on the end of the chain could go over that cliff and not leave some mark!

Nor could a wolf or any other animal of that size stand much chance of getting down over that cliff without breaking its neck!

The end of the trail was at the bottom of the cliff. There the final story of Rags or whatever wolf might be in the trap would be written, a period placed for all time to the end of its career with a .25-.35 bullet.

Haste, anxiousness, the suspense of not knowing what he might find at the bottom of that drop carried Caywood forward as fast as his horse could travel. His own feet were not yet sufficiently healed from that break to trust his weight on them more than a few yards at a time. He hobbled painfully when he walked. So the bay had to do the traveling.

The bottom of the cliff was reached. Swift glances showed no gray-tawny form of wolf lying at the base. Caywood felt a tug of disappointment. But his pulse picked up the exultant throb again when he found that indelible scar of the drag hook weighted down with the chain and the trailing trap.

Through sage, around oak brush, over little sandy stretches, by cliffs where red and yellow rocks vied with each other in their coloring, down a little draw, then over an open space, the trail led. Again the drag caught. The ground was torn up. Then the trapped wolf forged ahead, dragging the steel weight on his foot.

The horse lifted his head, cocked his ears. Bill peered ahead along the trail. He thought he saw the wolfish figure of the captive in the brush ahead. But he could not be sure.

The trail entered a narrow arroyo formation where the cliff stood up on either side, in sheer walls. There was just room for one horse to follow that trail between the upstanding cliffs. The trail branched, Bill peered ahead. Then urged the bay into the narrow left branch of the arroyo.

Suddenly the horse stopped, snorted.

Ahead in the trail was a trapped wolf. A big one, shaggy, gray, powerful.

Bill urged the horse forward. The bay was reluctant. It was so narrow he could not turn back, so plodded ahead. The hunter loosened the .25-.35 rifle in the saddle scabbard. He encouraged the horse. The bay took some more lagging steps forward.

The wolf started away, stopped, looked back out of level, unshifting gray eyes at horse and man. There was no wild plunging, no bellowing, no howling.

Again the wolf started ahead. He was moving slowly, not in a hurry, not plunging. Caywood forced the horse farther into the narrow place. Then, realizing that it was rather a ticklish place to have a horse if the wolf should turn and with the fresh recollection of the weight of the horse on his broken leg a few months earlier, he swung with difficulty to the side of the trail, pulled out the hunting rifle, and started ahead. The horse behind snorted. The clank of the traps and the drag hook were clear in the stillness that suddenly settled on the scene. Bill edged forward. The horse followed, wide-eyed, breathing terror at being left unmounted with the killer in view.

There was no question. It was Rags. Big, brawny, ragged in coat, rangy in body, potential death to any living thing that might cross his path except a superior killer, he stalked away, hunting freedom by escape.

The drag caught. It held. It was on a tiny twig in the trail. One more step would take the big wolf clear of this futile obstruction. One lunge would crack a branch many times as tough as the one that held the drag.

But he did not move. For a long moment he stood immovable, looking ahead to the open trail. Then slowly he turned his great wedge head. His red tongue lolled from the fatigue of the fight he had made. His gray eyes sought those of Caywood.

Then slowly, ever so slowly, he turned. He faced Caywood. Their eyes met. Held.

With no hurry, with no expression of fury, the big gray started a slow, measured step back toward the hunter. The drag hook came loose from the twig. It rattled, twisting in the trail. There was nothing for it to catch on and impede that stalking walk of the big killer.

Caywood felt a shiver creep over his spine. The words of Coats about Rags eating human meat came flashing to his mind. The warning of Neal came pounding into his ears as though the rancher had been standing but a few feet away and calling to him.

The unbelievable had happened! Caywood, wolfer supreme, was being stalked by his catch!

Then there came a great wave of relief. He had almost forgotten the gun he held in his hands. The turning of the wolf, so unlooked for, so unusual, had held his attention completely.

He brought up the rifle. His thumb sought the hammer. He pulled it back. IT DID NOT CATCH!

Frantically he pulled at it again. The first try had been as good as this second. The hammer would not stay back. It slipped under his thumb.

Seventy-five yards away Rags had turned. His measured steps had not retraced more than twenty-five feet of that distance. He was still coming in that unhurried, slow walk, so deadly, so like an inevitable Nemesis bearing down on the hunter.

Queer fear leaped through Caywood's heart. There was no real chance to fight. Bill's crippled leg would never permit him to climb up the steep side of the arroyo. Hampered as he was by the trap, Rags could lash a man to shreds in one driving attack. One snap and a leg would go helpless; a snip and blood would spurt from severed veins. Then the end.

But still there was that forty, no, thirty foot space between Caywood and the old lone lobo.

A strange new vision came flashing fleetingly to Caywood. A vision of a lonely, heart-hungry old wolf, without mate, yearning for some fondling touch, perhaps the kindly caress of his arch enemy, the trapper. The vision was stalking down that trail toward him. Something, something tremendous, indefinable, about Rags caught his attention and held it for the flash of a great understanding.

Could Rags have acknowledged his defeat? Was the old wolf coming to the hunter because he knew that Caywood was master? Was heart hurt and loneliness driving Rags to stake his life while seeking the friendship of the outdoor soul that lived in big Bill Caywood?

There was no growling, only a great, deep, low rumbling in Rags' throat. His hair bristled, but it bristled as it might on the back of a dog, shy, beaten, crawling back to the feet of its master after it had done something wrong and by fawning sought forgiveness. And yet there was regal bearing in Rags of Cathedral which declared his kingship in his kind.

Fascinated, Caywood gazed at the wolf.

Slowly, ever so slowly, those padding steps were coming nearer. The flash of fang in the big mouth caught Caywood's eye. The spell broke. Nervous fingers again clutched the gun hammer. But the trigger was jammed!

The horse snorted, began to back down the trail. The thirty-foot space was twenty.

Again Bill tugged at the trigger, for what seemed to him the hundredth time. The hammer would not hold, would not click and catch.

Fifteen feet away the wolf still came toward Caywood, in that march of death—or life. The hunter felt a sweat break out on his body. He wondered if he would have the steady nerve to plant a sure bullet if the hammer would catch. He tugged vainly.

Then a new thought came. He would let the hammer slip from under his thumb. It would explode the shell, send the bullet whining at that stalking wolf.

Twelve feet—no, ten—with traps clanking, the determined, unhurried wolf was coming.

For what?

Forgiveness, company, sympathy, release, recognizing Bill Caywood, wolfer, outdoors man, kindred spirit, as his master? Could he be coming, seeking release from the trap, sympathy for the injured paw?

Or was it murder, revenge, the final summation of the hate he had held for years against man? Was there blood lust in that wolf heart, deep boiling spirit of revenge against the man who had trapped him, deprived him of liberty?

The flash of fang, those steady eyes, that clanking, unhurried tread!

With all his understanding of the wild and its inhabitants Caywood could not tell whether Rags came seeking friendship or was stalking along that trail intent on killing.

Not an instant remained to speculate, to try to analyze the emotion throbbing through the heart of Rags.

Bill Caywood yanked, yanked as he had not before, at the hammer on the .25-.35! It clicked! Held!

Up came the gun. Snap sights were taken. Bill's finger pressed, pressed, pressed while his aim steadied.

Eight feet! Just eight feet left between Rags and the man who had mastered him.

A snap! Quick, sharp, spitting death! The bullet had but scant distance to go.

Quivering, struggling still to come on, Rags slumped in the trail, a bullet through his heart!

For a moment Bill Caywood stood in the trail, staring down on the jerking body of the great lobo wolf. One instant there whipped through him keen, agonizing regret. The next he was thanking his lucky stars that the bit of a splinter from the stock of the gun had not held that trigger from catching when he made the last frantic pull.

Life flickered feebly in Rags, the lonely killer eyes looked up at the man in front of him. The horse, swinging his head from side to side, snorted, moved uneasily. In a last shaky effort the great gray form raised itself, encumbered by the gripping tentacles of death, weighted with the traps of steel and tried with the last flow of strength before his life finally slipped away, to reach the feet of wolfer Caywood, his master.

Almost with his quivering nose touching Caywood's boot he fell, quivered, stiffened.

"You poor old devil!" cried Bill huskily as he stooped impulsively. "You poor, lonely old murdering devil!"

Unaweep

I: WELDING OF THE PACK

At the edge of a grassy open space, hidden from general view by oak brush thickets, a lanky gray wolf lay stretched in the mid-spring sunshine. About her raced four fuzzy whelps in mad play. Recently they had been coaxed out of the den by the mother. At first, timid and leg-wobbly, they had shivered in wonderment at the immensity of the little glade when compared to the confines of the dark, smelly den. They were still shaky on their baby legs, but had amassed worlds of confidence—so long as Unaweep, their gray mother, was on guard.

A game was in progress. One was forced into playing a part which resembled a steer running from a wolf pack. With erratic rush, a little dog wolf galloped in pursuit, attempting a semblance of hamstringing the victim. He that had played steer to the others of the pack lacked a relish for the game. He turned on his little mates. In an instant there were quick, sharp baby snarls. The "steer" wolf bared his fangs and lunged. His nearest antagonist slithered away, yelping in surprise. But the little dog wolf who had been playing leader budged not an inch. He yapped, leaped, snarled, refused to retreat. For a moment there was tense quiet. Then the little leader moved forward in tiny instinctive imitation of the strut of the challenging king wolf. The other lost courage and, tail between legs, scuttled back toward the mother.

Deep in her throat Unaweep growled, half in warning, half in approval. There was no disapproval in her eyes when she looked on the little dog wolf leader. He already dominated the pack. They all were cowed by him. He bullied them unmercifully. Proud in having whelped such a wolf, Unaweep had given him preference in all of the food she had given her babies, had watched him with more tender care. Her eyes followed him in their play. For here was a future pack leader.

Several times the whelps had fought furiously in the den. Such a general battle royal had always ended with the little dog wolf driving his comrades into a corner and then daring them to come out to a further attack. He never seemed the worse for the family quarrels, but during one wild free-for-all fight had bitten off the tail of one of his sisters in a quick, clean snap. Bobtail wolves are not uncommon, and usually when they are so marked have had their tails snapped off by a fighting litter mate during whelphood.

From babyhood the wolf king develops. In each litter, one usually is born to command.

Unaweep, the wolf mother, now knew that her mate would never come to help her train these whelps. Weeks back, she had left him on the trail far to the south. The old leader had started off on a foraging expedition with their eight yearlings. Unaweep, knowing that a new family would soon be nuzzling her breasts, had then loped away to the Uncompahgre plateau highlands. At the head of a little upland draw she had located an old badger hole. By much puffing and throwing of dirt with her front paws, kicking it away with her powerful rear legs, she had fashioned a den.

Four whelps had been born. Before this time, the father wolf should have sought out the den. Unaweep had listened often for his sniff at the mouth of the hole. When she foraged alone she had sought sign of him. Some of her yearling wolves came by, followed her for a few hours on the hunting trail, but then ran along about their own affairs. The big dog wolf was not with them. Nor had she found his scent at any of the wolf scent posts.

Unaweep could not know that the bullet of a high-power rifle in the hands of one of the hands of the Club Ranch leagues southward, had clipped through the thread of the wolf father's life.

Unaweep would manage. She had a great country in which to rear her brood. The Uncompahgre Plateau is a bit of the Old West, unsullied by the breath of man's mechanical machinery giants, unmarked by vandal tourist horde. The plateau is just old-fashioned, typically western cow and sheep range.

Like an island this plateau stands out in the sagy flats westward from the mainlands and headlands of the Colorado Rockies. To the eastward is the broad mountain valley of the foam-mottled Gunnison and its mysterious, twisty Black Cañon. Near Delta it joins the Uncompahgre River, which is born high in the jagged, gold-ribbed hills that encompass the little mountain town of Ouray. Fertile farms, old Indian hunting grounds, border these streams. Beyond are old, old mountains.

Westward from this great island of the Uncompahgre Plateau are sun-pelted plains billowing to where they finally drop into the Grand Cañon to the southwest, rise in the blue-hazed sides of the La Sal Mountains to the west, or climb in sweeping cadence to the majesty that crowns the Wasatch range.

On the sides of the Uncompahgre weather has gouged and pried at the rocks, splitting out tiny cañons, deep clefts, craggy gullies. Below are slopes finally fanning out into broken plains. Above the battlements of the plateau's walls there is a kingdom of outdoors—real West. Here are parks, bordered by aspens, boggy places from which seep cool springs, spruce thickets, little cliffs where cling stunted alpine or long-leaf fir, beds of blazing wild flowers that rival the splendor of the vivid Colorado sunsets. At other points are open parks bordered by stately yellow pines, veteran trees that were left when the country was logged years ago. Among the trees are sage, mountain mahogany, or the spiny twigs of Fendler's ceonothus.

Through aspen thickets bordering parks, finding some easy way up barrier cliffs, there are old wood roads, trails, almost obliterated paths that are traveled by the shy or cunning wild things that live in this skyland forest of the rock table—a giant rock table it is, fifty miles long and twenty miles wide, with a whole little commonwealth of nature on its high-lifted surface.

Spring had romped along to the door of summer before Unaweep decided that the time had come to abandon the den altogether. By the first of June the whelps had been on several day or night excursions, hunting small rodents and gorging to grogginess on an early range cow killed by their mother. The time had come to lead them away from their babyhood home altogether.

The whelps knew when the break came. They were eager for the big trail. Scampering, tumbling, nipping at each other, chewing ears, stumbling in puppy awkwardness, they raced after their gray wolf mother.

Yellow color flashing against the blue, yellow green in the sky, then burnished brass that deepened to gold and to deepest red copper, finally glowing and fading into saffron and buff shades, pulsed in the heavens, and then dusk came. They traveled among deepening shadows at an easy lope.

Darkness fell. They dropped to a walk and ranged slowly. It was a night for wolf raids. A watery moon hung low in the west and upland summer was in the air.

They traveled easily for an hour. Then as though a definite point in their journey had been reached, Unaweep trotted out to a spur ridge, clambered up on a rock, tested the wind, whined a little. Some sense of leadership gripped her and for the first time she lifted her head and bellowed forth that pack call, the wolf howl summoning to the hunt. It is the howl of the leader, the call of the king wolf, very rarely voiced by the females of the wolf family. She was calling her whelps of the last year. They had strayed far when the leadership of their father was lost. Now they must be called back. Contrary to wolf law, Unaweep, a she-wolf, would lead them!

The young whelps, startled at first, came yapping around her, excited by this old hunting call.

The whelps quieted, again Unaweep howled, listened, sniffed, then howled again, while the cliffs echoed. A few moments passed. The whelps whimpered, foraged, then came scampering back.

As though taking form from the shadows, there came into the little park below nine ghostly gray forms, gliding with airy tread through the dusky night. On they came, up the slope to the ridge, then trotted to within thirty feet of where Unaweep and her whelps huddled.

With stately tread Unaweep stepped forward, sniffed. Low in her throat there was a stifled growl. Quick to recognize the scent of individual wolves, she knew that in that pack there were all of her last year's cubs. But there was another wolf, a dog wolf, an alien.

With mincing tread out came that foreign wolf. He was rangy, a well-formed young male, brawny, strong, a leader, a possible mate.

Something within Unaweep leaped in instant rebellion. Deep-seated mother love for her yearlings, for the lost mate, welled up within her. Quick, fiery hate flamed at this dog wolf who had usurped her rightful mother place as leader. For had the old mate lived, he would have been leading these eight husky yearlings, training them, teaching them the wolf lore that he and Unaweep had gathered in years of life on the plains, in the La Sal Mountains, and on the Uncompahgre Plateau.

This usurper strode forward like a cavalier, a dandy on parade, in his wolf pride sensing no antagonism from the lanky she-wolf that stood so rigid a few inches above him on the ridge. Then the low growl in the throat of the mother wolf warned him. He stopped.

Quick as a flash, Unaweep dived. There would be no other than herself to lead her pack. This foreigner was unwelcome, hated, a challenge to her own leadership.

The dog wolf stumbled, dived away, turned, snapped, threw himself on the fighting demon. It was unbelievable that a she-wolf should attack him this way!

She drove at him as a rival dog wolf would, growling, snapping, the very person of fury. The meeting of her white teeth was like the snap of a target pistol. His reflex counter attack threw the dog wolf into the fight.

Up they came on their hind legs. She reached for his neck. He nipped her paws. With a quick shake she threw him. She pounced upon him as he fell.

Up again, in quick attack, their bodies thumped together. Pack leadership was in question. There was one orthodox way to settle that. The dog wolf with the ambition of a pack leader in his breast, struggled for supremacy.

He sank his teeth into her flank. She snapped at his back, cut the skin, ripped until blood was on her fangs. They reared, paws thrashing against heaving chests, snarling, wrestling for a hold. Again the smash of the collision sent the dog wolf rolling down the little slope. There was a super fury in the mother wolf's attack. She would lead her own!

He got up. Unaweep stood poised for another leap. For a moment he stood, crouched, looking at her. Then some queer chivalry that rules among the wolf packs whipped through the dog wolf. She was a female, a fighting demon female, but the mother of pups nevertheless. He whined, offering peace, comradeship, perhaps matehood. The answer was a low-toned growl; there would be no quarter, no friendliness.

The dog wolf edged a little farther down hill. The baby whelps whimpered. One of the yearlings nosed out of the pack that had been milling about at safe distance from the contestants, started to follow the dog wolf. Unaweep turned on him in a flash, snarled. The yearling slunk back. She had a new grip on her pack.

A moment passed. The foreign dog wolf, still stirred by that wolf chivalry which recognizes the homage to the female, finally turned, trotted a few steps, then loped away.

Unaweep, queen wolf, terror of the Uncompahgre Plateau, had attained distinctive, peculiar heights in the wolf nations. Through this battle she had become the rarest of all wolf killers of the West. She, a female wolf, had fought to secure and now would fight to hold, the leadership of a pack. No other wolf would train those youngsters. United again under their dam, these young wolves would receive expert training in the slashing, bloody butchery that is typical of gray wolf killing.

II: THE WHITE CALF

For the fifth consecutive season, Charley Bowman's grade shorthorn with the roan spot on her shoulders had borne a white calf. Four white calves had preceded this one that bawled hungrily for its mother on the Cold Spring ranger station meadow. These four had not survived their first season. Wolves had slaughtered them.

Charley Bowman and Forest Ranger Elmer Reed were standing near the corrals talking.

"There bawls that white calf again," observed Bowman. "Darn it, if the wolves would only take that shorthorn calf and leave the rest alone, I'd not kick. They just make eatin' that roan cow's calf a regular order of business and then go lunching around on some of the other cattle something awful. That white calf is doomed; it'll be wolf meat before autumn. Got no chance in the world."

Reed grinned sympathetically.

"Maybe the calf's got a chance this summer, Charley," said the ranger. "You know it's along the middle of June, and we were told we'd have a Federal hunter in here by now. When I was down to the Super's office last week he said they were about to send in a fellow named Hegewa. He's just cleaned up on a bad bunch of wolves over in the Burns Hole country. Maybe that calf has a fightin' chance this season."

"No chance, none at all," replied Bowman. "That white calf is a goner. But this hunter may stop other raiding."

Thus news of Hegewa preceded him. So when he stopped at Bowman's cow camp a couple of days later, he was greeted with hearty hospitality.

"Heerd you-all was goin' to come in and clean up on the wolves hereabouts," drawled a lanky cow hand, as he helped the hunter ease off the pack from the sweaty pack horse. "Damned tough bunch of lobos around here fo' sure. Got a job cut out for you-all."

Hegewa grinned in his weather-bleached beard. All wolves were tough customers or all were easy. They were all wolves, each renegade with a different personality, but all running true to general wolf form. This usual gossip did not make much of an impression.

"I'd give a nickel if you'd get that old she-wolf that is runnin' with the pack down in Unaweep Cañon; the Unaweep Wolf, we call her. I think she is the one who gets that white calf. I'm just obstinate enough to want to raise that calf this year." Charley Bowman squinted his eyes as he watched Hegewa.

"Tell me more about this calf," suggested the hunter.

Charley Bowman did. He told of the white calves that had made meals for the wolves the four previous seasons. He told of wolf raids on other stock, of the runs of the packs along certain woods trails, the tracks he had seen, and particularly, he mentioned the peculiar cross-toed track made by the Unaweep Wolf.

"Got her toes crossed over like this," asked Hegewa, crossing his middle over his index finger, "left front foot?"

Bowman nodded. "Pick her track out of a thousand."

"I know that old sister," declared Hegewa. "Know her awful darned well." He lapsed silent.

"They've never had a Federal hunter in here before," protested Bowman. "How come you know her?"

For a moment Hegewa stared into the muddy residue of cow camp coffee that swirled turbidly in the bottom of the heavy tin cup he was holding between both hands.

"Eight years ago," he said slowly, "eight tough years, too, I was in here as a bounty hunter, on my own. I trapped my darndest for that old girl. I caught her. Just clipped hold of her toes. Broke one of them when she pulled loose. It grew well, but crossed, like it is now. I caught her again later, but a stick wedged in the trap allowed her to pull out. I guess I've got a grudge to settle there. Besides, I've got a sort of hankerin' to give that white calf his chance. It's just too much to sacrifice any more white calves to that wolf pack." Hegewa grinned a little.

"Well, I've lost this shorthorn's calf annually. Expect to again."

"I've held a full house with queens high and been beaten by a straight diamond flush in a four-handed game. I've made some other bets that didn't turn out. But doggone me if I don't offer to put up a new hat that that white calf lives this year," declared Hegewa, laughing. "Any takers?"

"Sure," said Bowman, smiling a little. "I'm on."

The others laughed good-naturedly at the wager. From that moment the calf became a symbol of the fight between Hegewa and Unaweep, the queen wolf of the Uncompahgre.

With pack horse, saddle horse, his regular trail equipment of tarpaulin bed and camp cooking outfit, Hegewa established his base camp near the Cold Springs ranger station. It was a good place in which to live—clean, sheltered, bordered by flowery meadows through which tinkled high country rivulets. From here he rode northward to Unaweep Cañon, and southward toward Nucla and the Club Ranch. Here he heard of the lucky shot which had blotted out the life of Unaweep's mate.

In the higher country south he found fresh tracks. Occasionally they were of a lone dog wolf. At other points the trail showed a pack had traveled that way. Often lone tracks would be following the pack, flanking it, seemingly tagging along as though the dog wolf were trying to make friends with this herd of wolves, but was denied any kinship. Always in the lead of the pack was that telltale cross-toed track of the female, Unaweep.

By Dillard's ranch, near the V Bar cow camp, by the beaver dams that are on the head of the middle fork of the Escalante, along the ridge near Musser's and Shreeves' cow camp, and over the ranges where the stock of Bert Ennor fattened, Hegewa followed the trail, every day finding new evidence of the wolf pack, locating their scent posts, every day getting just a step nearer to the capture of Unaweep, the renegade.

"Real war starts to-morrow," said Hegewa as he met Bert Ennor on the trail near Cold Springs.

"War?" asked Ennor.

"On Unaweep's pack," replied Hegewa. "First step in eradicating 'em. Charley Bowman's white calf and a new Stetson are at stake and I've got enough information to begin operations."

"What you plan to do?" asked Ennor.

"Poison," replied Hegewa. "Most of them wolves are young 'uns. Oldest are not two-year-olds. I've seen that in the trail sign."

"Believe you're off," protested Ennor. "No youngsters could do the killin' this pack has."

"They've got a real leader, that old she-wolf, Unaweep," replied the hunter. "First time I know of a female leadin' a pack. Trainin' them whelps, too. I've seen it in the trails and about the kills. Wouldn't believe it at first, it's so contrary to wolf law for a female to lead. Now I plan to poison as many young ones as I can before they all get wise to poison. Then I'll have less to deal with."

"Well, more power to you!" cheered Ennor as he touched his horse with the spurs. "Something needs to be done pronto."

The next morning Hegewa rode to Bowman's camp. At the hunter's request Bowman contributed an old, worn-out pack horse that had been nosing around the camp, for bait. Hegewa then asked for the use of the spring wagon, the team, and one of the cow hands.

"I'll be back to-morrow morning early," promised Hegewa. "I'm going to scout the poison line to-day, and see where I want to locate the poison stations."

Early next morning Hegewa and a cowboy drove away from the camp, leading the old spent horse. They rode for perhaps a mile over unused woods road.

"Here's first station," said Hegewa, stopping the horses.

A bullet ended the fading career of the poor old pack horse. He was a martyr, like many of his kind, that other range animals might be rid of the menace of predatory animal fangs.

Butchering went on apace. After cutting the body up into head, neck, two shoulder-blade pieces, two rib pieces, the two hind legs, and separating the belly and flank fat from the carcass, Hegewa directed that all but the paunch be loaded into the wagon. He then cut a number of squares of the tender flank fat, an inch and a half square and a quarter inch thick. These he threw around as dummy baits, carrying no poison. With bailing wire he tied the bloody horse head back of the wagon, mounted, and drove on.

The head formed the bait for the next set. This was wired to a bit of brush so it could not be carried away. Around it were thrown other dummy baits. This time, in pulling away from the station, the ribs were allowed to drag along the ground.

"Don't savvy, quite," said the cowboy, looking down at the chunks of fresh horse flesh. "And the little squares of fat—no poison in them?"

"Well, this dragging meat leaves a line when we pull it, and a wolf crossing it will often follow it. Leads 'em right to the poison station. The baits are just to whet their appetites. Makes 'em think this is the cowmen's free lunch for wolves."

Eleven stations were made. Then they returned to the cow camp. Gathering up the hunks of fat that he had left in the wagon rolled up in a piece of the horse hide, Hegewa returned to his camp near the ranger station. That evening he prepared poison baits.

The keen nose of the wolf can detect the faintest of foreign or man scent. Fat is quick to pick up such a scent. So Hegewa, following the best practice, scrubbed his hands thoroughly, then greased them to further insulate against leaving scent.

Dexterously he cut squares of fat an inch and a half to two inches on a side and about a quarter of an inch thick. With deft skill he sliced into the side of the squares, leaving each with a hinge line so they would open like a book. After all were out, Hegewa took out the can of poison and quickly apportioned out a dose for each square of fat, placing the deadly chemical in the fold and then sealing the edges. The wolf or coyote that might gulp the deadly sweet morsel would have the poison well inside of him before the flaps opened and permitted action of the poison. For if wolf or coyote might taste the bitterness of the poison in time, it would be as fatal to its efficiency as the detection of man scent, for the intended victim would spew it out quickly.

After the baits were finished Hegewa packed them in a two-quart screw-top can which had air holes in the top. Pet cattle dogs might find those baits and gulp them wolfishly unless so protected. The poison bullets were not aimed at helpful dogs, but at the pack of Unaweep.

The next morning Hegewa visited the poison sets where the dummy baits had been spread. At the first one there had been no change. The baits were gone, but there were no wolf tracks. Magpies swarmed in the near-by brush.

"May have to get you black and white mischief-makers if you keep stealing baits," growled Hegewa, looking at the chattering birds. "I haven't any magpie poison along this time, but I'll bring you something to eat next trip."

At the horse head there were wolf tracks. The baits were gone. Hegewa worked quickly, methodically. Under the edge of a dried cow chip he slipped a bait; another he placed under the edge of some grass in a little depression; another below some leaves and twigs. A dozen baits he hid thus, handling them with gloves from which scent had been removed. They were clean gloves used only in handling fats. The poison pellets were placed from ten to thirty feet away from the piece of carcass. They were supplemented by new dummy baits. A wolf approaching the line would first encounter a harmless dummy bait or two. Then the next bait between him and the chunk of horse would be several baits carrying death. If he ate the first two harmless baits and was reassured by their not causing him trouble, the wolf would be certain to eat a fat square loaded with processed strychnine. The whole surroundings were left as though no one had visited the place, except for the baits, cunningly hidden.

III: THE STEALTHY ENEMY

Cattle had been on the Uncompahgre Plateau for several weeks. Unaweep, laboring with her youngsters, had led the kill, demonstrating by example the technique of hamstringing steers, throwing heavy, lumbering cows.

After the kill the cubs would scatter to sleep off the drugging effects of the fresh meat feast. For a day the pack would be deployed in open glades, on sunny ridges, in cool, shadowy thickets. Then when evening came, and when there was just the suggestion of hunger, Unaweep would clamber to some high point and, lifting her head, would sound the hunting call. Out from the dusk the wolves would come like silent gray wraiths of destruction. Within the hour some steer, heifer, or calf would be struggling in the grip of death while the pack, gibbering and snarling, ripped and tore.

Confronted with acting in the capacity of both parents, Unaweep had risen to the occasion. At one time she would chastise some cub. Again she would whine encouragingly at another which had made progress in his schooling. Even the youngest that had been whelped in the enlarged badger hole but a few weeks before were growing lusty, acquiring true wolf habits, becoming a part of that grisly army warring on the stock grazing on Uncompahgre Plateau.

Several dog wolves had tried to join the pack. Wolflike, they had sought out the largest, huskiest male to battle for leadership. But each time the visitor received a surprise when a powerful she-wolf drove at him with all the ferocity, the battle tactics of a dominant dog wolf leader. Awed, beaten before the fight started by that universal diffidence to the female, they slunk away, became pack followers, waiting for rutting season, when Unaweep might pick a new mate.

Running true to wolf form, Unaweep had led to a fresh kill every other night. Long ago, when she was a young wolf, she had committed the sin of eating from a dead carcass. The poison it contained had been weak and poorly placed. She had spewed up that bitter, sickening dose in time to save her life. Like other renegades that have learned their lesson, she had since refused to eat of carrion.

Now the unvarying law was not to touch any meat that had not been freshly killed by the pack.

The young wolves were curious, investigative, of an inquiring turn of mind. The world was new to them. Traps, guns, or poison had not yet entered their lives to make them bitter, mold them into renegade killers with knowledge of man enemies. With twelve such young rascals to manage, Unaweep was kept on the alert.

Loping along a woods road near the Cold Springs ranger station, Unaweep suddenly stopped, sniffed, dropped her keen nose, circling to catch the scent. The pack started milling, instinctively imitating the movements of their queen mother. One little wolf yapped excitedly. There was the taint of fresh meat on the ground.

More from curiosity than from any idea of finding food, Unaweep turned and started at the trotting wolf lope. In an open park, tied to a scraggy low pine, they came to the horse head lure wired to the tree. Unaweep stopped, sniffed. At first the pack surged forward. Then, following the movements of their leader, they started circling, edging toward that bait, sniffing suspiciously.

Growling, Unaweep advanced toward the interesting bit of horse carcass. She was suspicious, testing every bit of ground with keen sniffing. She found a square of fat. A little wolf found another. The little fellow gobbled it greedily. It was easy food, tempting and sweet, that had not come from the gruelling work of cattle killing.

With a growl the leader mother dived at the offender. The whelp scuttled to safety. Another of the pack yapped excitedly as he found another square of fat, gobbled it. Another went directly to the horse head. Discipline was disorganized completely.

Circling, afraid of some unseen, unsensed danger, Unaweep rushed at her followers, snapping, snarling, driving them away as best she could. A moment later, still with that dread of the unseen enemy stirring in her wolf mind, she led the pack away. No ill effects followed. The young wolves continued to romp and play, raced in the slaughter of the cattle that night, and then went peacefully to sleep off the meat jag. Still Unaweep was uneasy. Instinctively she dreaded any repetition of that incident.

The damage had been done. The youngsters had tasted the teasing fat squares at the old horse head, had wolfed them down, and had relished the tid-bits placed there as decoy baits by Hegewa. No bitterness of smeared strychnine was on the surface of those decoys. Any other fat bait, as sweet, as tempting as those, would now lure them into the forbidden act of eating of meat that was not of their own fresh kill.

Night came again. Unaweep, uneasy, realizing that the faint man scent, the scent of shod horses, that had been around that horse head forecast trouble, lifted her head and sent forth the call to the pack. Some of the youngsters came hurrying along the trail. Minutes passed. Never before had that call been disregarded by the pack. For nearly an hour she waited, occasionally howling in summons.

Four whelps only came—the four youngest. Something told her that at the horse head she would find the rest of the pack; here, gathered by curiosity, lured by the taste of the fat squares, would be the truants.

Unaweep and the young whelps loped to the horse head poison station. Around the little open park circled the yearlings. At the head stalked the largest dog wolf of the group. It was he that would ultimately question Unaweep's leadership if she did not take a new mate soon.

Timid, held back by some instinctive fear, realizing that a horse head could not get to this point by itself, the yearling wolves had not yet advanced to the area covered by the newly placed mixed poison baits. Unaweep snarled, growled, charged the yearlings. They scattered.

Intrigued by the fascinating chunk of dead horse, the old queen stopped, then went carefully forward. She passed a tempting bit of fat. She dropped her nose, sniffed. Violating those years of careful abstinence, assured by the fact that similar fat had been eaten the night before, Unaweep picked up the bit of fat, mouthed it. Then she spit it out quickly. There was some taint on that fat, some foreign taste, some indescribably warning flavor. She had almost disregarded that terrible lesson of years before.

She turned, started away. But back of her slunk the truant dog wolf yearling. In a flash he reached the fat that Unaweep had spit out, now covered with wolf slaver and washed of that faint foreign scent. He picked it up with his white hard teeth, jerked his head as he threw it into his mouth, did not stop even to puncture it with his incisor teeth as is generally done, but gulped down the poison-laden fat greedily.

He stopped, sniffed at other fat, then in bewilderment growled, turned in a daze, wobbled to the side of the little park. He tried to heave out the thing that had leaped into life in his belly. Unaweep saw that quick rising of the hair on the dog wolf's back. She had seen it before in other poisoned wolves. She knew that death had flashed out from some unseen point and jabbed its talons into her son.

With running steps the mother wolf was at the side of her yearling whelp. There was nothing to be done, but she instinctively moved to shield him from further attack. The dog wolf snarled, whimpered, tried again to throw that rampant tigerish thing that bit at his vitals, out of his body. The other wolves, awed, scared, slunk away, tails between legs, frightened by the quick, unseen attack on their brother.

The dog wolf staggered. He fell. Then, with a mighty effort, his rough, bristling hair raised, his every fiber taut, he partially disgorged the contents of his stomach.

But it was too late. For he had swallowed a full dose of Biological Survey poison, processed strychnine, made purposely for killing predatory animals. He fell in jerking, convulsive writhing.

Grim, stalking, growling, Unaweep stood over him. For a long moment the dog wolf twitched, jerked, snarled, bit at himself as though to tear out the death thing that was ripping through his fiber. Then he lay quiet for many moments.

Unaweep went forward and sniffed. Faint odor of that bodiless killer that had nearly snuffed out her life years before was in that mess which the dog wolf had thrown up. She growled, bared her teeth, then nosed closer to the stricken wolf.

Slowly, staggering, the young dog wolf got to his feet. Unsteadily he started to trot, dropped to a walk, then weaved along through the brush. He was blind; the poison was tearing at him. But sheer will of the wolf kept him going away from the point where he had been stricken. Painful, wearing feet lengthened into yards. Slowly, weakening, but driving on with determined, faltering steps, the wolf finally passed beyond the quarter of a mile mark. But even the flesh of young wolf sired by a leader, mothered by the one wolf queen that the Survey has known in Colorado, could not stand the creeping monster that was striking at his life from within. He fell, struggled up, staggered a few feet more, then, a convulsive shudder, a sudden stiffening of the muscles and the truant leader of the yearlings let go his grip on wolf life.

Whining, upset beyond comprehension, torn by fear and mother love, Unaweep moved cautiously toward her dead son. Killer, unmerciful executioner of quadrupeds that came in her way, Unaweep was still a mother. She nosed about the dead body of the yearling that had the year before been her pet of the litter.

Nor was that the only night that she stayed with that stiff form in the brush. She came back the next day, the following night, then circled that dangerous horse head and its tempting death baits. In a few days flies, the forces of disintegration, stinking rot, finished the job that the poison had started. The potential dog leader of the pack was moldering into the earth that had housed him as a pup, furnished a place to live and things to live on when he was a lusty yearling.

Then Hegewa, tracing the odor of rotting carrion, found him.

Unaweep tried again to round up the pack that had scattered during her preoccupation resulting from the death of the yearling. But others were missing. The pack was now but six. Nor could she find the other wolves. For those missing had dropped out of sight as quickly, and by the same route, as the dog wolf.

With vicious, lusting blood hunger, with new cruelty, Unaweep drove into the herds of Ennor, the Club Ranch, Bowman, and the other cow owners of the Uncompahgre mesa. With uncanny, sure-footed precision she led her pack around trap sets at scent posts, blind sets, ambushes where rifles might be hidden.

New solidarity came to the pack that Unaweep led. It had been tried and had learned its lesson, at the cost of six yearlings. Unaweep drove them at her will, marshaled them when kills were made, directed their every step when they ran together. Her leadership was never more questioned. She was their queen and their mother.

Unaweep had found a new, definite enemy on the plateau. It was the enemy that left man scent. And that man scent was the same as had been on two traps that had nipped at her legs years before; scent that had been around the place where she had broken her toes that had grown back crossed and deformed.

New caution, greater cunning, fiercer hate of man things came to Unaweep after the day she found that man odor near one of the pack's scent posts. With uncanny knowledge she reasoned that traps were about that scent post. At her silent command the whole pack forsook their usual trails, abandoned their established scent posts, which had been used by wolves for years, became wolves that did not follow wolf procedure, proving the axiom that when a renegade leader is being hunted, all wolf law, all wolf habits, may be upset. Anything may happen—or not happen—which is more baffling.

IV: LONG LIVE THE QUEEN!

Hegewa had labored early, late, incessantly, marshaling all his wolf lore in the drive on Unaweep and her pack. High country summer had passed in the brief, flowering days of July and early August. The white calf still fed near the ranger station, and Hegewa was beginning to twit Charley Bowman about a new Stetson.

The calf was still alive, but Hegewa was baffled. The old queen had evaded him. It was time to have outside counsel. That was why Stanley Young came from Denver, and with George Trickle, field foreman of the Survey stationed at Montrose, started for Hegewa's camp.

Hegewa's letter asking for help had also given directions for reaching his camp.

"Will be glad to have you visit me," he had written to Young, "and get some puzzlers straightened out—and help with the wolf problem at the same time. You can get to my camp with car by doing a little road work in places. Anyone in White Water can direct you how to get to the Cold Springs ranger station O.K. I will have an order of grub put up by the Mahannah Mercantile Company to bring with you if you will do so, as travel is light just now and all means have to be employed in order to get grub on the hills.

"When you leave White Water take the Gateway mail road. At the bottom of the long hill you go down, take the dim road to the left at a bridge, follow south and west to Keith's sawmill (signboard), thence south to Cold Springs ranger station. My camp is the only house along the road (on the right) before getting to the Cold Springs station.

"You will have no trouble finding camp—the only trouble will be high centers in the road and a couple of steep hills to climb. Cars have been up and back lately, though, and got through O.K.

"The dugway road out of Unaweep Cañon is washed out and a car cannot get up that way—don't try it."

Young and Trickle followed directions. But Hegewa's assurance that they would have no trouble finding camp proved unfounded. Grub and pack outfit loaded the little car so it had to pull ferociously. The gas got low. It could not get the explosive juice into its carburetor. It stopped, coughing.

"Turn her around, quick," suggested Young. "We'll have to back up the hills like an ant." With its head down hill, the carburetor got gasoline, and with a great to-do, they climbed the first steep grade.

Night spread over the plateau. Then came a hill where the woods road seemed to climb up among dark timber as though taking a running start to leap into the sky. The flivver ground in reverse. Young shouted directions to Trickle, blocked the wheels when they had gained a few feet. Sweat, short breath, a few cuss words fitting the occasion, came further to complicate or ease the situation. The auto stalled, rear high in the air, steaming at the radiator.

"No use, George," said Young. "I'll go up to Hegewa's camp. Can't be far. Come back with a saddle horse."

Young started up the road through the thick darkness that had filled in between the trunks and branches of the spruce. He slipped in muddy places made slick by seeping springs, fought his way up sharp little pitches where the stones rolled under his feet, lost the faint track and forced his way back to it through thickets of alpine fir.

At length he began to call Hegewa's name. It echoed back from tiny cliff and tree trunk. An owl hooted mysteriously through the aisles of the forests. The spectral breath of the high country night wind rustled the spruce boughs and dashed past Young, touching his cheek with elfin caress. He called again, repeated the shout; no answer. He pegged on, knowing that the hunter's camp could not be far away. Up a steep pitch he labored, then stopped to breathe in puffing gasps of the rarified air of the plateau.

On every hand was wild. Cow camps, a few cow waddies, Hegewa and Trickle were almost the only human inhabitants of that vast table-land. It was an eerie place, filled with the night things which eons ago sent prehistoric man scuttling to the shelter of his cave. Even as much as Young had lived in the wilderness, this dark, lonely, ghostly woods road gripped his nerves. With every sharpened faculty alert, he stood listening, hoping to hear the horse bell on one of Hegewa's ponies.

Like a hurtling javelin there leaped through the blackness a cry, piercing, wavering, high-pitched, then low. Young shivered. As many times as he had heard it before, it never failed to make his muscles tense, his heart pound faster. This night the full-mouthed, yarring howl of the queen wolf reached into Young's imagination, gripped it. It was as though his coming was challenged. Again the high, quavering blare of the pack call lifted from the breaks a mile back in the timber, echoed in the woods, died away in hoarse, deep-throated reverberance.

"Go to it, old girl!" exclaimed the Federal man. "Yell your fill while you can."

In defiance that chilling signal to the pack lifted over the top of the plateau again.

It was still pounding in the ears of Young as he groped his way into the camp of Hegewa, which he located by the bark of Hegewa's trap dog. The cabin was welcome, a veritable citadel, though consisting only of moldering logs.

With the yammering of Unaweep's pack in the excitement of a kill filling the still night, Hegewa and Young threaded their way back to the stalled auto. Trickle had given up hope of aid that night and had made his bed beside a camp fire. With Hegewa's saddle horse straining at the tugging lariat, the little car was yanked over the hill and close to the camp. Late supper, bed, and then morning broke with mists lifting before the attack of the countless sunbeam army. Young and Hegewa squatted before the door while Trickle sat near by, smoking thoughtfully. It was a council of war.

"Won't pay attention to scent post trap sets. What remains of the pack fights shy of poison. I get coyotes and magpies, but no wolves. Most of all, I can't seem even to make a good try at this old she-wolf, Unaweep," declared Hegewa. "She keeps out of trails, follows hard ground where there would be a chance to set a trap. I've made every sort of a trap set that I know, strung out every kind of poison bait. The whole bunch under her leadership seems to melt away and drop out of that part of the country, only to show up with a whalin' kill somewhere else on the plateau. I'm licked to this point."

"But you're going to get her?" said Young, with a note of question in his voice.

"Get her!" snorted Hegewa. "You damn know I'm going to get her; and the rest of her kin."

"That's the stuff!" cheered Young. "Stay with it until you do, Burt. Wolves are wolves, and some day you can outthink her."

"I'll be thinkin' faster than I have to date when I do."

Days of riding followed. At a number of points the men found the cross-toed track of the old queen. There was no mistaking it. Every time they met it Hegewa would growl in his beard and curse his luck of eight years before when Unaweep ripped loose from his trap.

"You've done about everything I would have done," commented Young, after several excursions over the trap lines, poison sets, wolf runways. "This she-wolf seems to know all about our work all as well as we do. Pretty spooky."

"How much blind setting have you done?" asked Trickle.

"Everywhere a set could be made in a runway. Cattle have sprung a lot of my traps. You know, they nose around scent posts just out of curiosity, stumble into the traps, tear up the ground, and ruin the location. Most of the scent posts sets have been spoiled that way. But this old girl won't visit them anyway; torn up or not torn up.

"Trouble is, there are a darned few places on the runways of this bunch of wolves that has earth deep enough to make blind sets. Seems like I've had a try at all of them."

"How about that open aspen-bordered park near Keith's sawmill," asked Young. "Seems to me that is ideal and you've not put in any traps there yet. That's one place she follows the regular trail."

"Too much stock in that park. I could put it off to one side of the main trail, but that wouldn't catch any wolves. Her tracks there have always been right in the dust or muddy parts of that loamy trail. At either end of the park she gets out of the trail altogether—clear away from it. There's just that one stretch that she follows regularly. But so do the dogies."

"Get the cowmen to move the stock out," suggested Young.

"Think they'd do that?"

"You bet they would."

The stockmen readily agreed to shove their cattle out of that section of the range and keep them out. Young and Trickle departed. Hegewa prepared to make the trap set for the one big last try. For several days the riders were busy gathering the cattle from that portion of the range. They were being held in a pasture near the ranger station. The white calf and his mother were in the bunch.

"Looks like a new Stetson for me," chaffed Hegewa as he rode with Charley Bowman.

"Season's not over yet," gloomed Bowman. "But I'll give that hat willingly if you get that wolf."

Night came. Hegewa turned in early. Sleep had wrapped him in rest for several hours when he suddenly sat up, listening. Murder was being committed in the cow pasture. Hurriedly slipping on his boots, Hegewa grasped his rifle and slid out into the night. It might be a gorgeous chance at the pack if there was light enough. Anyway, it was a chance.

High carnival of slaughter was galloping with the wolf pack over the cow pasture. The gray killers raced and howled in excited frenzy. Hegewa reached a little ridge above the pasture. He stopped to listen. A calf was bawling frantically. The herd was milling crazily. There was more death bawling from the calf, the ripping of staples from the fence as the animal in blind fright plunged through the barbed wire heedlessly. The wolf pack yawed and yapped. Through the brush beyond the pasture they raced. Swiftly, moving in silent trot, Hegewa hurried forward. For a few moments there was more grisly noise beyond the pasture. Then sudden silence fraught with tragedy.

For an hour Hegewa stalked. Black night, clutching tree branches, impeded his progress. Then, certain that the pack had made the kill, eaten, and then been frightened away by his own coming, the hunter found his way back to the cabin.

In the morning he followed the tracks of a she-wolf with crossed toes leading a pack of leaping hound devils to where Charley Bowman's white calf had finally bawled out its last breath in a bloody, frothy death gurgle.

Hegewa stood impotently above the remains of what had been a symbol of his contest against the queen wolf. He cursed helplessly and then stubbornly set himself for the next drive against the gray raiders.

"Sure as death," remarked Bowman as though a load had been lifted from his mind. "That calf was marked from its birth as wolf meat. White coat made it a special target in the night, I guess.

"But if you can stop her this fall, I'll not begrudge this one more meal to that wolf and her pack."

"I owe you a hat," reminded Hegewa.

"Get that wolf so I can see her with traps on her feet and a wire muzzle around her jaws and I'll forget the hat!"

The few strays that had broken out were gathered and the cattle shoved down into other ranges. When they were all out, Hegewa carefully made his trap set.

All his care, his training, his lore, were put into setting the first two traps in the aspen park.

Grimly, he went back to the camp, bundled up other traps in the setting cloth, buried all for the night in the ranger station manure pit to kill the man scent. The next day he visited the first trap set, passed on when it appeared undisturbed, then made two other sets in the park.

Days of watching followed. No new wolf tracks appeared in the park. It was disheartening. Hegewa finally came to the conclusion that the wolves might have left the high range and gone into the sage flats below, to the Utah border. Then came word that their sign had been seen near a fresh kill ten miles to the south. Hopefulness came to the hunter. October first approached. Another few weeks and the wolves would not be following the high ranges any longer, but would be loping away to the southward into the La Sal Mountain country beyond the Utah border. If luck and persistence did not do the trick now, it might take another whole season to catch the Unaweep wolf and by that time she would be leading another litter of whelps, have another mate.

The last of September came with blue sky, golden aspen, crispy clear atmosphere. Another kill was reported.

"Come on up," urged Hegewa to Bowman when the latter had visited the cow camp, ready to make it tight for the winter. "Make it about day after to-morrow. I think I'm goin' to get results after all."

"How can you tell?" queried Bowman.

"Feel it in my bones. Living like an Indian, I can come near telling what is goin' on just by the feel of things. And something tells me those old trap sets that have been in that park for the past two weeks are going to do something within forty-eight hours."

Bowman scoffed laughingly.

"I'm not joking," cried Hegewa, half angrily. "I mean it when I say I've got this hunch. I'll have that wolf before the end of the week."

But it did not take that long. Hegewa came hurrying into Bowman's camp in time to stop the cowman from leaving the following morning.

"Got her," exulted Hegewa. "Got her with two traps on her feet. Gosh, it was lucky. Stepped dead center on both traps. Can hardly move. Come help me muzzle her."

Challenging, howling, snarling, daring the two men to come near, Unaweep thrashed in the trap. It looked like a fight to subdue and muzzle her. But once the light pole was across her neck and the rope around her free legs, with Hegewa moving methodically out on that pole to slip the haywire muzzle over her jaws, she gave up.

The queen wolf of Uncompahgre had fallen. Reprieve from death had come to other animals on the plateau.

Forty-eight hours later Hegewa got a wire from Denver.

"Ship skull and skin of Unaweep carefully and at once. Colorado Museum Natural History needs female wolf to complete wolf family group. Young."

Bigfoot, Terror of the Lane Country

I: DEAD OR ALIVE!

$500 REWARD

A Reward of $500 is Offered by The Cattleman's
Association for The Notorious Outlaw, Bigfoot

DEAD OR ALIVE

A bounty was on Bigfoot's life. He was marked for death. He
was outlawed from Red Pinnacle, where it stands as a headland
of the Flattop Mountains all the way to Utah. Any trail rider
who sighted him would shoot him on sight.

The life of an outlaw is hazardous. The life of a wolf is brimming
with danger. To be both outlaw and wolf and still escape
the snares, traps, bullets, poisons of man, or death by fang, requires
cunning.

Bigfoot was both outlaw and wolf, and he was cunning.

He was born far up on the austere shaley slopes above Roan
Creek near De Beque. This country was then dominantly frontier.
It has not changed materially since.

Bigfoot had grown prodigiously through the stages of the
awkward cub. When three years old he had started campaigning
to become pack leader. At first he had been whipped. But
he would not give up. He was a brawny four-year-old when he
first led his pack through the sagy flats and shaley slopes that

drop away from the Flattop Mountain country, to where they finally blend out into the plains that border the Green River in Utah. The Lane Country, it is called, named after the Lane family, pioneers.

Big of bone, with dynamic sinews that never rested when awake, with powerful frame and broad, intelligent head, Bigfoot was a wolf leader. Gradually he accumulated knowledge of man. Some of it had not been pleasant. Bitter poison had seared his throat when he was little more than a pup. He had thrown it from his stomach and staggered away to recover from the quick poison sickness. It had made him poison-wise.

Years had passed. Each season he had led a pack of killers. His track, the great footprint that would barely fit inside of a number two horseshoe, was the trademark of this four-pawed cutthroat and his murderer crew.

More clashes with poison had taught that he dare not eat of anything but that which he had slaughtered. Each meal required a new kill; this very part of the education of the renegade wolf not to touch questionable meat is the cause of his greatest destructiveness.

Traps in trails, around scratchings or scent posts; younger, less wise wolves lunging in traps, and the loss of mates to these steel demons made Bigfoot trap-wise. He knew, too, when a man had a rifle and when he had none. New tricks tried by trappers fooled less canny wolves. Avoiding these pitfalls had further sharpened his wits. In man lore this wolf was a very wizard. Each new effort of the bounty hunters, the ranchers and the cow hands added another bit of learning to his store without injuring Bigfoot.

Seventeen years is a long time for a wolf to run the same range without being touched by some form of man-made death machine. But Bigfoot had succeeded.

With his mate Bigfoot had denned in 1919, 1920, and 1921 in the breaks above Roan Creek. Fuzzy babies had come, suckled at the breasts of his mate while Bigfoot foraged or kept guard. Then riders had located the den and the wolf babies had been dug out. Their scalps taken to town had brought to the bounty hunter who had found the den fifty dollars per whelp. It was a profitable annual income for the lucky hunter. In spite of these losses, that instinct of the wild thing which pulls it back to its old range again had drawn Bigfoot and his mate to the Roan Creek watershed.

A false spring had come. Little gullies carried water turbid with gray silt washed from limestone and shale cliffs. Buds swelled and the early Easter flowers sent forth haunting dainty perfume that barely touched the air with fairy-like sweetness. Then winter rushed back for a farewell visit, making mud into rocklike hardness and stopping the sap flow.

Bigfoot and his mate sought some safe den. They sniffed nervously at the old dens from which their babies had been taken. They sensed danger there. Instinct pulled them back to their favorite denning ground. Other instinct warned them away. Their wolf minds were in a quandary of unrest.

Northward they ranged. Bigfoot led, his great gray body swinging easily to the trail trot. His mate, three-legged, maimed by a trap years before and subsequently trap-shy, followed laggingly. They foraged beyond the Book Cliffs. Then they headed northward to the country where Rags had ranged. They even swung eastward to Sweetwater country, the edge of Old Lefty's domain. Back again their trail turned. For a few days that instinct to den in the old whelping ground held the upper hand.

It was then that Bigfoot found an old coyote hole near the head of an arroyo and started digging a den. The she-wolf helped, but her three legs were no match for the brawny four of her mate and master.

The print of a shod horse in the trail, the imprint of a cowboy's boot in the soft earth, the smell of man and a crude trap set made them abandon that den.

Again they ranged. Hunger came and was appeased. Calves and yearlings were slaughtered by Bigfoot. Satiated, they found their way to some high bench and there slept until hunger or restlessness came again.

And when Bigfoot fed, the cattlemen frowned.

Tom Currier, rancher, hung over the counter at the De Beque bank, talking to his friend Wilcoxson, the banker. Both had stock ranging near the Book Cliffs. Both had recently felt keenly the killing by Bigfoot.

"It can't go on, Tom," declared Wilcoxson determinedly. "This cattle industry near De Beque simply can't carry this burden."

Tom Currier, short, mustached, dark, wiry, tanned, with good-humored, determined face, gazed out of the window along the street of De Beque where a rider was trotting his horse away from town back to the range.

"Yeh, I know. We've said the same thing before," he replied. "But you and I both know that with a bounty of $500 on his head and no one to take him at that price, there's no use offerin' more. A thousand bucks would not bring him in any quicker than five hundred.

"Every man on our outfit had a try at Bigfoot last year. The way he cut into our calf crop was simply scandalous. We've probably been the heaviest losers. But even with our givin' those fellows all the time they wanted, with a five-hundred-dollar reward up an' all, this old wolf still goes his way, feeding on veal and stepping wide of the traps."

Gloomily, Wilcoxson looked out of the bank to where the rider was disappearing from view. To these men the menace of the killer was very real and of magnitude. He had slashed through their herds. They had come to fear his forays.

"Well, I'm goin' to Denver during the stock show week and I'm goin' in to talk with the fellow that is the head of the Biological Survey there. You know him— Young. He had a man north of here that trapped the wolf, Lefty, and another over southwest of Grand Junction that caught out a whole pack. He ought to have some fellow that knows enough about wolves to catch this old fellow."

Like many another rancher, Wilcoxson came to the office of Stanley Young in the gray old Custom House Building in Denver. The shaggy end of winter had whipped across Colorado and its capitol city, leaving dirty patches of old snow, plastering down splotches of soot, making buildings, streets, sparrows and even people a bit dingy, ready for the fresh cleansing snows and showers of spring.

"Sure, I can get a man in there," declared Young when Wilcoxson made his request for help. "Hunter down on the Picketwire, near Thatcher, cleaning up on the last of a pack that an old renegade wolf named Whitey had running with him. I can shift him over pretty soon."

"How long?" Wilcoxson had asked.

"Can't tell," was the reply. "Maybe a week, maybe a month—all depends on what luck he has."

"But these wolves are on our range now, just raising the devil," remonstrated Wilcoxson. "Can't you send him in right away? I can show him their tracks within ten hours after he gets on our range, and a fresh kill within forty-eight, certain."

"We'll put in every hunter we've got if necessary," Young assured Wilcoxson. "I'll send this fellow, Hegewa, right away. He knows wolves like a book. But there's one thing you fellows will have to do. You've got to take off that reward and you've got to get those bounty hunters out of there, pronto. We can't have any amateurs messing up that den, smearing the trails, putting in clumsy trap sets and scaring these wolves."

This Wilcoxson promised.

"But if we take that bounty off and exclude bounty hunters from our cow ranges, you've got to do your part and get that wolf before you quit."

"We'll get him," replied Young.

Snow squalls rushed down cañons, swept over the Flattops, blanketed the valley with thick, heavy snow that melted in a few days only to be followed by another deluge of frozen rains as Bigfoot and his mate continued to hunt for a safe den. With coats starting to shed, wet, bedraggled, disheartened by fresh tracks of cowmen, the wolf pair started southward toward De Beque. Down the cañon of Roan Creek they went by night. Twinkling lights marked ranch houses. From a high butte they looked at the winking lights of De Beque. From there they turned northwestward, still seeking denning country, where they might raise a family in safety and peace. Bigfoot was old, and if there were to be any young wolves to carry on in that section, he and his mate would have to raise their puppies to maturity this year.

Another den was started. It was in the ledgy oil shale which here stands in giant blocks miles square. Again the scent of man on the trail, the imprint of a shod horse hoof sent a tingle of fear through the she-wolf and caused Bigfoot to bristle and growl in misgiving and anger. Man enemies seemed to threaten wherever they turned.

Now came the peak of late winter. Cold gusts whipped down in sweeping dashes, bringing sleet, cold of the high country, slushy, wet snows. A sunny day came. Then snowy winds howled until it seemed that winter never would let up so den making might proceed.

With that lurking, burning fear for their unborn pups' safety driving them, the two wolves traveled ridge, draw and cañon. Finally, with new purpose, Bigfoot started one morning through the bluster of the storm, heading westward. He did not look back. The she-wolf, hesitant at first, finally followed. Bigfoot trotted hour after hour away from the old denning grounds. He was deserting the old home on Roan Creek.

It was at the very beginning of this uproarious farewell of Old Winter that Hegewa landed in De Beque. He found Wilcoxson awaiting his arrival anxiously.

"You're not afraid of superstitions, I guess," remarked the banker-stockman after the greetings.

"Nope," returned Hegewa, laughing. "February thirteenth, nineteen twenty-two, is just like any other day to a wolf, and so I guess it is to me."

"We'll pull out to the camp," suggested the banker. Hegewa assented.

Grub, traps and outfit loaded on pack horse and then sixteen miles of fighting mud took Wilcoxson and Hegewa to the former's winter cow camp west of De Beque.

"Give him every bit of help you can," Wilcoxson told the cow foreman. "Just everything he wants in saddle stock or anything of the kind."

II: MUDDY TRAILS

Burt Hegewa whistled in a "plague-take-it" manner as he saddled his horse. Two days before he had established poison lines. It was time to check up. Mud or no mud, the campaign against the wolves must go on.

His horse grunted and hunched down as he felt the weight of the saddle on his back. He walled his eyes at Hegewa as though to tell the hunter that any human was an utter fool to take out a horse on such a blustery day. Burt continued to make preparations to take to the trail in spite of the lumbering winds that galloped around the forlorn corral of the Wilcoxson cow camp.

Cinch tested, bridle adjusted, Hegewa threw himself into the saddle and headed the bay out of the open corral. The horse, realizing that wordless protests were useless, no matter how eloquent, started dejectedly along the trail.

Foggy clouds curled over the edges of the Book Cliffs. They were ghostly streamers, eerie drapes for the blocky, grotesque, misshapen cubes that are the foothills near Roan Creek. Oil shale breaks away in stratified cliffs which often rise step after step until the tableland above is reached.

This formation, now partially clothed in the cloud banks that were spitting spasmodic rain on rider and horse, had been a factor in some of Hegewa's operations. No wolf could get up or down the cliffs except at the heads of the cañons. Bigfoot and his mate must stick to definite runways in this country. When on tablelands above the cañons they were free to roam over broad surfaces. On the plains below they could travel in many directions. But when going from lower to higher levels there were certain strategic runway focal points the wolves had to pass. Toward some of these Hegewa now rode. There were ideal places for trap setting and poison stations.

Sullen, lead-colored sky hung a few feet above lower clouds. It was so turbid, so solid, it seemed that if he mounted to the head of a cañon it would be possible to reach out and sink his fingers into that gray canopy. As he climbed he was enveloped by thick fog. Moist fingers of the clouds swished wisps of gossamer mist across his face and hands as he rode. That heavy sky seemed to rise and stay just beyond reach as the trail climbed. It was a clammy, disheartening day, and Hegewa, in spite of the whistle he continued to force from his lips, felt dejected.

On all sides cliff, brush, and stunted cedar were made unreal by the gray robes of the swirling vapors. The sloshing plod of the horse barely drowned the drip-drop of spring tears that splattered from branch and twig. Several times the horse stumbled because of the insecure, greasy, wet adobe footing. Then the whistling stopped; but in a few moments it would come back tenaciously challenging the day.

Long hours in the saddle, the leather under him wet with little seeping streams that came through tiny holes in his slicker, his hat heavy and wet on his head, the horse steamy, smelly, tired from the extra work of keeping on his feet while laboring through the mud, finally ended as Hegewa came back to the cow camp. He took care of the bay and came sloshing into the little cabin.

"No luck," he said in greeting to the cow-puncher who was frying bacon over the sheet-iron stove. "Not a wolf track around the bait sets."

Hegewa followed the poison lines on subsequent days. His eyes kept keen watch of the trail. He sighted no wolf track.

"They're denning," he declared one night as he sipped coffee. "I'm goin' up to-morrow mornin' and look over those old dens near the head of Roan Creek. They may be in that country. Pass the cow."

The puncher handed the can of condensed milk to the hunter. It is the invariable cream supply of the cow camp. Seldom do cow-punchers milk cows. Tin cans are the extent of the dairy industry in most cow camps.

Fortified by hot coffee "strong enough to float a railway spike," Hegewa took the trail next morning. Denning season was on full swing. These wolves had stopped running the trails. He must find the new den. There was no use to try to trap now in the sea of mud that was spread over the uplands and cañon floors. Later, with the den located, he could make a trap campaign.

For a whole day Hegewa scouted around the old denning section. At one point he found a little new sign, but not a new den. The next day, not satisfied, certain that there was a den somewhere, he again rode the trail. When he came in to the cabin the night of his final checking up on the old denning sections, he was whistling cheerily.

"You must have found that den," suggested the cow waddie, as he yanked open the door of the little red-cheeked stove and hauled out a pan of crispy, golden-brown baking-powder biscuits.

"Nope. No den," replied Hegewa, smiling as he sought the questionable cleansing powers of cold water, laundry soap, and a much-abused camp towel. "But I'm just plumb sure that they're denning—and not in this country. Thought first that my work here was not much use, but I've come to the conclusion that if I drift west to-morrow, down on the desert over a portion of the Currier Brother's range maybe I'll run into something. So I'm goin' to pull for there."

March winds snorted and puffed as Hegewa left Wilcoxson's camp for Currier's. It was slow going. But he was light-hearted. He had eliminated one possible section from his operations. As fine a country for wolfing as the Roan Creek section might be with its forced trails centering at the heads of cañons, it was now definitely out of the campaign against Bigfoot, for Bigfoot was not there.

Harry Knight, foreman at the Currier cow camp, welcomed the hunter.

"Not much luck in the upper country?" he questioned as they unloaded the pack horse.

"Gosh, no," replied Hegewa. "There ain't no wolves up there. Anyway, the runs were so full of mud that it was impossible to plant a trap anywhere without churnin' up the whole country."

"Well, it's dry enough 'round here. We've been at the edge of the storm but not in it. It's hung up there on the range for the past ten days."

"Don't I know it. It sure raised cain with my plans up there. Believe it drove those wolves out as much as anything did."

"Going to try poison here?" asked Knight. Hegewa wrinkled his brow as he stopped to roll a cigarette.

"Hardly think so. Old wolf mate of Bigfoot probably has had her whelps already. Better to find the den first."

With a Colorado sun coaxing the tiniest bit of green up in the grass, Hegewa the next morning hit the trail in the first ride of many which circled out from the cow camp through the surrounding empire of alkali, sage and greasewood. He was positive the den of Bigfoot and his mate was not far distant. His conviction was strengthened by the report from Harry Knight that wolves had recently killed several calves and yearlings.

"He's an old wolf," declared Hegewa after hearing Bigfoot always preferred calves. "His teeth are gettin' worn down. He can't kill big stuff. But there are probably several seasons of calf killing in him yet. And if he gets to raise a family, he'll fill this country up with yearling wolves for next season that would sure play hell."

Harry Knight nodded agreement.

Now started a great game of hide and seek, with the wolf on one hand, the patient hunter on the other. At the end of the first day Hegewa came in with his horse's head drooping. The day-long ride had produced some results. He had found fresh wolf tracks.

"Matter of a few days I'll have his den located," he declared to the several riders and Harry Knight, as they sat at supper. "Gosh, though, if he is as big as his track he's almost the size of a yearlin' steer. Is he just a normal size wolf?"

"Yeh," affirmed one of the riders. "I've seen him once. Then went over and looked at the track. Didn't seem extra large as a wolf. But when I looked at that track—oh, boy, my hair bristled up."

Another day of riding followed. More tracks were sighted.

"Not yet," replied Hegewa to the cow hands' questions that night. "But in a day or so, I'll have that den located."

"And then what?" asked Knight. "Dig out the whelps?"

Hegewa looked up in slow, squinting gaze.

"Nope," he replied. "I should say not. Never go near the den."

"What's the idea then? We usually get the whelps quick, 'cause the old mother'll move them soon as any rider goes around the den."

"I'm not going near that den," declared Hegewa. This was a new side light in wolf hunting for the cowmen. They had never heard of not molesting a den after it had been found.

"Well, what are you going to do? How in Sam Hill are you goin' to locate the den if you don't go to it?" asked Stub, the short, fat youngster that was riding for Currier's for the first season.

For a moment Hegewa puffed at his cigarette in silence. Then he shifted his position in the old board chair.

"Wolves in denning season have two ways of traveling," he said seriously. "They go out from the den and then they come back toward it."

The group smiled. Stub was being chaffed. Hegewa noted the mirth. He grinned.

"That sounds a bit funny, I know. But what I mean is that when a wolf goes away from his den he travels differently than when he is coming back to it. After they den up the old male wolf does most of the hunting. When the pups are maybe a week old the mother wolf may hunt a little, too. But mostly it is the old he-wolf that does the killing. That's an instinctive habit, I guess, for if she got killed or hurt it might mean death for the babies.

"They always sort of scout around before they ever leave the den. Then after they are sure that they are not watched they start out just as straight as a bee flies to water. There is no switching from that straight line unless something unusual happens. They travel that way for several miles. Then they start rummaging around for a kill.

"After they start back to the den they don't go in straight lines. Their tracks are circlin' around. When they get toward the den they snoop around more than ever. It's not so hard to tell about whether a wolf is goin' from his den or toward it. If you can pick up his line goin' out from the den all you have to do is back track. Then you'll find a lot of these tracks coming together and you're near the den."

"Yeh," laughed Stub. "Perfectly simple. Anyone could see it in the dark."

"But then what?" asked Knight.

"Blind trap set in the runs out from the den far enough away not to bother the old scamps and let 'em walk right into the traps."

Two days later Hegewa reported the den located. "It is in shaley slope below an old rotten rock cliff in some choppy country over northeast from here. They cover a big territory. I've found in tracking them that they come within seven miles of Grand Junction. But this is their den sure. Going to make some trap sets to-morrow. Better come along, Harry."

Knight accepted the invitation readily. The next morning Hegewa hauled out an old pair of moccasins from his pack and handed them to Harry Knight.

"Guess they'll fit well enough for to-day," he remarked.

"Oh, I can wear my boots," replied Knight.

"Don't kid yourself," said Hegewa. "No cow-puncher's boot tracks around my trap sets to scare these lobos away. You put on those moccasins and do like I say or you can't go along; savvy?" Hegewa grinned. Knight looked ruefully at the soft-soled footwear. "And don't handle those any more than you have to. They've been cleared of man scent and wrapped in an old, descented canvas setting cloth, so be careful not to get sweaty hands on them."

Going to the barn, Hegewa dug out from the edge of an old manure pile his own moccasins and traps. He also took out a queer assortment of other objects. Among them was a calf hide. He handled it with cotton leather-palmed gloves that had been buried with the rest of his plunder. There was also an old wolf paw and a wolf tail that had been skinned out and a stick inserted where the tail bone had been removed. He wrapped all within the calf hide.

Returning to the house, he bade Knight remove his boots and socks. Hegewa washed his own feet, carefully sudsing and drying them. He bade Knight do the same. Then clean woolen socks and the descented moccasins were put on. In a few moments they were on horseback. Knight grinned broadly and winked wisely at Stub, who was smiling at the careful preparations of the hunter.

For several hours they rode, then dismounted.

"Here, you can carry these traps," Hegewa directed, handing them to Knight. "Use these gloves. Don't let your bare hands touch the traps. Be careful you don't brush up against things too much with your clothes."

"Why don't you ride over to where you're going to make the set?"

"Well, it ain't the best plan. Heady old wolves hop out of a trail quick as a wink if they find the track of a shod horse. Boot tracks make 'em shy, too."

Hegewa led the way to a place where an old cow trail crossed a low saddle in the sagy hills. He kept out of the worn trail. After a few steps he pointed silently at a track in the soft trail. Big and deep, the track of Bigfoot was outlined there.

At a place where thick oak brush hedged a little open space Hegewa stopped. It was certain that anything following that trail would pass here. Knight threw down the traps and watched.

With a trowel that was part of the kit he had taken from the cow camp manure pile, Hegewa carefully dug up an imprint of Bigfoot's paw. It came out intact, and Hegewa laid it carefully on the edge of the calf skin on which he knelt.

"What you plan to do with that?" asked Knight. "Send it to the museum in Denver?"

"You watch what I do with it," chaffed Hegewa. "By the way, most fellows don't savvy this calf-hide setting cloth. You know, some of the boys use canvas. But I'd rather use a calf skin. Some way it still carries calf scent. That helps kill man scent.

"'Nother thing, we keep all the excess dirt on this setting cloth. No dug soil is left near the trap set. Wolves just too darned suspicious. Guess if other trappers would have done this they would have snagged this old codger before. But they won't do it. Think they're wiser than the wolf. Go ahead their own sweet way. And the wolf just outthinks them."

Hegewa hollowed out a place where the number fourteen wolf trap would set comfortably. Then he dug a place where he could hide the chain and drag hook.

"I'm puttin' this point in the trail a bit lower than it was," he pointed out to Knight. "We often make a little depression over the pan of the trap so when the old wolf comes along, he'll throw more weight on it. You know how it is when you put down your foot in a little hollow in the ground you've not been expectin'. Well, that's the way with Mister Wolf. He socks his foot down harder, sure to set off the trap and at the same time shoves his paw down farther between the jaws. We get less nipped toes that way and higher holds on 'em."

Hegewa sprung open the trap. The strong steel jaws gaped wide, held by the trigger on the pan. He lowered the trap carefully to the bottom of the little hollow.

Then, straightening up, he carefully walked a few feet down the trail, stooped, picked a bunch of dead grama grass with its dry, stiff, wiry stems, broke off a half dozen of these, then came back to the trap. Carefully he placed the tiny dry stems under the pan of the trap as minute vertical grass stem pillars propping up the pan. Any light weight thrown on the pan would not set it off until the tiny grama grass stems collapsed under the pressure.

"What's the idea?" asked Knight. "Never heard of that sort of a stunt before."

"We do it quite often," replied the hunter. "It keeps rabbits and chipmunks from setting off the trap. I have another reason for doing this. It's that wolf track I dug up where I started this set."

As he talked, Hegewa placed a canvas cloth about four inches in diameter over the pan of the trap, called a trap pad by the Survey man. This prevents earth and sticks from interfering with the action of the trap pan and trigger. He filled in around with soft earth, carefully keeping the trap jaws in the clear.

Then he lifted the little slab of earth he had dug out at first. Carefully, he trimmed off the excess soil until he had a flat pancake-shaped piece, in the center of which there still remained the original track of Bigfoot.

"He can't object to having that sort of a trademark on this trap set," laughed Hegewa as he lowered the wafer of soil into place over the trap. "See now, this is held up by those grama grass stems. We'll fool him with this, sure."

The next move was to sift dusty earth around the trap, fill in the corners, and pack cracks where they were still visible, covering the set in such a way that not even the keenest man eyes could detect that the soil had been moved or disturbed. This is the art of successful trap setting.

"Now for the finishing touches to what I call a real trap set," said Hegewa.

He picked up the old wolf tail with its stick handle and the dried wolf paw that he had brought rolled in the calf skin. He carefully pressed the pads of the wolf paw into the track left by Bigfoot, freshening the old track, defining it more clearly. With a quick, whisking motion he fanned over the earth with the wolf tail, blending the little particles of earth that still did not seem just right. The effect was as though some wind had come along and laid light fingers on the soil, brushing it back and forth. Nothing seemed disturbed. The old wolf track appeared as though it had not been lifted from the trail. Trap and chain with drag were hidden beyond possible detection.

Getting to his feet Hegewa picked up the setting cloth containing the loose earth which had not gone back where the trap had been buried. This he carried with him.

"I can see now how come some of the fellows around here didn't get this old sinner," remarked Knight. "If you have to go to that sort of measures to get him. None of our punchers would take that trouble. They'd set a trap and if the wolf blundered into it, all O.K. If not, still O.K."

"Well, you can catch common wolves with ordinary trap sets, but the amateurs and bounty hunters have trapped at this old cuss so much they probably have him so educated he can tell a common trap as far as you and I can see."

Three more traps were placed before they returned to the cow camp. Each was set with meticulous care. They circled away from the den on every trip between trap sets. Once they topped a little ridge and the hunter pointed to a little, low, shaley cliff below which there was a slope covered with sage and stunted cedars.

"Den's there," he declared. "The old lady and her whelps are in some snug hole just under the edge of that cliff. Bigfoot's around somewhere, soakin' up the sunlight and watching."

Night had fallen when they reached the cow camp, and biscuits, strong coffee, the inevitable condensed milk, steaming steaks, sorghum for the biscuits, fried potatoes, and canned peaches were on the oilcloth-covered camp table. The men were making prodigious inroads on the food when the two riders entered the cabin and proceeded to scrub faces and hands.

"How many lobos to-day?" asked one of the riders.

"None to-day, old-timer," replied Knight. "Maybe all-same big wolf to-morrow. Anyway, I'm not bettin' on this wolf lobo no longer. He's goin' get his'n pronto and Burt here is goin' to be the boy that does it."

"I've known that wolf for nigh five years," remarked one of the hands. "I've tried to trap him myself. Want to bet anything on that?"

"You damn betcha," replied Knight. "Make it five pounds of chewin' plug and I'll take you on."

"I see where I chew on you for the rest of the year," replied the rider, grinning. "You're on."

III: THE DEN UNDER THE CLIFF

Bigfoot had found ideal denning country. It was dry, rock-walled, not like the old denning places. There was easy digging between more solid rock. A good hole could be scratched out in the loose earth. And above the place where he and his mate had chosen to make their den there was an ideal lookout point.

Both worked at building the den. Dirt flew as they hurried to get it done to receive the new whelps. It would be but a few days before the little family would arrive.

Bigfoot dived into the partially dug hole. Puffing, his red tongue lolling out, panting until his sides heaved, he worked in the tunnel of the den, scratching and clawing. Out he came, backing, kicking loose earth behind him until finally it was all shoved to the mouth of the hole. Then it was the turn of the she-wolf. In spite of her having to depend on three legs, she worked lustily, grunting, snorting, kicking dirt in great clouds.

Finally, the den was done. And none too soon. Within a day after it was finished their pups were whimpering and blindly groping for their mother's breasts. It would be some days before their eyes would open. In the blackness of the room at the end of the tunnel the wolf parents had dug they would not need sight. When, after two weeks, they got ready to come out of the den, they would have their eyes open.

Meanwhile there was ample room for the cubs within the den. It was a good wolf den, built as instinct had dictated, according to the hereditary specifications of wolf dens. First there was a short tunnel about seven feet in length, through which a crouching wolf might walk. Then a narrow place was reached. Here a wolf could just comfortably squeeze by. It is the point of defense against invaders. Back of this narrow place the den widened and there were a series of enlargements where a grown man could have crouched. At the far end was the biggest room of all, large enough for Bigfoot, his three-legged mate, and their growing family.

Proudly the she-wolf licked the fluffy, soft coats of the whelps. Throatily she welcomed Bigfoot as he nosed into the den, sniffing, inquiring. Proudly the father came out of the tunnel and went rocking away in his trail trot to make a raid on the calves of Currier Brothers.

Several days passed. The she-wolf came out from the rooms of the den, ready to hunt. It was a relief for her to stretch her limbs after lying on the dirt floor of the den for hours.

The two loped away to a kill. For several miles they loped away from the den. Usually the dog wolf does the killing when there are whelps for the mother wolf to care for. When the father is away during the season when the whelps are young, the she-wolf will kill closer to the den. When she does, she will sometimes eat of dead meat for several days after the kill, provided it has not been disturbed. These wolf habits all tend to protect the mother so she can care for the babies.

In an unhurried manner Bigfoot and his mate cornered a calf that bawled lustily for its mother. With quick drive Bigfoot threw the little body to the ground. He slit its throat and the warm blood spurted with the beats of the dying heart. Hungrily the she-wolf licked up the warm blood, ripped at the tender, quivering flesh. Satiated, the two trotted back toward the den, circling, stopping to test the wind with their nostrils dilated, then flying like daylight ghosts through the brushy draws and sagy hills.

At the den the she-wolf again sought the dark, smelly room at the end of the tunnel, where the whimpering, fuzzy pups had been huddled on the dry earth floor while she was hunting. There she gathered to her body the little ones that drew from her breasts the strength she had derived from the warm flesh of the calf she and her mate had killed. Until they were well developed and left the den she would mother them, rule them, as does any mother with her children. This is the rule of wolf families.

Bigfoot, cautious, suspicious of every unusual sound, sight or smell, climbed up on a little low bench that topped the rotten rock cliff above the den. Here he took his post as guard. Through hours he lay dozing in the sun, sleeping off the effects of the last kill.

When he felt he could leave the den he would lope away, scouting the country. The bump of inquisitiveness is well developed in the wolf. He must know what is going on. So Bigfoot looked for other dens, watched the coyotes as they sneaked through the brush, eyed the riders that loped over plains and down draws. With his curiosity satisfied concerning these sights, he would start along the trails like a lone buck Indian, scouting, hunting, picking up trail knowledge of what is going on in the neighborhood.

It was an ideal place, this den under the cliff, and Bigfoot was contented as he had not been before this spring. Perhaps his cubs would follow him that summer in the training season when he would instruct them in how to throw a steer, how to slit the throat of the tender veal calves.

Then came the time when the wobbly whelps came out of the den. Some of them ventured forth on their own initiative. Others came only after they had been lifted by the scruff of their furry necks by their mother, hauled, squealing, then quiet, to the mouth of the den and deposited on the earth that was spread around the door of the wolf home. Their eyes were open now. During sunny hours most of their time was spent near the mouth of the den in play.

At these times Bigfoot would look down on the playing whelps in all the pride of a wolf father. Invariably one little dog whelp would lead the others in coming out of the den and then would be the bully during the play. The she-wolf would gaze at him with great pride, as though to say he was already the future pack leader. Bigfoot would dream wolf dreams of the time when that cub would be strong, lusty, and merciless in driving into the bloody confusion of the kill.

Nearly three weeks had gone by since the whelps were born. Nursing time was about past. For several days Bigfoot had brought home meat. He had not carried it in his jaws, but had swallowed it; then upon his return he had disgorged it within the den. The she-wolf had done this, too. This method of feeding the whelps their first meat soon gets the den filthy. Sometimes as much as two hundred pounds of disgorged meat which the whelps have been unable to consume have been found in and around wolf dens. The stench from spoiling disgorged meat is one reason for the whelps spending much of their time in the open, and is also a reason why wolf mothers often move their family to a new den, miles distant, when the old den gets too foul with rotten flesh.

It was on a sunny day when the whole family was out of the den and Bigfoot was in his usual sentinel place, fulfilling the denning season obligation of the wolf father to keep watch, when the wind first carried new man scent to him. Bigfoot raised, his ears cocked forward.

"Gerwhuff-ff," he cautioned his mate. "Gerr—r—r." It was a warning to hunt cover.

Quick apprehension assailed the she-wolf. She herded the cubs toward the mouth of the den, picked up the first one, unceremoniously carried it to safety, then hurriedly came back after the others.

Bigfoot sniffed. He lost the scent. Then it came again, wafted by a loitering breeze. With the man scent came the smell of sweaty horses. Bigfoot, his heart thumping at the fear which these odors brought, dropped swiftly to the mouth of the den. This scent of man and horse mingled had always been present when their other dens had been raided. Now it made Bigfoot desperate with anxiety. The she-wolf had caught that second scent-bearing breeze. Her hair bristled as she tucked away the last of the whelps.

For the next few days Bigfoot was doubly cautious. Then, reassured, he became less suspicious.

It was a heart-warming sight for Bigfoot to watch the youngsters playing from his sentinel cliff. They were awkward, roly-poly little things, but with great wolf blood in their veins. Bigfoot could see their every move, though the point at which he kept watch was more than fifty feet from them.

At night, with the whelps packed away in the den, his mate now went night after night to help with the kill of the Currier calves. For a time after that man scent had been detected Bigfoot had deserted his regular runways. Now he returned to them again, keeping his eyes open for the imprint of shod horse or other man tracks.

So hours, days, a week passed, without any disturbing incident. Bigfoot again felt that this den of cubs might reach maturity, might follow him to the kill.

IV: THE MOTHER HEART

For three days Hegewa had set traps near the den. Then passed a day that he scouted in another direction. Calves had been slaughtered in the pastures, within a few hundred yards of the cow camp, and in far ranges where the cattle had been turned out for the summer. Bigfoot's tracks were always around those kills. Calf meat was his particular specialty.

"Nothin' new," Knight had assured him. "Regular thing every spring to lose calves like this. Maybe we'll be doin' it again next year."

"You'll not," declared Hegewa. "You know damned well you'll not, even if Young has to send in the whole army of the Survey hunters. I know my wolf. We've just as good as got him and his whole family."

"I just can't quite give up the idea that we ought to get those whelps while the gettin' is good," observed Knight.

"I can poison them," said Hegewa. "If it comes to a final showdown, I can get poison into a yearling wolf. Even a two-year-old will take it. But it's trappin' that old he-leader that takes the pains. And as long as there is a chance to catch him on his runs from the den, I'm goin' to stick to that plan."

Knight shook his head and walked away. A touch of gloom came to Hegewa when several days passed and he did not find the big-footed renegade in his traps.

Nearly a month had gone by since Hegewa first started on the trail of Bigfoot. It was time to get results. Methodically, exerting all of his hard-earned wolf lore, he had doggedly trailed the big fellow. Somewhere the trail had to end. And the end of the trail was the extermination of Bigfoot and his family.

On April fourth Hegewa hit the trail as usual, riding his trap lines. He did not go to the traps. Rather, he kept away from them, looking down from an open place on some near-by ridge. He had left the cow camp for nearly two hours when Knight saw him coming back on a fast trot.

"Need your help," cried Hegewa, as he came jangling up to the corral. There was triumph in his voice.

"Catch anything?" asked one of the riders.

"You bet! Old boy himself."

"The hell!" exclaimed Stub, the rider.

"Want you to come along with me, Harry," said Hegewa, addressing Knight. "Bring your lariat and I'll want some hay wire to make a muzzle. He's thrashing, roarin' bloody murder, and just churnin' up the whole country where he's hung up in some brush. I want some tools, too. Pick, shovel, and all the stuff we need to get those cubs. We'll have to move fast as the dickens now that the old he-wolf is snagged."

In less than an hour they were back to where the great gray form of Bigfoot was lunging in the trap.

Quickly giving directions, Hegewa soon was easing out on the pole he had rested over the neck of the wolf while Knight held taut the lariat that was snared around the untrapped legs of the wolf. A few quick turns of wire and the wolf was muzzled and then hog tied.

Gingerly one of the riders who had accompanied them loaded the captive Bigfoot on his horse. Like other wolves, Bigfoot acknowledged defeat when he was finally trussed up. Where a few moments before he had thrashed and bellowed defiance, his powerful jaws snapping like the crack of a black snake whip, he now lay quietly across the saddle, the very picture of defeat.

A short ride brought Knight and Hegewa to the den. As they came in sight of the hole under the cliff Knight asked a question.

"What's that rag on a stick I see up there in front of the den?"

"My handkerchief," replied Hegewa. "Not knowing that kink has cost a lot of bounty hunters many a scalp. I was afraid the old she-wolf would come to that den and get out those whelps. She might never hole up again this season. Just keep on the move. But if she didn't get them out right away after Bigfoot was caught, they're still in there. No wolf will go back to a den with a cap or rag on a stick stuck up in front of it. You can't block them by filling in rocks or dirt in the mouth of the den. They'll dig right through that. But this mysterious rag with the man scent will keep 'em away for hours—and keep the whelps in, too."

"See here," said Hegewa as he dismounted. "Here are some fresh tracks of the old girl. Probably stayed with Bigfoot until I showed up this morning. Then she came back to the den right after I put up this flag. See how she has run back and forth and around in a circle. But she's not ventured closer than this. The whelps are in there, all right."

Digging, working with pick and shovel, finally getting into a chamber of the rocky cliff, the two men labored in getting to the whelps. It was rough working after they got in some eight or ten feet. Quarters were cramped; there could be no swing to the pick.

Finally Hegewa hitched into the hole, head first, sliding along on his belly. In his hand was a grain sack. In a moment he came out, crablike, hitching backward.

"Just one more little stretch before we get all the way to the end," he reported. "Can't get there without a bit more digging."

The digging was done, then he eased in again, with thick leather gloves protecting his hands against the needle teeth of the wolf babies. Smelly, dark, earthy den odors filled his nostrils. It was nothing new. He had raided wolf dens for the pups for years. Shivering, the pups were huddled together in a tight knot. With quick, diving hand Hegewa grabbed them, felt for the scruff of each tiny neck, or a leg, yanked them away from their brothers and sisters, and shoved them into the mouth of the waiting bag.

"Six," he said as he stood up after backing out of the den again. "In another week they would have been gone. But we've got the whole family now but that old she-wolf. And we'll have her soon."

There was rejoicing in the cow camp of Currier Brothers that night. Hegewa grinned when congratulated. He listened with amusement as wolf stories were told, tales of raids by Bigfoot in years past, yarns of phantom wolves, of packs that yawed and yammered in the night. It was an evening of celebration, and Harry Knight fried the last of the supply of ham and eggs for the feast that ended with sorghum and biscuits because the canned fruit had run out.

"You got the old devil," remarked Tom Currier at the camp the next forenoon when he looked down at the cowering Bigfoot. "He's been the terror of the Lane country as long as we can remember. Well, the Lord so willeth—but I'm plumb glad he was on our side and not with that old codger."

"There's still a bad one loose," reminded Hegewa. "The old she-wolf mate."

"Goin' to try for her?"

"You bet."

For several days Hegewa did not ride the trap lines as before. He did go back to where Bigfoot had been captured. And he visited the den also. The first trip to these two points he found tracks of the female wolf scattered everywhere. Then they ceased. She had left the country.

"She'll be back," he declared to E. J. Currier, when they talked at the camp. "And when she does, I'll nab her."

To this end Hegewa made preparations.

Seldom can a wolf be tamed if captured after its eyes are open. Few can, if captured before they can see. There is no place in to-day's civilization for the gray wolf except in fur shops, museums, and zoos.

So the whelps were killed. Then with a sharp knife Hegewa dissected their tender little bodies and removed their scent glands. From these he took a small bottle of scent, which he carefully wrapped and protected.

With the same care he had given the setting of the traps along the runs followed by Bigfoot, he went to points near the den and made new sets. Around them he placed the scent taken from the little wolves.

The three-legged mate of Bigfoot had gone far, driven by the big fear. Through the lower country, west from Grand Junction, she wandered. Terror had whipped into the peaceful life at the den and robbed her of Bigfoot. At the same time the den had been rifled and her puppies had disappeared.

Restless, with heartache eating at her, with fear nagging her limping steps, the wolf sought some place of solace otherwhere than near the range of the Curriers. She had killed a steer single-handed in a pasture west of Grand Junction. But there had not been the zest of killing as before. No babies were back in a den whimpering for her to come and nurse them.

Rain squalls, biting winds from the range, soft, enticing breezes that came boiling around the end of the Uncompahgre Plateau to the south, whispering of spring that was creeping up over New Mexico, ruffled her shedding fur. But the invitation to roam did not meet and equal that pull that lay back in the rifled den under the oil shale cliff.

Finally the mother instinct could no longer be denied. She must find out if there had been just one woolly cub spared from that man raid.

Night covered the Currier ranges when the she-wolf of Bigfoot came "home." She trotted to a point near the den. Then she left that, wary, and scouted the place where she had last seen Bigfoot striving to free himself. Finally she trotted toward the den.

Evening had come to cover the movements of the she-wolf. Limping, she trotted eagerly along the trail. She reached a ridge above the old den. She mounted the outlook point on which Bigfoot had rested on days when the puppies played outside the den. Here she stopped, sniffed, lifted her nose and whined for the dead mate.

For a long moment she stood there in the darkness, listening, looking, sniffing the breeze. Faintly, ever so faintly, there came to her the scent of whelps. Excitedly she nosed forward, stopped, took a few more steps. Then a slow little breeze brought it plainly to her nostrils.

It was the scent of her own whelps, fresh, pungent, definite!

Caution could not hold back the she-wolf after that. Still wary, but urged forward by a love universal, overpowering, she moved forward. She came to a bit of grama grass that held the scent stronger.

She trotted a few steps, stopped, circled, started away, whined to call the whelps; then, when no answer came, sniffing the scent again, she turned determinedly and started toward the mouth of the den.

It was inevitable that Hegewa should find her the next morning. Bedraggled by the fight in the trap, weary, heartsick at the disappointment from not finding her whelps, the mate of Bigfoot was whipped, subdued, when the hunter reached her.

Gleaming with the shadows of hate, with the cloudiness of mother love still filming their brightness, she looked up out of her amber eyes at the hunter. But there was no fight. The world had lost its call for the she-wolf. She submitted without struggle to the hog tying, the wire muzzle.

"I kinda hate to do it," declared Hegewa at camp later. "They're just the know-in'est brutes on four legs. Sometimes they're almost human. I've heard 'em cry night after night just outside my camp when I had their whelps in a cage. Look at this old girl comin' back for her whelps, then losin' her head when she caught that scent I put there. Never would have caught her but for that scent. Actually, I sometimes feel sorry for them, wipin' out whole families this way."

"How about their wipin' out nearly forty percent of my calf babies last year?" exploded Currier.

"Well, that is what makes me stay on the job when a bunch of bad wolves like this are up for extermination. After all, they sign their own death warrant in the blood of cattle."

Three-Toes of the Apishapa

I: MATING CALL

For many weeks Three-Toes, mate of old Whitey, had followed the trails on Bear Springs Mesa and north to the Apishapa. She was alone. Like some racing blight the campaign of the Biological Survey had whipped through the wolf pack, obliterating all but Three-Toes. Fate had decreed their doom.

The old she-wolf did not know why this had happened. She only realized the loss of her running mate and the pack. At first she had thought that some far call had beckoned them to other ranges and that Whitey, leading the pack of yearlings, had swung many miles south and would return.

June had passed. Three-Toes first had busied herself teaching the young whelps to stalk victims and to make kills. Had Whitey been there, he would have led this schooling. Then the mysterious hand had dropped on the young pups. Within a few days, Three-Toes had been robbed of the last of her kind.

The trails that summer were lonesome ways. Old familiar runways no longer were marked by wolf footprints except her own; her peculiar three-toed footmark, made by trap-maimed paw. In desperation she had swung north to where on clear nights she could see the flaming beacons of the Pueblo steel mills. Her way had led westward and upward to where the Greenhorn Mountains break from the plain, the first vanguard of the Rockies. She had loped up to the base of the Spanish Peaks, among the cool, green fir and pine trees. She had skirted the peaks, gone up the valley of the Picketwire, had slunk by the crowded little coal camps between Walsenburg and Trinidad, had even gone to the southward beyond square-headed Fisher's Peak, sentinel mountain above Trinidad, the city of the Trinity.

Everywhere there was coyote scent. These yapping prowlers infested every range. For years wolves and coyotes had inhabited the plains regions, had even fought at the same kills. But never has coyote and wolf mated.

Coyotes may be camp followers of wolves licking up the remains of some kill, but wolves will not associate on even terms with coyotes. Three-Toes, although tremendously hungry for wildling's company, did not break traditions. She would have no coyote associate.

She found much dog scent. This interested her. Although usually opposed and ready to fly at each other's throats, dogs and wolves may become running mates.

Recollections of Whitey lingered, leading her on in the search for wolf companionship. Over trails shaded by dusk or bright in early morning light she traveled, or when the moon spread a lacquer of silvery plating over trees, rocks and cliffs, she followed the beckoning spirit of her lost wolf baron, the leader of the pack that had passed.

Weary, lonesome days passed. Three-Toes would lie under the meager shelters of sage brush or piñon and with tongue lolling, rest from her quest. At night she was lured ever onward by the becking ghost calls of the lost pack. At times, heartsickness, yearning, would burst restraint, and she would mount little cliffs or jutting rocks and howl. In the stillness of a windless night mocking echoes came rollicking back from cliffs or cañon walls.

The baking heat of summer passed. Winds with the pointed nip of fall chill came stealing from the high peaks where the first white sugary snow had dusted the gray old heads of the mountains. Flecks of new gold on the sides of the hills were seen from the mesa. Actually these were acres of aspen groves that were changing the soft green mantle of summer for the regal robes of fall. In the foothills the oak brush lost its glossy green. Then came several nights on which Jack Frost hurried through the tree and shrub colonies, painting their leaves with sharp, quick strokes. The oak blazed forth in a riot of color. Cottonwoods on the banks of the streams echoed the gold of the aspen in the hills. Signs of fall were on every hand; winter was but a few days away.

It was mating season for gray wolves. For days the knowledge that she was alone had oppressed Three-Toes. She knew there was no other wolf in this region, yet instinct relentlessly drove her along the trail, seeking a new wolf lord, a masterful, powerful, dog wolf that might be father of her whelps. But her quest was fruitless.

Then came a day when Three-Toes was lying relaxed under the shade of an overhanging piñon, looking under drooping eyelids at the valley below. Stock was grazing peacefully in a pasture beyond which were ranch buildings. As she watched a buff and white form came leaping and barking from the ranch, ran around the herd of cattle, and with deft precision huddled them and started the group toward the corrals. Instantly Three-Toes was all attention. She raised up, growled a little, then whined. The collie dog raced and bounced at the heels of the steers, diving in to nip if they were slow, heading them when they threatened to break and scatter. He was all life, bouncing and biting as though the task of cattle herding was the most joyful thing in the world.

The sun caught the glint of his yellow coat, threw shadows in the deep fur as his springy muscles rippled. Suddenly the cattle broke, swung, and headed back toward the cliff where Three-Toes crouched. Like a flash of tarnished sunlight came the collie with long nose outstretched, with every fiber leaping and alive. He dived, nipped a steer, barked threateningly, then boisterously. He was a very army of energy beating the truant cattle back toward the barn by the big intensity of his romping attack. With a flourish he headed the cattle through a gateway, and then a man came and put up the corral bars.

From her distant lookout point Three-Toes saw the collie disappear at the heels of the man. First there had been only interest in her eyes, then as the cattle broke and drove toward her, she had raised up, nervous and excited. Funny little whines filled her throat. Her lower jaw had chattered until her teeth clicked. She could hardly hold to her place of concealment. Approval had come as she watched the last of the cattle go galloping into the corral, driven by the racing dog.

For many moments after he had disappeared, after the man had gone into the house beyond the gray poles of the corral, Three-Toes lay with eyes wide, staring, looking toward the ranch building.

Evening came. The clear red of the sunset was followed by the translucent tints of a cloudless afterglow. In the pale green-blue of the western sky a crescent moon hung above the teeth of the ragged crest of the Rockies.

Three-Toes arose and stretched. Throughout the afternoon she had kept her eyes on the ranch in the hope of again seeing the collie dog, but the afternoon had passed without the bronzy gold of his coat again flashing in the landscape.

Slowly Three-Toes started along a trail. It was one of the old wolf runs. Every tree, shrub, rock, arroyo was familiar. Memories of the lost days when the old pack, ten strong, had raced along this way flooded back. She whined, started along the road, then stopped and looked to where the deepening shadows of night were blotting out the last reflections of the sunset.

Then with new definiteness, new determination, Three-Toes started along the runway. Mating instinct that would not be denied was driving her irresistibly to seek her lost mate or a new one. Resolutely she loped away on the old wolf trail. She topped a rise, stopped, whined, stood quiet, motionless, then turned and slowly, with stately tread, retraced her steps to the cliff overlooking the pasture and the ranch beyond. For many moments she stood on the little rocky outcrop looking toward the west. Queer emotions whipped through the old wolf's breast. New thoughts, old yearnings, a fierce flood of hunger for companionship surged through her. Restlessly she looked from side to side, and peered at the light in the ranch house. Finally giving way to the irresistible force, she raised her head and in trembling crescendo sent forth the cry for the pack. This she had done before, but now there was a new challenging command in the call. Again and again, her throat vibrating with the ghostly wolf howl. Then she was silent, listening, her ears pointed forward, her head dropped slightly between her hunching shoulders. In faint staccato came the answering bark of the dog at the ranch. A door opened, light flamed out, then there was quiet. Cautiously Three-Toes crept down from the little overlook cliff and across the pasture, crouched as she went under the lower wire of the barbed wire fence, then slowly, watching every sign of the night, she circled toward the corral and the barn beyond. Finally she was within an eighth of a mile of the ranch house. Before this her keen nose had picked up the scent of the dog where he had raced that afternoon. It had set new emotions surging through her. Whining, stopping to sniff the air, Three-Toes approached the corrals.

For many moments she stood watching the blinking light in the window. Then without sound except the rustling padding of her feet, she raced toward the mesa, back to the old wolf run, back to follow the beckoning call of the old pack, the phantom pack and the ghostly leader, the spirit of old Whitey.

Morning found Three-Toes miles away from the ranch of Monroe Brothers and Henerson, the home of the collie dog.

But as the sun set the next evening and the crescent moon shone like silver inlay in the darkening sky, Three-Toes was back at the little rocky cliff above the pasture, her eyes centered on the lighted window in the ranch house kitchen.

—❧❧—

II: SHEP

Shep was a ranch dog. From puppyhood he had known only the buildings and pastures of the Monroe Brothers and Henerson ranch near Thatcher. His mother had been a grade collie like himself; his father was a great, imported Scotch collie with long, slender nose and thick, shaggy, golden-hued coat.

Shep was part of the ranch organization. In his own mind, the dog was quite certain that the routine of the place would not go ahead without him.

He gathered the cows in the morning, then herded them back into the pasture, ran at the heels of the ranch foreman when he went out to round up some of the saddle stock, and after the morning chores were done, he would tag along with the men in the fields.

For the most part there was nothing but business in Shep's schedule. Occasionally the monotony of daily tasks would be shattered by the leap of a jack rabbit from cover in an alfalfa patch. Shep would give chase, yapping and barking until the rabbit would leave Shep yards behind.

These were great occasions. The excitement of the chase would send Shep's heart pounding, his breath quickening and sighing in his throat, and in his mind there leaped up visions inherited from some forgotten experience of his ancestors when they hunted in the wilds, depending on their own ability to bring down game and not having to eat food scraps thrown to them by man.

Another daily event always gave the collie a thrill. It was when he rounded up the cattle and with his quick, driving run headed them into the corral. There was a flashing of hoofs, the dash and drive of running the stock, a feeling on the part of the collie that he was master of the situation. Of all thrills there was that occasional quick dive he made, nipping the heels of the cattle. Sometimes his hereditary instinct would dominate, and he would nip deep into a steer shank. Then there was always the exciting leap away from the flaring hoofs of the kicking steer.

Altogether, Shep's life was a fine dog's life. He knew he had the confidence of his human associates. He found pleasure in working with and for them. They, in turn, provided him with food, his choice of shelter, encouragement in his work, and an occasional whipping when he disobeyed orders.

But with all of these a ranch dog's life may be lonely. The nearest dog to the ranch was some miles away over a ridge. Very occasionally Shep would run away and hunt with this other ranch dog. Those were great holidays. Still there was lacking some dog companion. Lonely spells would come, and Shep would crawl under the kitchen stove or lie in the sun in front of the barn with far-away visions shadowing his mind. Then would come a picture of a sly, roguish dog he had met on one of his few visits to town. He always thought of her when thus dreaming. His other dog was quite all right, but he would not take place of this intriguing stranger of the town.

On nights when wolves howled Shep was restless. At the yap of a coyote he would always go scouting, for there was no tinge of fear in his heart. But when wolves crouched on the mesa and sent forth their pack call, Shep would bark, his hair would bristle, he would growl, whine, and finally seek the protection of the nearest human.

Then came the night when Three-Toes in her loneliness came back to the little limy cliff and sent out her wolf call filled with its yearning for a mate. As usual Shep growled, barked, put his tail between his legs, and slunk around the buildings, but there was something unusual in this call of the she-wolf. He felt it tingling within him. It beckoned him to the open trails, to the alluring life of the wild. Shep ran out a little distance in the pasture, stopped, barked. The call came again. It was a wolf call, even though it carried the big invitation, and Shep's instinct, smothered by associations with man and the habits formed in his ranch life, made him race back half in terror of the wildness in that call and partly in fright from the cajoling cry of the she-wolf.

He stopped at the door of the house, whined, barked, in short, choppy little barks. Mr. Henerson, one of the ranch owners, let him in.

"What's got into that dog lately?" asked Mrs. Henerson.

"I'm plagued if I know," replied Henerson. "He seems all upset and nervous. Guess he's just afraid of the wolves howling up there on the breaks."

Shep looked out from under the stove with his inquiring eyes, seeking from these friends something which might give him the key to the curious enigma that confronted him.

The night passed and another came. Three-Toes would not be denied. She was seeking a mate. The drive of her instinct for perpetuation of the wolf pack was forcing her ahead into the conquest of the heart of Shep. Night shadows had blended the detail of the ranch building into one black mass and Shep was on his usual scouting tour around corral and sheds when the mating call came. He stopped, whined, sniffed the air. Something clutched him. He trotted beyond the barn, around the corral, then out a little into the pasture. He did not bark to-night, but stood whining. It was the call to the pack, and yet hidden in it was a mating call filled with loneliness, yearning, almost a command to the listening dog.

Shep was more upset than ever. He raced ahead for a few hundred feet, stopped again, whined, and for many moments waited nervously, trotting back and forth, peering in to the darkness.

Then like a gray shadow came Three-Toes.

Slowly, pacing sedately, she approached the collie. She stopped, sniffed, then whined invitingly. Shep answered and took a step forward. The wolf stood her ground; the dog hesitated, trotted away a few paces, then came back and whined again. The gray wolf started toward him at a little dog trot. Suddenly fear, gaunt, stark, compelling, leaped through Shep. With a quick little short yelp he dived away, racing back toward the corral and the barn, where would be found the protection of the humans.

Quick as a flash Three-Toes was after him. For a hundred yards Shep ran desperately. Three-Toes made a valiant effort to head him away from the ranch, to shy him back into the open pasture where his misgiving might have been overcome. But Shep, driven by a fear accumulated by his dog ancestors through years of civilized life, was endowed with fleetness never before attained.

They were within two hundred yards of the corral when Three-Toes, catching the man odor quickly stopped, all four paws braced. Shep continued his wild run by the corral poles and clear to the door of the house before he stopped. Then he turned, looked back toward the open field and whined. He got up, faced the place where he had last seen Three-Toes, then was startled by the quick opening of the door.

"What's the matter, pup?" asked Henerson.

Shep nodded his head up and down, licked his lips rapidly, struck out with his front paw sheepishly. Had he been able to more definitely express his uncertainty, he could never have told concisely of the turmoil of compelling emotions that mastered his dog mind.

Two nights later Three-Toes again sent out her call to the collie. This time Shep trotted out into the open pasture. In the voice of the wolf there was an imperious demand that he answer that call.

Shep raced toward the cliff, slowed, stopped, stood waiting. Then from the darkness came the she-wolf. She walked slowly, cautiously toward the dog. Shep stood nervously sniffing, his tail between his legs, his hair bristling, his mind whipped by a flood of uncertainty.

Three-Toes whined appealingly, barked gruffly. Shep broke, started to run, but in the first few leaps he was headed and turned back toward the country. He stopped, skidded, all four feet braced, and then stood taut. Three-Toes stopped in the same instant. For a moment they stood rigid. Then the she-wolf put her nose forward and whined ever so little. She dropped on her front feet then danced away in light, doggish play. Shep trotted a few steps, started back toward the barn, but was headed by the wolf. She again invited him to romp and play in the open pasture. With hesitation at first, the dog started trotting with the wolf.

They stopped, touched noses, sniffed, and then as though queer understanding had been reached, they romped away through the pasture, dived under the barbed wire fence, and galloped out over the old wolf runways of the mesa.

New music was beating in the heart of Three-Toes as she led the collie over the old wolf trails. Here was a new leader for a pack. She, herself, would teach him wolf lore, the knowledge of traps, of how to kill, of how to avoid the pitfalls that men set for killers. In the heart of Shep there was chorusing a song of the open. He raced madly with Three-Toes over open parks, by sagy flats. The vision of the little she-dog of the town was blotted in the spectacle of this dominating female wolf that ran with him along the trails.

"I believe Shep is running with some of those wolves," said Henerson a few days later.

"Ah, come now," taunted Mr. Monroe. "Shep is too steady an old dog for that sort of stuff."

"Well, I'm not so sure," said Henerson. "They all listen to the call of the wild, and when it gets strong enough they break loose and are gone. Whether he is or not, I'm going to lock him in the old chicken run to-night. Maybe if he is fooling around with the wolves they'll come down and we can get a shot at them."

Fierce revolt filled Shep that night when he was dragged protesting into the gate of the chicken run and left there. For many moments he stood looking toward the disappearing figure of Henerson. Something told him that he was mistrusted, that his jailing had something to do with his wild free life with Three-Toes. Man was demanding undivided allegiance to civilization.

Shep had reached a point where this was impossible!

With dog companions at the ranch, Shep might never have sought comradeship with the wolf, but he had tasted of that strong, stirring life of the open range, and now nothing would ever blot it from his memory. The killing of steers, the taste of fresh, warm blood, the excitement that came before the animal was downed by the driving snap of Three-Toes' powerful jaws had transformed him. Along with these moments there had been others in which the two played gloriously.

Wire and wood of the chicken run made an effective jail. Shep looked off to the field where he had met Three-Toes and whined.

Some moments later the call came. Shep barked. For many moments he stood watching and waiting. Again he barked and howled. Then through the dusk his keen eyes saw Three-Toes. He whined, calling to her to come to him. Slowly at first, suspecting some trick or trap, she advanced. Long moments passed while she was reaching the side of the chicken pen. Both were in a state of nervous excitement. Three-Toes ripped with her teeth at the wire. It had no effect. Shep bit at the boards. Then suddenly the wolf began to dig. In a moment the same idea had been conveyed to the collie. Desperately, with quick little soft yelps, they kicked the dirt away with their feet. Soon the hole under the fence was complete. Shep squeezed through and away they went, racing across the pasture, away toward the open country.

III: NEW BLOOD

Never again did Shep go back in peace to the Monroe Brothers and Henerson ranch. In raids, quick, driving, vicious, under the guidance of his new wild mate, he visited his old home and, mad with the excitement of the kill, helped her slaughter the beeves that he had driven in happy fun, days before.

One taste of warm blood and the collie became an outlaw. Latent wild flame leaped forth. He was more clumsy than lithe, quick Three-Toes. But he swiftly acquired some of her tricks in killing. Happy, care-free, led by the spirits of the wild, they played in open sunny places, and then on dark nights trotted through the dusk, slaughtering and gorging in a bacchanalian orgy of blood feast. At other times the ecstasy of their wild wolf-dog love swayed them.

Puppies would come about nine weeks after mating. Three-Toes began to look for denning country. Shep took more of the brunt of the killing. With approving whines Three-Toes watched his increasing skill. Her heart thrilled at the thought that here was the beginning of a new race of wild leaders that would dominate the mesa, would be filled with wolf craft and the keen learning acquired by dogs. The great buff collie, with his handsome body, his long, shaggy hair that streamed when he ran, with his quick intelligence, was to be leader of the new pack.

Three-Toes would teach him the lore of leadership. Together they would train their whelps in all the varied knowledge that both had amassed.

Then new fear came to Three-Toes. There was a man on the range with traps. Hegewa, who had stopped the raiding of Old Lefty, who had smashed the pack led by Unaweep, Queen Wolf of the Uncompahgre, and had caught Bigfoot of the Lane Country, had been sent to get this last wolf of Bear Springs Mesa.

Pale moon was spreading faint light over the late winter landscape as the collie and Three-Toes ran together one evening. They were racing down a woods road. Suddenly Three-Toes stopped. Her keen nose had detected the scent of man. She whined to Shep. He stopped, looked back inquiringly, then trotted ahead as though to run away and leave her.

Quick as a streak of gray light Three-Toes threw her body against his. With a half bark, half snarl she knocked him out of the way. Shep bristled, snapped. It was their first quick quarrel.

But Three-Toes was not inviting combat. Instead, she had sensed lurking trouble, and had thrown her body between it and the collie.

Slowly, head dropped, sniffing, Three-Toes edged toward the cleverly concealed trap. Her hair bristled. Her teeth bared. Collie sensed danger, whined menacingly, edged beside Three-Toes, then threw back his big body and trotted away quickly, nervously. Suddenly he howled, with all the challenge he could muster, daring, threatening, inviting the unseen to come to combat. He now fully realized that man taint, formerly a friendly odor, now meant deadly enemies. He had begun to learn the death that hovers over the lives of four-footed murderers. Keenly Three-Toes watched the collie as they went trotting more cautiously down the trail. The next trap set she gave a warning whine. Collie stopped, sniffed, stepped out of the trail.

New pride in this mate she had picked came to the she-wolf as they went on through the night seeking a kill. He had learned the menace of a trap set in a night.

Then quickly, without warning came the catastrophe that again robbed Three-Toes of a mate. They had gone back scouting around an old kill. Curiosity alone brought them there. Collie had stubbornly insisted on this digression from the run they were following. Three-Toes had been uneasy, but had followed.

They came to the little open space where the rack of steer ribs showed dimly in the night light. The collie stepped forward cautiously. He would have eaten of that carrion if the wolf had allowed it.

Shep scented something tempting at his feet. He dropped his head, and in one quick gulp wolfed the square of flank fat that had been set as a dummy bait. It was sweet, luscious, tickling his dog palate.

In little circles he began quick excited scouting. There might be other squares.

Three-Toes growled, started away, came back, whined invitingly. The dog continued to hunt.

He found what he sought. It was another square of fat. He gobbled it.

Three-Toes growled angrily.

Then the thing which had been skillfully hidden in that second piece of fat stirred within Shep's stomach. It gripped his bowels until he staggered, sunk its death claws into his inner flesh and became racing death fire in his veins.

The processed strychnine left there by the hunter for any killer beast that might find it, swiftly did its work.

Three-Toes again faced the coming of her puppies and the hard job of rearing them without the aid of their father.

Many times she returned to the chilling body of Shep. Many times she whined for him to come back to life and follow her. But he did not move after that first frantic fight against the poison.

As morning dawned Three-Toes turned, lifted her head, wailed with her whole wolf heart. It was a cry of anguish, a sorrow-laden challenge to the man tribe that had torn from her through trap, rifle and poison, her mates and her puppies.

There was new hate, new viciousness, new striking back at man in the attacks the lone she-wolf launched at the cattle on the ranches.

Collie, once trusted, man's friend, companion, helper, had chosen to live by the law of fang. Lured away by the mother of killers, he had become a lusting slaughterer. Through his own acts he had brought the sentence of the killer, the penalty of the renegade beast, which is death.

Then Hegewa, living true to his name, proved a disappointment. He broke stern rules of the Biological Survey and dismissal followed.

Days later John W. Crook, blocky, tanned, with range-worn clothes, stood by the corral at the Monroe Brothers and Henerson ranch, talking to Roy Spangler. Crook was one of the field assistants of the Survey working out of the Denver office. Spangler was wiry, with that sinewy build that suggests slightness, but which embodies resiliency as does slender steel. His eyes were blue, there was the continual deep burnt red of range tan on his slender face, his keen blue eyes were steady and alert, his small ears were close set, accenting the effect of sinewy strength, and as a purely irrelevant feature suggesting that there is with all a bit of the romanticist about him. Roy Spangler's blonde hair tried to curl.

"Of course we've got to get someone on the job here, now that Hunter Hegewa's gone," declared Crook. "After what I've told you about the game you still want to try it?"

"You bet," declared Spangler. "I can get this old female wolf."

Crook eyed the man for a moment. He had told Spangler of the trying work of the Government hunter, the need for self-sacrifice, that when a man is set on the trail of a killer wolf there is no let-up until the wolf is dead. Tales of blizzards, of fighting through mud, rain, wind, hail, keeping the traps at work at all hazard, had been spread before Spangler, applicant for the job of Survey hunter.

But Spangler had grinned good-naturedly. For several years he had punched cattle, and hardship and application to duty were a part of that steady program. Crook saw in the cow-puncher a likely candidate for a Survey hunter's job. Approval crept into his eyes.

"I've a mind to put you to work," Crook commented.

"Now look here," Spangler protested, "I've told you all you've got to do is give me a trial. You admit this Three-Toes wolf is one of the hardest wolf problems the Survey has at present; that Hegewa didn't get her in spite of his knowledge of wolves. That's all fact, isn't it?"

Crook nodded.

"Well, I'll repeat my offer," declared Spangler earnestly. "I'll go after this wolf, and if I don't get her you don't need even to pay me for my time. No wolf, no job, no pay. I know this old girl well—have for several seasons—and I know wolves. Give me a chance and a little time and I'll prove this. If I do show you I know this game I get the job. Isn't that fair enough?"

Crook smiled. "I reckon nothin' could be much fairer," he agreed. "Tear to it, Spangler. If you bring in that hide we'll want you steady."

Crook left the ranch after he had checked the Government outfit of traps and equipment over to Spangler. The new wolfer of the Survey hurried to the little house that stood not far from the main ranch residence.

His entrance was greeted by a chorus of childish voices. Inez, six; Evelyn, five; Reba, three; and even Georgia, who had seen but a year and a half of this life, all scampered toward their daddy. Spangler smiled, then turned to his wife. Her slim face lighted, her blue eyes flashed happily as they caught the significance of Spangler's grin.

"You got the chance, Roy?" she said, half in confirmation of her own surmise.

"Yeh, shore did."

"Did they put you on steady?"

"Not exactly. But it's comin'. If I get this old Three-Toes I get the job for sure."

Mrs. Spangler smiled. "Well, Roy, you can catch that wolf if you have the time to put into it, can't you?"

"You bet I can!"

Then followed talk of a happy vein, a mild celebration of good fortune ahead. The Spanglers had come to Colorado from Missouri nearly seven years before. Roy had started to wrangle cattle for the ranchers in the Thatcher section. He had gone as far as was possible as a cowboy. Now there came the chance to work up in the Survey, become one of their regular staff. Loving outdoor life, wishing for just such an opportunity, Spangler made ready to prove that he was qualified as a hunter. Nor was his slender, blue-eyed, twenty-three-year-old wife any less happy.

It was the big opportunity. It was the portal to a new, big, better future.

Spangler did not lose any time in setting in motion his campaign. As he rode away from the ranch the next morning Paul Henerson waved to him encouragingly.

"Go get her, boy," he called. "You'll make my heart glad when that old killer's hide is hung up. I've done my best to get Young and Crook to let you have a try at this game. Now show 'em your stuff."

Spangler grinned. "I'll get the old devil," he assured the ranch owner.

But Three-Toes had become more canny, more elusive, more filled with man-hatred than before. It was three days later that Spangler came into the ranch yard with a slight cast of worry on his features.

"Never saw anything like it," he declared to Henerson. "She knows most as much as a human. I set traps in the trail back of the second ridge, using every bit of care I could. She came right up to them, sniffed around, knew where those traps are and side-stepped 'em, neat."

Henerson looked serious. "She's killing cattle worse than ever," he declared. "Just raiding all the time. Couple of our calves last night again."

"It's the pups. They're runnin' with her now. She's teachin' 'em how to kill."

Henerson turned away, his brow a bit dark. "Confound that fool collie of ours," he exploded. "Now there's a new kind of a beast loose on the range—half wolf, half dog. Worse than either. And with that old killer, Three-Toes, to teach them all the devilment she knows, too!"

It was a week later that Spangler found where Three-Toes had passed unusually close to one of his trap sets. That trap had been in the ground for five days. The day previous Three-Toes had avoided another trap similarly, but more recently, set. It showed to him that a steel trap in the ground where the earth is moist will lose the man and steel scent in five days.

Acting on the knowledge, Spangler reorganized his campaign. At an old stack yard where hay had been stored in years previous he made a new trap set, carefully concealed in the moist ground.

That evening he found new trouble at the little home. His wife, normally healthy in spite of her slender, hundred-pound body, had given up before the attack of a maddening headache that made housework impossible.

"It's nothing, Roy," she declared optimistically. "Just you never mind. If you can get the kids their supper I'll be all right in the morning."

But the next morning found Mrs. Spangler still suffering from illness.

"No, you'll not stay home," she declared, with flash of determined vehemence. "Don't mind me, Roy. You go ahead with your job."

"But maybe I better stay home," he still protested.

"Please, Roy, go ahead with your work. You know what it means if you get that wolf—or don't."

Reluctantly Spangler left the house. But new impetus was given his determination to get Three-Toes as he left the ranch. It came from a brief conversation with Henerson.

"Roy, you've got to get her," declared the rancher soberly. "She's just gone crazy for killing."

"Something new?"

"Yes, she killed six calves last night." Henerson's face was cloudy. "That can't keep up. It would just knock the stuffing out of our herd."

For a moment they were both silent.

"I made some pretty strong recommendations concerning you to the Survey, Roy. I still think I haven't misjudged your ability. I'd give a whole lot if you can stop this old brute soon."

Spangler now had a new worry. His friends were beginning to wonder why he did not succeed.

Whipped by anxiety, spurred on by the necessity to kill Three-Toes, obliterate her pack of half-breed wolves, Spangler hurried away from the ranch with new, driving determination. Nothing would be left undone to stop the raiding of the wolf. He even switched horses this day, for he had found she recognized that his own horse meant traps ahead, and that she would get out of any trail where his horse traveled.

But in spite of the significant talk with Henerson, his thoughts kept returning to the little home and his plucky little wife. Worry added its burden to his work.

Ahead the trail wound, beckoning. On every side stretched the plains. Overhead the blue of the sky dome spread until it dipped to the horizon. Chipmunks, prairie dogs, magpies chattered and barked at him.

Roy Spangler barely sensed these usual surroundings. His thoughts were fully taken up with the big problem of capturing the wolf and anxiety for his wife.

The horse passed over a sandy stretch in the trail where hoof beats were muffled. Roy swung easily in the saddle. The trail dipped, came out of a little swale, topped a bit of a ridge and then emerged from behind a screen of cedars.

With rapid, nervous reflex movement Spangler reined in his horse.

For a moment there was big, quick silence. That picture and what followed will remain in the memory of Spangler as long as he lives.

In the trail, with all the joyous abandon of a mother playing with her children, with happy frolic, Three-Toes was romping with her seven half-wolf puppies.

They dived, rolled, nipped, dodged, leaped, yapped a little in excitement, bit playfully at one another. The old wolf was the happiest of the group, the leader. It was as though she was finding here the solace for her heartache.

All this happened in vivid flashing movement in that fraction of a second before Spangler reached for his rifle that hung in the saddle scabbard.

With a quick dive his hand dropped for the butt of the gun. Here was the big chance, the one great opportunity to stop the renegades, the great chance to reach his goal and then get back to his sick wife and his own babies.

A quick, sharp qualm flung through Spangler as he realized he was about to smash that picture of wild happiness. But it was followed swiftly by the exultant knowledge that here lay the end of his quest, here might be the termination of the ferocious career of the old renegade wolf.

As he yanked at the gun there came a quick break in the tableau. Three-Toes caught sight of the rider on the big horse.

With a wild cry, a sound filled with warning, thrilling with fear, she flung herself behind some sagebrush.

Like phantoms the wild pups scattered.

Spangler jerked the rifle to readiness.

He spurred ahead frantically, seeking one of the pups. With one scalp of the wild half-dogs to bring home there would be less chance of criticism falling on him.

He peered hopefully for one good look at a whelp.

Then his attention was whipped away from the puppies. On a small butte, just beyond the reach of the light, high-power rifle, at a point she knew was safe, Three-Toes had found a station. She came out in plain sight, inviting Spangler's attention.

Howl after howl she hurled at Spangler. In him she saw the force that was warring on her kind. Instinctively she knew that here was the man that was making her life one succession of pitfalls, poison, snares.

If ever a wolf of the wild talked to a man, Three-Toes talked to Spangler. In her language there was every bit of venom, hate, vindictive, passionate anger that she carried against man. She dared him to come and get her, threatened him, poured forth the surging, boiling madness that had filled her wolf heart.

Spangler, excited, hoping to get one long shot at her, spurred his horse toward the butte.

The horse crashed through the sage, stumbled, recovered, and galloped forward. A hundred yards more and he would be within striking distance. The horse snorted in fright.

Three-Toes continued howling. There was nothing of fear in that mad cry. Just that dominating anger.

The hundred yards was almost covered. Spangler reined in his horse.

Like a wraith the wolf dropped out of sight.

She was gone. Her ruse had worked. The man had been tricked. And at that instant Spangler knew she had outwitted him.

Spangler quickly turned to follow out his original plan to catch one of the pups.

But they were gone. They had followed the command of their mother, voiced in that first wild cry.

It was then that Spangler realized fully how neatly he had been fooled by the wolf. When she realized he might be getting within rifle shot she had scurried to safety. But had left her post only when she was sure her puppies were safe.

"The darned old she-devil," Spangler breathed in half admiration. "She knew. She sure knew."

IV: TRIUMPH—AND DEFEAT

Spangler's encounter with Three-Toes left him groping for new methods of attack, brimming with fresh resolve to succeed. She had dared him, taunted him, urged him to come and get her, and then had disappeared.

"You must get her, Roy," declared his wife that night, as he told her of the incident in half-awed tones. "I know you can. I just know you can, Roy."

"Well, with that faith back of me I will," he declared, mustering a smile.

The next morning he protested leaving his wife.

"Just one day, dear," he said. "I can stay home here to-day. You shouldn't try even to think about housework and I know you do when I'm not here to do it."

"Now, no more fussing around, Roy," she said, with as much cheer as she could bring to her tired voice. "You go on with your work. Think what it means to us. I'll be well in a day or so."

"Don't you think we ought to get the doctor out?"

She shook her head. "I'll be all right. You run along to your traps."

A driving demand for results rode with Roy Spangler that day. He was grave, determined, whipped with the necessity for bringing his campaign against

Three-Toes to a close. The day before he had had success almost within reach. Only the swift, uncanny mind of the wolf had thwarted him. Her lightning flash of thought after sighting him, her daring threatening, had robbed him of that chance to score against her.

Now he must find some other way, and quickly. His whole future was at stake.

The day passed without incident. Night approached.

He turned his horse down toward the old stack yard.

He reached the yard. There he leaped to ground. He hurried forward.

His heart bounded with new rhythm as he recognized the imprint of Three-Toes.

The trap was gone! A song of triumph welled up in his heart as he saw the scarred trail where the wolf had fought her way across the open ground and into the arroyo that dropped into the Apishapa!

Quickly Spangler unsheathed his gun. At a fast dog trot he started on foot down the arroyo.

Eyes alert, his pulse beating, his nerves atingle, he hurried along, his gaze seeking every bit of sign.

He reached a point where the wolf had hung up. The ground was ragged and torn. Brush was beaten down on every side. Scrub trees as big as a man's wrist were snapped off in the fight between the wolf and the trap. Everywhere the track of the wolf with three toes assured him he had caught the old renegade, the elusive wild killer.

The arroyo broadened. He hurried along. Dusk crept into the shadows. The sun was setting back of the distant mountains. The arroyo came to the junction with the broad mud-walled channel of the Apishapa River. Snow was melting in the hills and dirty water swirled in several channels that spread over the broad bed of the stream. They would run for a few hundred yards as independent streams, then would come to a ledge, would unite, boil over the limestone into a little frothy pool, and then meander over the wide, muddy stream floor. On either side arose the adobe earth walls.

The trail of the captured wolf skirted the bank. It disappeared into the stream. It went through a pool where Spangler looked in vain for sign that the dead wolf might be there, drowned.

A new dread came to him. Three-Toes might thrash into the pools in the stream, become entangled with the trap and the accumulated trash that had become knotted in the chain, drown, and then sink from sight. He could never prove that he had caught the wolf.

He might be cheated after all.

He went ahead warily. Every time the trail swung into the river channel his hope waned. When it climbed out again in draggled scrub brush at the side of the stream he found renewed courage.

The unconquered she-wolf had fought along indomitably, through every obstacle.

His progress was slow. He could not overlook one chance to find that dead wolf body in the pools or rapids of the Apishapa.

For several miles he worked down the stream, carefully. Shadows deepened. Yet Spangler could not hurry. He dared not overlook any chance.

Night came. He was balked. He could travel no farther.

Discouraged, disheartened, fearing that the river would at last cheat him of the chance of proving his catch, he turned back to the ranch.

There things were not any more encouraging. Mrs. Spangler made a brave effort to be cheerful and bright. But she was not so well. Spangler worked around the house, straightening things up as best he could, cooked, washed dishes, scrubbed, and then put the babies to bed.

Morning came. Fever was hovering over his wife. Spangler was torn between two duties. There was the certain knowledge of the tradition of the Biological Survey. Nothing must stand between the hunter and bringing in his renegade wolf. Out there in the choppy breaks above the Apishapa or along the dun-colored banks of the turbid stream was Three-Toes, the renegade, fast in a trap. He must get back on the trail immediately or someone might find the wolf before he did, steal it, obliterate the evidence of his catch. But he also should stay at home and help his mate, his plucky wife.

"You must go, Roy," she insisted. "It would be worse for me to lie here and keep you from getting that wolf than to have you away out after Three-Toes."

"Well, I'm going to phone the doctor to come out," he insisted. "I'll get out and get that wolf and be back before he leaves."

Spangler picked up the trail again beside the roily summer flood of the Apishapa. Carefully he worked along the edge of the stream. Several hours passed. He realized that the doctor had come and gone at the ranch. But he could not give up that trail that lay ahead, demanding his immediate attention, imperative in its requirements that he stay with it until the end came.

The trail deserted the side of the stream, climbed over a sloping bank, threaded up an arroyo. Three-Toes had traveled through tangle after tangle, fighting her way in an effort to attain liberty.

Spangler hurried. He realized that this trail to higher ground assured him that the wolf was probably still alive and in the trap.

The trail climbed to the sagy flats, threaded through piñon and scrub cedar. It was plain. At points there were circles where the wolf had thrashed while the trap was snagged in the brush.

He approached a stand of brush where there were signs of the wolf having been held by the drag hook and chain. His nerves were taut with the intensity of the drive he was making in an effort to find the end of the trail.

But caution dictated that he move slowly. Keen wolf teeth, bloodthirsty, ready to snap the veins in the throat of man, were at the end of his quest, and he could not come within their reach until they were made harmless.

He stepped forward slowly. His rifle was held at ready. It was cocked. The brush cracked under his feet. Wind rustled eerily.

With a quick, nerve-wracking leap Spangler threw himself back, then laughed nervously. A tiny bird, nesting in the undergrowth, had flown in terror. Its quick, darting movement had started the reflex jump instinctively.

Spangler, doggedly determined, trudged forward. At one moment he moved cautiously. At the next he could trot across the open without hindrance or caution.

He reached the edge of a little mesa and climbed up to its tableland. He skirted some scrub cedars, eyes, ears alert.

Then came reward!

Ahead, in a thicket of scrub cedars, there leaped a gray form. It was Three-Toes in the 4 ½ wolf trap. Heart pounding, exultant, Spangler trotted forward. Here was the triumph, the end of his campaign, the certainty of his recognition that he could do the work of the Survey hunter.

Frantically the wolf lunged. She threw her body out until the chain snapped. She lunged back in another direction. She seemed almost to try to climb the scrub tree in her frenzy to get away from the nearing doom.

Then of a sudden she quieted. Fate, inevitable, certain, unavoidable, had followed this killer for months. Spangler was its agent. She quit. She lay panting, as docile as a dog.

Quickly Spangler strung out new hay wire, ready to muzzle her. He had brought his lariat with him. He made a quick loop. Three-Toes ducked as the rope swirled in the air, snapped at it as it fell short.

Spangler jerked the rope out of the way of those keen teeth, made another loop. Quick, positive in its action, the loop fell over the wolf's neck. Spangler jerked with precision. The loop tightened. The wolf thrashed a moment, then was still.

With another scrub cedar as a snubbing post Spangler stretched the gray form between the drag hook where it was caught in a cedar and the rope.

In a moment the man had straddled the wolf's neck. He made quick turns of the wire. Her nose was encased in a muzzle of metal, preventing those slaughtering jaws from opening.

Spangler eased the tension of the rope a little and slipped the loop.

"How old are your pups, you old vixen?" he said, talking to the wolf that was watching him with baleful glare.

He reached under her belly to feel of the wolf breasts. For there he would find evidence of whether those wolf pups were still sucking or not.

Quick as a flash, with vicious, nerve-shredding snarl, Three-Toes leaped.

There was no indefiniteness in that plunge. She knew what she was after.

It was Spangler's life or hers!

Spangler staggered back as her nose slammed into his windpipe. His scalp tingled. His blood raced. The vision of bloody death that had flashed up in that last wild dive of the wolf left him surprisingly weak the next instant, as he realized that only the haywire muzzle had saved his windpipe, his arteries from being clipped.

Three-Toes, Killer, had had a real try at murdering a man!

"But you didn't make it, old girl," declared Spangler grimly. "Thank God for that haywire!"

With the wolf on the horse, he made his way back toward Monroe Brothers and Henerson's ranch. Optimism had returned. Still there lurked the specter of the sickness that had laid its hand on his wife. But here was encouragement for her. There would be years of work together. She would have the rearing of the four girls, their training, the keeping of their little home which they could establish with the salary of the Survey hunter.

And Roy Spangler would hunt wolves, coyotes, predatory cats and other destructive beasts, out in the open under the blue skies of Colorado. Triumph beat in Roy Spangler's heart. Three-Toes, who had fooled even the best, had fallen before his persistent campaign. And from such work emerges the real star hunters of the Survey.

He was to be one of them.

He reached the corral. He came to the barnyard. No one was in sight. He unloaded the wolf that was hog tied with the wire and muzzled.

Spangler, unable to contain his triumph longer, yelled. The door of the ranch house flung open. Paul Henerson came running out. He was followed by Mrs. Henerson.

"I've got her, folks," cried Roy exultantly. "Snagged the old brute. No more stock killing for her. And I've made good my promise."

THE LAST STAND OF THE PACK

Quick exclamations came from both of his friends. Then curious silence came, blanketing their exuberance.

"I've got to tell the wife," said Spangler excitedly. "She'll sure be happy."

Then the strained silence caught his attention.

"What's the matter? What's wrong, folks?"

Spangler whipped around and looked toward his little house where his wife lay ill. A big, new, yellow sign on the door caught his eye.

"What's that?" he gasped. "What's that card?"

Fear had leaped into his voice. Shattered was the gladness of his triumph. His heart almost stopped beating.

"Not smallpox!" he demanded, a quaver in his voice. "Not the black smallpox!"

Wordlessly Henerson nodded affirmatively.

Harbinger of death, like a specter, this dread disease had entered Colorado that season, and now, fatefully had laid its hand imperiously on the home of Roy Spangler.

Night came, and in the dusk that settled Roy Spangler sat by the bedside of the plucky little woman who by her own courage had spurred him on to the goal of achievement. Long, dark hours passed. Perhaps it was a day or more. Time was of no consequence to Spangler as he sat at her bedside. The crisis came; fate stalked into the little ranch home with the grim reaper. As the spirit of his mate entered the valley of death, Spangler's brave soul traveled with her.

Uncounted time passed before his spirit came back, alone.

Then the hunter, benumbed by the blow that had fallen, bewildered, as had been Three-Toes the day her mate, the collie, had suddenly given up earth-life battles, groped toward the doorway of his little ranch home. There he looked out over the broad sweep of the dark, silent prairie and mesas that spread on every side of the ranch. His soul filled with their bigness.

Three-Toes, wolf, had not given up. Unconquered, she had battled odds to the last ditch. Hers was a fighting heart.

Roy Spangler, man, was now battered, bruised by invincible, silent, stalking shadows that had entered his home. But within him beat a heart as brave, as true, as any wolf had ever possessed.

He straightened his shoulders, turned, stood a moment above the four sleeping babies. His eyes were misty but his heart was full of big resolve.

He would carry on!

Gray Terror

Blizzard gods chortled over the barrens where the shoulders of the hills splay out. It was fierce Wyoming winter in the northern spurs of the Neversummer Mountains. Dizzy ghosts formed of swirling snow were caught in the arms of the storm and danced away while the wind demons howled in glee.

The mountains were lost in the colorless void where the court of the wind and the frost was arrayed in a stupendous up-piling of cloud, ice-crystal, and gusty squalls. Only the hardy might brave this without feeling death hands. Weaklings would be buffeted, battered, overwhelmed, and finally cradled in the lulling embrace of winter death; would fall into the long sleep.

Lean, tough, sinewed, with thick coat of fur sheltering his powerful wolf body, Gray Terror faced the storm. It was his country. It was his kind of a day. He was as vicious as those beguiling snow images that faded in the gusts of ripping winds.

Gray Terror was an old wolf. He had seen many such winters. He had always gloried in them. Even when it meant hunger for several days while the other life of the range dug out, the old wolf would range through the rack of the storm, becoming a part of the vicious revelry.

Long, long before, when he was a yearling, he had known other country. There was a place where winter came with more moderation. The southern slopes of the hills kept fairly open during the snowy weeks. Stock could weather through on ranch lands without being frozen stiff by some swooping sub-zero blast. That other country was great wolf territory, for there were cattle and wild game to kill, a place to run on the slopes and through cañons, and—other wolves.

But this also was great outdoors, here where the storm raged. Gray Terror sifted along with the wind, keen nose and eyes alert. Wild, lashing, domineering turmoil billowed and streamed around him.

The wolf turned into the face of the wind. Something strange, new, laid quick grip on him. Some fighting instinct of the wolf leader suddenly made him revolt at this rough handling.

His teeth bared, his lip lifted. He thrust forth his long nose, snarled. The flowing wind current caught his hair and brushed it back.

Suddenly Terror howled, bellowed defiance against that thing that a moment before he had considered a kindred spirit. For subtly it had challenged his right to live; threatened his supremacy. Hate of this thing that had worried him, that he had before considered almost a thing to play with, to run before and consort with, filled his soul.

Half bark, half howl, his challenge was lost in the louder baying of the winds.

For many moments he stood there, his nose outthrust, his gleaming, long tusks bared, heading into the wind. The intangible new enemy continued to be all about him, whip him, caress him, then slam him with cruel icy hands and with shouting boisterousness throw handfuls of the snow into his thick coat.

Gray Terror suddenly wanted to fight this ruling storm spirit. It was too near like his own. It was almost as though he were challenged by one of his kind.

Slowly he started forward. Then he broke into a trot. Into the teeth of the wind, retracing in part the steps of a few moments before, he bored his way through the ruck and riot of the blizzard, seeking something, looking for fight to ease the vicious anger that boiled within him.

Nothing loomed up before him but those eerie snow figures. They whipped into the air, swayed, danced, beckoned, and then melted into the white inferno that stewed over the earth. Something tangible, something to sink his white teeth into, was what Gray Terror sought. Fighting, killing, murder mood was on him. It gripped, swayed, dominated him.

In all the whole white expanse of the flats in the high mountain swale he could find nothing to attack.

Through the fading white dusk of the late sunless afternoon the wolf loped along the hunting trail, stalking a thing which he could not find. Midnight found him still hurrying. But his direction of travel had changed. He was journeying at an angle with the storm. His nose pointed more southward.

He had suddenly recalled vividly that country where there were fat beeves, wooded slopes, craggy, blocky mountains and—other wolves to romp with, to master, perhaps to mate with.

Almost without respite he traveled, always southward, seeking that country of his whelphood. The old home had called its own, and Gray Terror, baffled, worried, still defiant, but beaten by the storm gods, had given heed to that call.

No other thing of the western wild could cudgel the Terror to submission. It was death for one or the other. And now that he had realized suddenly, after years of association with the storm spirits, that they were his master after all, he would leave their range, would find a new place where his strife-hungry spirit would be appeased in fighting for leadership on the old range where he was whelped.

II: THE RETURN OF FEAR

For full two years the range of Old Lefty in the Burns Hole country had not been trod by wolf feet. Hegewa had eradicated the remnants of Lefty's pack. Four-legged dwellers in the region had not cringed to the cry of the hunting wolf and ranchmen had breathed easier.

There had been forays on sheep flocks by coyotes, chicken coops had been raided, and tawny death in the form of mountain lions had ripped the life from buck, doe, and fawn. But the master murderer, the wolf renegade, had not been on the range.

Weasels had fattened their lithe little bodies on birds they killed. Magpies had robbed, eaten carrion, and quarreled. Foxes had caught nesting grouse.

This was mostly normal wild life on the range. Then came back Fear!

The coyote pair that had dug their den in an old rabbit hole on the head of Milk Creek watched this new ambassador of wilderness death on his first trip through the sloping breaks of Castle Peak. They knew if they kept their place they would not be molested. They rejoiced, even while worried by the stranger's coming, for they knew they now would have more cattle carcasses on which to feed, less work in getting food.

The magpie rabble chattered raucously, celebrating the return of wolf killers.

Over the ridges, the cañons, through the aspen groves and under shady spruce boughs the rumor spread, as rumors will in the land of the wild, and before that long, rangy gray form of the invading wolf had completed the swing of his first circling scouting trip in the Burns Hole country the woods and mountain creatures of fur and feather knew he was there.

Selfishness of the bully pulsed in the cruel wolf heart of Gray Terror as he traveled through Burns Hole, his old, old home. It was HIS country. He would be its tyrant. He sought any that might question his leadership. But there were no other wolves.

When he realized this, loneliness first, followed by demoniacal glee, swept through Gray Terror.

He was king. Nothing could stand before him. This domain of Old Lefty was his exclusively. Before him lay a carnival of killing, murder, ghoulish mistreatment of other animal life without the demand that he fight his kind for supremacy.

With quick fiendishness the killer struck. He raided the Mayer ranch. William P. Mayer shook his head when he found the ripped and torn bodies of three young beeves. One was still alive. The other two were dead. Little was eaten from any one of the three. Instead there were lacerations, chunks torn out, rips in the hides of the cow brutes.

After this, man, as well as the wildlings, was warned that a wolf had again come to the old stronghold in Burns Hole.

Snowy patches were mottled on the south slopes where the winter sun had warmed drifts until little rivulets raced down hillside or soaked into the earth. The north slopes were still solid white. Snow was banked on the north side of the buildings in the little town of Eagle, that is headquarters for a vast sweep of the country between the Mount of the Holy Cross and the Colorado River. Spring was not far away.

Three men stood in front of the bank, talking. The first was short, broad-shouldered Ben White, who had the year before served as president of the Colorado Stockgrowers Association. He wore weather-bleached hat, duck coat with sheepskin collar, dark trousers tucked into riding boots. His reddened face, round and cheery, was troubled and serious.

"I don't agree with you, Mayer," he said, turning to the tall, broad-shouldered, round-faced rancher. "That doesn't sound a bit like wolf killing. What do you say, Brown?"

The third man in the group squinted his eyes a bit. He was of medium height, and wore the uniform of the forest man. He had charge of the Eagle district of the Holy Cross National Forest. Both of these ranch men were permitees on the Forest and the killing of their stock by any predatory animal was of concern to ranger Brown.

"Well, it don't exactly sound like wolf work," replied the forest man. "More like dogs."

"That's what I think," agreed White positively. "You know how a wolf kills. He hamstrings."

"Well, there's always an old she-wolf with whelps to take into account," suggested Mayer slowly. "And there sure were wolf tracks at those kills."

They all considered a moment. Then Mayer contradicted himself.

"No, it couldn't be a pack of whelps very well. They'd be too small now. But this is for all the world like some young pack bein' trained. Cattle ripped all to pieces and not killed. Just ripped. They'll die, a lot of them, but they'll drag around for a week or so before they give up the ghost."

"I just can't help believing it's wild dogs," declared White positively. "Sounds just like their tricks."

A fourth man swung around the corner of the bank, caught his stride almost in mid-step, stopped, stuck out his hand to first one of the group and then to the others.

"You're just in time, John," declared Ben White. "Heard about this stock killed at Mayer's? Wolf killing, he thinks."

"No, I should say not."

John Welch, treasurer of the State Board of Livestock Inspection Commissioners, with a ranch up Wolcott way, was instantly all interest. Welch, rancher, stockman, among the leaders in his field of activity, knew what loss to ranchers a new wolf drift in the Burns Hole country would bring.

"I claim it's a pack of wild dogs," said White.

"Tell me about it," suggested Welch.

Briefly Mayer told of the killings, how the cattle were torn and lacerated, going around with great chunks of their flesh ripped out while they still lived, of bitten noses and chewed ears, almost sure sign of dogs doing the killing; of tails ripped off and rumps cut up, leaving the steer or heifer to die a lingering death or get well, as fate might decree.

"Well, whatever it is, dogs or wolves, we've got to stop it, pronto," said Welch. "Twentieth is the monthly meeting of the Inspection Board. You'll be in to Denver for that, Ben. We'll meet Young there. Don't know if you fellows know or not that the Inspection Board has been made the coöperating agency of the state to work with the Biological Survey on predatory animal control. Took it out from under the Game and Fish Department. We intend to give the Survey men real coöperation every step of the way."

The group broke up. More immediate business called them and engaged their attention. But following the agreement, Welch and White did meet with Young in Denver.

"I can't help you right now, boys," declared Young. "But if you'll wait until Big Bill Caywood gets back from Kansas, where he is mopping up on a bunch of coyotes down in Rawlins County, I'll shoot him right over there. I haven't another man that I could send now. But Bill is one of the greatest authorities living in Colorado, on trapping wolves, and if there is a wolf in there he'll get him."

The stockmen agreed, and Stanley Young wrote to Caywood that a queer killer that slaughtered, butchered, cut and maimed instead of killing and eating, awaited his return.

Meanwhile cattle were cut and torn by this strange four-legged demon. Deer fell before his driving attack. Calves suffered most among the domestic stock. Ranchers became more worried. The sight of the stock sick from their wounds teetering on the verge of death, or slowly getting well, was more disquieting than dead carcasses.

Through the forest clearings, under cover, slinking and dodging, the wild folks crept, with eye cocked open for that leaping gray killer that had shattered their relative peace.

The range knew what was going on, while the stock growers were still puzzled. Its citizens snarled, growled, or cowered, as their spirits dictated, and got out of his way.

Lefty and his pack had been killers. They had killed for food. But this newcomer killed, slashed, and maimed for the very love of it.

Blood lust, killer joy, the sheer brutality of the animal bully had stalked into the old range of Lefty, with Gray Terror, the wolf from the north country.

III: BULLY OF THE RANGE

Wolves are like men. There are brave wolves, there are cowardly wolves, others that are sneaking and there are bullies. They know fear, jealousy, hate, love, hunger, and all the other man emotions. When they go "bad" they are like brutal two-legged criminals.

Man is likely to have sympathy for animals. Even when they are renegade he is likely to excuse their faults as he does sometimes excuse the viciousness of his own, saying that they know no better. But the wolfer knows. He will tell you that renegade wolves are brutes, that they kill for the joy of killing.

That is why the Survey hunters, men of the open, lovers of all outdoor life, scowl or are sober and thoughtful when they hear of a wolf renegade, and why they drive into the wilderness, silent, grim, determined to "get their wolf."

Gray Terror, the butchering wolf of Eagle County, was one of the most fiendish, most heartless killers that ever engaged the attention of Biological Survey hunters. Anyone who can muster sympathy for the genuine killer wolf after knowing of Gray Terror's forays, or who can blame the Government hunters for their unwavering efforts to shoot, poison, snare, trap wolf renegades, after acquaintance with the history of any bad wolf, simply is sentimentally blind, does not see the situation from the side of the game, wild life and stock.

No mercy dwelt in the heart of Gray Terror.

Had there been a wolf pack he would have companioned with them. He would have found a mate. There would have been whelps to think of. The law of the pack would have held him somewhat in check. Killing would have been for food, except when steers were lacerated while young whelps were taught the art of murder. But alone, with no other thought to dominate his mind, killing became his greatest pleasure, his constant pastime.

His gluttony for murder brought anxiety to the stockmen of Burns Hole. Beef was his particular target. They were senseless things. Buck deer might fight. Their flashing feet would cut and wound when they were cornered. Terror had no taste for inviting bruises.

Steers ran and bellowed. They looked so ridiculous when he rolled them!

Gray Terror lay looking over the slope of a rolling, sagy hill, watching a group of cattle in the pasture below. His lips drooled, his nostrils quivered with brutish anticipation.

Slowly, stealthily, he raised from the grassy bed on which he lay. His lower jaw chattered as he skulked forward. The fact that he had been enjoying this ghastly sport for weeks did not lessen his excitement. He lived in a state of semi-intoxication from the excitement in the fearful game he played.

Sage brush, mountain mahogany, some scrubby native currant hid the death-walk of the wolf. His shoulders hunched, he crouched, his legs—springy, tense—doubled under him as he wormed his way down the hill. His mouth slobbered.

Emboldened by the lack of challenge, he had come to this killing in the full light of day. It was more fun to see plainly the herd milling in fright than to stalk in the dusk.

The wolf stopped, peered out from blazing tawny eyes at the cattle. He could not restrain himself.

With a leap he shot through the brush, heading like a streak for a whitefaced, long yearling.

The steer sprang away clumsily. He bawled. The others scattered, milled in the space beyond, looked back, fascinated, watching the game of death between the whiteface and the wolf.

Rocks rolled, dusty little puffs of dirt were kicked up by the lumbering steer's feet. Almost as though he were running through a lane of air without any obstacles whatever, Gray Terror found his way through the sage and mahogany.

He leaped in ecstasy as his prey ran headlong down the slope. He threw his body from uphill, hit the steer head on, teeth closing over soft flesh of the inner flank.

Down went the steer as though he had been tripped. He struggled up. Blood oozed from his flank.

Terror licked his bloody lips.

Again he dived. He hit the steer at the head, caught his teeth in the gristle of the cow brute's nose. The steer stumbled, bellowing. His eyes were wide from the fright that comes when death is near.

Terror backed away. The steer sprawled on the ground, kicked, got up, lowered his head, dived at the wolf.

This was a new move. The wolf danced away. His grinning jaws were red with blood, his furry coat stained crimson.

It was a great life! Killing was gorgeous sport!

The steer bellowed, dived, stopped as the wolf again circled in quick leaps.

Teeth met in the tender, lighter beef that lies on the inner part of the thigh.

The steer squalled miserably, stumbled, fell, got up, and tottered away.

In the brush Gray Terror ripped and tore at the strip of quivering flesh he had pulled from the steer.

The wolf gulped a couple of mouthfuls of the tender, steamy meat. He abandoned the remainder. It was not his plan to eat his fill. Gorging would make him stupid, drunk from the fresh raw flesh.

All the viciousness, the roguish evil of the wolf brute, swayed his soul. It was his big religion, this lustful murder!

Away he drove through the brush, seeking that poor, maimed steer. The whiteface saw his fate coming like a gray streak. He started down the hillside, seeking the slight advantage of level ground.

Terror let him race. Then he plunged, getting that hold which in effect is so like the hip lock the cowboy applies to a calf when he throws it. The steer rolled in the dirt, bawling miserably.

The whiteface got up and shook himself. There was no fight this time. The pain in his lacerated nose, the hot, piercing agony that was the wound in his inner flank, had taken the fight from him. He sought sanctuary only.

Away again, down the hill they sped. Terror was exultant. Racing on the upper side, on springy, inspired legs, he yammered in his excitement. Then with a clean leap he threw himself clear above the steer, landing on the downhill side. He caught his hundred-pound weight on his springy, tireless legs, headed the steer uphill a little.

A gully got into the way of the death run. The steer saw it too late. He stumbled, went in, kicked up moist earth and dusty soil.

The wolf dived in. He snipped at the throat of the whiteface. Blood spurted over him. The steer struggled, lay still, then wallowed up and tried to get out of the little hollow.

White teeth tore at his nose. He felt the ripping of the scimitar fangs in his throat. He bellowed, death fright in his gurgling cry.

Again the Terror struck. In his plunge there was meanness, brutality, lawless slaughter. The steer fell forward on his knuckles, rammed his bleeding nose into the ground. His eyes rolled back until the whites showed pinkly in the goggling rims.

Terror ripped and tore. Juicy living flesh was between his jaws and he was intoxicated with it.

Leaving the kicking steer, Terror raced away at the staring heads among the other cattle that, fascinated, had watched the murder of the whiteface.

A yearling heifer broke away from the little bunch of long yearlings. Terror leaped into the killing run. In a moment he was by her side. He jumped, soared over her back, landed on the downside of the hill.

She bawled, tried to run uphill as he lunged at her head.

By her side, around her, inevitable death raced. Again Terror leaped over the heifer.

Oh, it was great sport to see these helpless things struggle to get away, to see them with big fright in their great, wide, staring eyes, to hear them bawl as he struck, ripping and tearing.

The wolf dived in, nipped at the tender flank meat of his victim. A strip tore away. The heifer fell, got up in a stumbling run.

In a flash the wolf plunged again. His teeth closed on the tail of the heifer. In a clean snip the bone was cut through, close to the body. Blood spurted from the wound. The yearling bawled, miserably.

Terror threw himself at her nose, ripped and tore, then backed away to look in quivering, nervous excitement as the heifer stood a moment, wide-eyed, helpless, facing the ghastly fate threatening her.

Then another frenzied run. Down the hill, up again as the wolf headed her and turned her away from the flats below.

It was a race, wild, violent, with death hovering over every leap of the murderer and his prey.

Blood streamed from the rump of the cow beast. This wound was the target for another plunging, hurtling dive. Wide-spread, red, foamy jaws clicked. The teeth fastened in the soft tissue at the tail. He threw his weight with tremendous force, ripping, tearing at parts unprotected by the tough armor of hide. He gobbled in fearsome gluttony at those shreds of soft meat tissue he had torn away.

This ghastly, repulsive trick is not uncommon among the renegade gray wolves.

The heifer sank to her knees, bawling in sick anguish.

The wolf stood for a few moments, dived in, harried the poor, maimed, sick creature for a moment, and then turned toward the others.

This had been but play, fiendish prankishness which delighted his wolf soul. Now he was ready for a finish job. The steer and the heifer might live, might die. It was nothing to the Gray Terror. He would never touch them again. They were but playthings in his wolfish sport.

Now for the kill!

A two-year-old, heavy, full-meated, was cut out of the bunch with machine-like precision. There was a run. The wolf headed the steer downhill. The flat was ahead.

Just as the sharp slope of the hill broke away from the dip and spread out in the flat, at the point where loose rocks gathered after rolling down the slope, where racing horse or cow would stumble, Gray Terror struck. There was no tarrying. He meant to down the steer.

His teeth closed over the hamstring, the great tendon of Achilles. They snapped. The steer rolled, bellowed, tried to get up, stood helplessly on three legs.

Again the wolf attacked. The other tendon snapped as his teeth clicked through it.

Now it was the throat. This was a kill! The others had been but a game.

Hot, gurgling, spumy, red, the blood gushed from the slit arteries in the throat of the groaning steer. With quick, snarling, ripping slashes, his teeth reddened, the wolf chewed at the flank fat of the animal. This was his own titbit.

Other wolves might prefer the kidney fat, eating it only, leaving the rest of the carcass to rot; still others might favor horses in foal, kill, rip open the mare and eat the tender little unborn colt, leaving the rest of the meat for the magpies and coyotes. But the Terror liked flank fat and for this he made many of his kills.

Hurrying stealthily, two gray forms approached the place where Gray Terror gobbled at the carcass of the two-year-old. They were the coyote pair from near the head of Mill Creek. For days they had fattened on the kills of this wolf, had become his camp followers. Nor had the wolf molested them, for they had kept their distance.

Called to this feast by the last bawling of the two-year-old, they came running. They raced into the slight opening near the Terror. They stopped, hesitated, then started forward a step or two. Following the wolf day after day, they had come to have less fear of him.

For an instant there was tense quiet.

Then gigantic anger thrashed through the Terror. It was quite agreeable to him to have these scavengers follow him. But to try to consort with him was gross disrespect. To attempt to feed with him at one of his kills was an insult.

With a leap he was upon the pair. The little female yapped and ran. The dog coyote made a brave attempt to threaten this sudden and unexpected attacker. Their bodies crashed.

The coyote leaped away in fright, yelping.

Terror sped after him. Their bodies thumped again. The wolf's teeth slashed mercilessly. The coyote dived away, his body bleeding from a dozen wounds.

The coyote cried for mercy. But there was no such element in the heart of the wolf.

Terror leaped, his fangs caught in the body of the coyote. He threw his weight away, twisting, pulling. The coyote screamed in death fright.

The wolf snapped at a new hold. The coyote fought feebly.

Blood-smeared wolf teeth clicked. The coyote quivered, died jerking and twitching.

Nor did Terror leave the coyote immediately. He ripped, tore, snapped at the bloody tangle of bones, hide and flesh, shook it crazily, until the mad anger that mastered him had been appeased.

With mane still bristling, with his eyes flaming with murder light, he stalked back to the interrupted meal. He tore a few more pieces of flank fat from the steer. But a new relish for murder called him.

He turned from the still twitching carcass of the one outright kill he had made. More crazy death races, other ripping, tearing dives, two more of the yearlings torn and lacerated by his cutting teeth, and the wolf sought a place in the higher slopes to sleep off the meat and blood drunk he had accumulated.

The next day Mayer stood looking at the sick steers and heifers with their blood-oozing sores, and swore deeply, impotently.

"I wish some of those sentimental fools might see what we've seen here to-day," he said, turning to ranger William Brown. "There's some that think it's cruel to trap a big gray wolf. I wish they could see the suffering of these cow brutes just for a little while. They'd change their minds."

"You know it," agreed Brown.

"It's got to stop," declared Mayer. "Wolf, dog, whelps, or demon, whatever it is, it can't go on. Young's got to get a man in here and get whatever it is."

IV: COLD TRAIL

Two men faced each other across a paper-littered golden oak desk. Stanley Young, his face tanned from his frequent field trips, was sitting in the tilted swivel chair, his body hunched forward, his pipe held between thumb and first finger.

Bill Caywood, the other man, gazed thoughtfully, silently, on the gray-white pelt of old Whitey, where it hung on the office wall. Bill's brown face was wrinkled into a quizzical half grin.

A quick, sharp pause had come in the conference between the two, which related to the butcher wolf of Eagle County. For a moment there was quiet in the room. Then Young swung the chair in which he sat into an upright position, planting both of his feet on the floor. He spoke crisply to Caywood.

"Go get him!"

Caywood's deep-set eyes switched their gaze to catch Young's.

"All right."

"When can you get in there, Bill?"

"Outfit's at Rio Blanco at the ranch. I'll catch the night train. Get there to-morrow morning. I'll be back to Eagle the day after with my wolf plunder."

"Good."

"If it's a pack of dogs, like you think, instead of a wolf renegade——"

"Clean 'em out, Bill. That's your job. Whatever it is, mop up and stop that killing."

"Bueno."

Young had waited with no small impatience for the chance to send Caywood into the former range of Old Lefty. Brutal, ghastly slaughter had ruled on that range throughout the whole of the spring.

Caywood, with pack animals, his traps and his camp outfit stopped for a day at the Mayer ranch. Here he heard more than Young had been able to tell him of the fearful slaughter wrought by the butchering wolf, Gray Terror. Cattle had been mutilated until there was no hope for their recovery and then left by the butcher to die. In one or two instances he had killed cows and had torn at their bellies until he had found the unborn calves they carried, and had eaten of that only. Other stock had been ripped so that their intestines protruded, and the ghastly sores which the killer had made meant inevitable, lingering, torturing death to the killer's victim.

"Wolf," said Bill Caywood. "A bad hombre. But wolf. It sounds like dogs—wild, bad dogs. But there's real wolf work in it. No hound in the country could throw a steer like this fellow does."

"Whatever it is, I hope you get him quick," replied Mayer. "This just can't keep up much longer. I've stood about all one rancher can absorb in that style of punishment. It's getting my goat."

Mayer spoke the truth. Just before Bill Caywood had come the butchering wolf had killed in two weeks seventeen young head of livestock—slaughtered them for the joy of killing—and had not eaten a pound of meat from any of the seventeen. There was no limit to the damage he might do if not captured.

The next day Bill Caywood moved to Mayer's cow camp. Before the setting of another sun he was on the trail of the heartless, ruthless killer that had cast a spell of dread over Burns Hole.

The forest ranger knows that unless he gets to the fire, smashes it, that he will be grilled officially for failing in line of duty. The Royal Mounted Police have a slogan that they get their man. Considerable romantic luster has been shed on these organizations because of the grim tenacity with which they fight against enemies of the community.

Never in any history has there been a more determined campaign against a criminal of any kind than that which Bill Caywood launched against the elusive, unknown killer in Eagle County. He was out to get his wolf.

Caywood, frontiersman by inheritance, loved animals. Unable to talk mutual language, able only to attain wordless understanding, he and his horses became real partners on the trail.

This love and understanding extended to the wild life. Deer, their fawns, camp robbers, chipmunks, all friendly life of the forests were fellow spirits.

Even for the big gray wolf, the killer, he had great compassion. He would let them live if they could be turned from their inherent instinct to murder.

But there was no hesitancy in Bill Caywood's mind when he started on the trail of a renegade. For he knew from decades of experience the limitless cruelty that fills the heart of the renegade wolf.

Without an hour's delay Caywood started to scout for the runways of the butcher of Burns Hole.

Early morning found Caywood on the trail. Late dusk and the bright flaming Colorado sunsets found the silent, grim rider guiding a weary horse back to the cow camp. On all sides there was the sprightly wild life of the range, the brilliant flower gardens of timber line, the elusive bird life of the undergrowth, the beauty of the cloud patches as their shadows moved in stately measures over the valley lands or the mottled hillsides.

Caywood sensed all of this. It was a reflection of his inner being. But the spirit of it could not dominate. He was trailing a renegade.

The usual wolf runway is established because of food conditions. It is often as much as fifty miles long—sometimes longer. It follows ridge, mesa, cañon or open valley. Its width is sometimes as wide as a quarter of a mile, sometimes narrows to fifty feet or less as it threads through cañon or over pass. The first move of the wolfer is to figure out the runways of the wolf he stalks.

Trails led over sagy flats where cattle lolled in the sun or sought the shade of scrubby cottonwoods in the draws, while magpies flopped away, their spiky black tails suggesting a bit of a black comet in flight. Or the trails threaded through little cañons where the granite rock dripped in the shadow of the douglas fir thickets and moss spread green cushions over the deep red tones of the stone. Again they would lead up where the straight-growing lodgepole pine stood so thick on either side of the trail they almost made stockades which would resist the intrusion of a large animal. At other times the way would take the rider far up where the last thinning bit of the tree army would finally blend through the scrubby stands of alpine fir into the bald uplands above timber line.

No other man has ever surpassed the knowledge of the renegade wolf possessed by Federal Hunter Bill Caywood. His knowledge of the wolf mind is uncanny. It has been amassed through years of trail riding, trap setting, silent, bitter campaigns against the cruel gray wolves. Into the work on the range of dead Lefty he threw every bit of his skill.

His deep-set, piercing blue eyes peered out from bushy, sun-bleached brows, looking for that wolf footprint which would be the starting point of his campaign. He must know the sort of a killer he dealt with before traps were set.

Dog tracks there were in plenty; coyote tracks, too. They did not interest him. He looked for the big, broad, elongated track, the size of a big Alaskan husky, but unlike the dog's in that it would not be so round in shape.

Nowhere did he find such a mark. The raiding, the mean, slaughtering attacks of the killer had ceased.

Ten days went by. But they did not stop that campaign.

Caywood still was positive that he trailed a wolf—a lone, hard-bitten, merciless big gray. With all the evidence of the moment pointing against him, he stuck to the theory that no other killer would do all the things that the butcher of Eagle County had done.

The tenth day had been long, wearisome, without any more results than those which had preceded it.

He was more grim than before as he rode this tenth consecutive day. Plodding, plugging, untiring alertness, attention to every sign on the pathway beneath the horse's feet was the price he was paying for the slightest shred of evidence. And it did not matter that the sun was dropping down back of Castle Peak and there were miles between him and the camp. If the next hundred yards would give him the information he wanted he would go that—more, too—if needed.

He guided his horse into an arroyo. Its mud-colored walls were vertical, as though they had been dug by a spade. The earth-wall arroyo blended into a little rocky cañon.

His keen eyes followed the sign of the trail. This trail sign was like news print to Caywood. A coyote had come down that run early that morning. Then it swung out of the soft dust. Cattle tracks of the day before were plentiful. Stock was spread over the range. This was perhaps the reason there had been no recent report of the butchering raider; he could kill in some far distant meadow, and his victim would not be found for days after.

Ten days! And thirty miles of trail each day Caywood had ridden. In all that distance no trail sign of significance had escaped his eye. Plugging, persistent, careful, trailing would bring him the fragment of knowledge he needed, just one significant track would start his whole campaign against the killer.

Reward for persistence came suddenly.

Caywood reined in his horse, dismounted, strode to a place where water had stood days before, and stooping over, peered at the one, solitary wolf track he had seen during all those days of dogged trailing.

It was in old adobe mud. It had been made by the big dog wolf, Gray Terror, days before. It was sunbaked, cracked from the heating, but as definite as though cast in plaster.

On that one slender bit of evidence that there was a wolf in Burns Hole, Caywood launched his campaign. The next day traps were thrown out. Blind sets were placed in the saddles, a few scentpost sets, sets in runways. These were all placed in locations that Caywood knew from experience rightly placed. Bill Caywood staked his whole campaign on one sun-baked track and his wolf lore.

"Do you think you'll get the old devil?" asked Mayer anxiously when Caywood reported the finding of the track and the setting of the traps.

For a long moment Caywood was silent. Then he bent over slightly and with methodical deliberateness projected a shot of tobacco juice at a horsefly that buzzed near the bottom of the log steps. He watched the disturbed fly hum away unhurt and then raised his eyes and squinted as he looked across the open park surrounding the cow camp. His jaws were grimly set, his eyes held a steely, determined look.

"You don't need to worry, Mayer," he assured the rancher. "It's a wolf. I'll get him. Maybe not first trip. But I'll get him!"

The hunter was silent again for a moment. Then he took off his stained range hat and scratched his dark hair, which was just shot with little silver streaks.

"I'll be just plumb thankful, Mayer, when I do stop this killer. Mean? Why, there's nothing more so. When wolves go bad like this fellow there ain't nothin' they won't do. Go crazy for blood. Just cut up anything they can get to play with. This one is just about the meanest wolf I've ever tackled. Just no decency about him. He's got to be stopped, that's all."

"Aren't all wolves bad?"

"N—o, not exactly. Can't truthfully say that all wolves are just blood crazy. Most real renegades are, though. All of them kill game and stock. All are butchers at heart.

"No use talkin', wolves and civilization can't bunk together. Man's too humane a creature, has too much respect down in his heart for other wild things and domestic stock, and squar' dealin' to let such heartless criminals as this big gray I'm after run free."

Bill bit off a big chunk of new tobacco to replace the one he discarded.

"I'll be happy, mighty damn happy, to see this old butcher thrashin' in a trap of mine!"

V: CAYWOOD MEETS A CRIMINAL

There were no illusions in Caywood's mind when he rode away from the cabin the day after he had talked to Mayer—the day after the last of his traps were set. Just possibly, he might catch the wolf the first time he came back through the country. Or the hunter might be there in the fall, still riding the trails, still looking for the sign.

Across the rolling hills, through a little, cool cañon where a crystal brook leaped, laughed and brooded in the mottled sunshine and shadow of a little rocky cañon, the trail wound. Later it climbed over a ridge, slanted across the side of a brush-covered hill, and then entered a broad upland valley.

Noon came, followed by the slanting shadows of the last half of daylight.

Then something Caywood saw made his nerves tingle; made him spur his horse a little!

In the soft earth of the trail there was the track of the big dog wolf.

Straight ahead, right in the line, there was one of Caywood's trap sets!

He urged the horse along the trail. Occasionally he glimpsed the track and knew that the wolf had not changed his line of travel.

The way seemed long to the next trap. He tried to peer ahead to see through shadows. He looked for that great rangy wolf body of gray to rise eerily.

He came to a point where the trail swung a little. His heart pounded faster. He forgot to chew the tobacco that nestled in his cheek, then nervously rolled it with his tongue.

The trap set was reached.

Bill Caywood let out a yell. The unbelievable had happened!

With the one track to go on, on the first trip through he had snagged the killer.

Wolf tracks were everywhere; the ground was torn; the earth was scattered where the surprised wolf had sprung into the air.

Caywood scrambled off his horse, yanked his light hunting high-power out of the scabbard.

The horse started to follow. Bill, crouching a little, worked forward, eyes alert.

He passed a thicket of evergreens, then a tangle of sage, stopped, waited, listened. He moved forward again.

This renegade would meet death the moment Bill Caywood could clap eyes on him. His death sentence had been written in the blood of his victims.

The horse snorted as he followed Caywood.

Quick as though released by a spring, the terrible, powerful form of the gray wolf leaped out of a windfall.

The butcher, Gray Terror, caught at last, made a single frantic effort to get away from his Nemesis.

In almost the same instant of motion Caywood's gun came up for snap sighting, cracked.

The wolf leaped, struggled, lay still.

Gray Terror, fiendish, wanton, lustful murderer, the bloody, butchering wolf of Eagle County, had come to the end of his criminal career.

→ ←

Back at camp Bill laid out the pelt and skull of Gray Terror. He knew, intuitively, that he had got the killer. There might be other wolves, or even some few killer dogs, but here was the worst. Subsequent riding did show that this had been the only killer—a lone wolf that slaughtered more than even a small pack.

Caywood called Mayer by telephone.

"Heard any more about that supposed wolf up here?" he asked, as Mayer answered the phone.

"Nope," replied the rancher. "I've just about come to the conclusion that he has left the country."

"He has," replied Bill with a chuckle. "I trapped him last night. Killed him this afternoon; got his hide here now."

"Wh—a—t?"

"Fact. Caught him in a set up near Hannewald's cow camp and—"

Caywood stopped to listen, for Mayer had dropped the receiver and his excited shouts to the others in his home were being swallowed by a rising tumult.

In the darkening shadow, with phone receiver glued to his ear, Bill Caywood stood and grinned happily. Much of his reward for the grim game he had played so successfully was being conveyed to him by the joyful noise that flowed over the slender metal wire stretching between the cow camp telephone and the Mayer ranch. All thought of the unhooked receiver at Mayer's had been blotted out. It dangled at the end of the cord. The hubbub, with all its spontaneous rejoicing, came to the happy listener at the cow camp.

Finally with a sigh Bill Caywood hung up the receiver. He turned to get his lonely supper.

For a moment Caywood stood looking down at the furry bundle on the floor. He touched it with the toe of his shoe. He turned abruptly to the little stove, stopped to bite off his customary chew of tobacco, and took up the coffee pot preparatory to brewing the nectar of the cow ranges.

Big peace was with Caywood in the little cabin as he ate his homely meal, by the light of the kerosene light.

The Phantom Wolf

North of the Colorado River, where it winds between the red walls of Ruby Cañon, east of the Uinta country of Utah, and west of the craggy battlements of the White River plateau, there is a stretch of country that is little marked by the white man's civilization. The browse is a little more closely cropped, the bunch grass has been over-grazed in places, there are few fences, and occasionally one may spy a man on horseback as his mount jogs along through the sage-draped landscape. Of course there are a few sandy, twisty roads that meander across the 'dobe-colored earth. Travel on them is infrequent. They would soon revert to wilderness if they were never used.

Bookcliff Mountain rises in ragged splendor from the choppy mesas, arroyos, and plateaus. Fat streaks of oil shale decorate its sides. Other strata carry colors. A band of red seems to glow as though heated by some hidden furnace. Another streak of color is cool and green as the sea, while soft gray and neutral tint blend all into a mountain cloak of beauty. These tints are again echoed in the sides of the arroyos and cañons.

On headlands, where showers, wind, and frost have worked their artistry, there are queer rock shapes. A squat imp may stand beside a caricature of a slender temple spire, or the bulky form of a rock resembling an elephant may stand guard over an outline which appears to be a sleeping Indian of gigantic size, or a castle cornice, depending on the imagination and mood of the beholder.

It is a spooky land, with all the lure, all the threat, all the beauty and cruelty of the semidesert.

Along the arroyos there are bushy scrub cedar. They hold to life in dry areas where other trees will not venture. In a few places there are piñon pine. Higher in the hills there are patches of scrub bull pine.

On the flats there is mesquite, yucca, mountain mahogany, sagebrush, twisted and years old, and some low-growing cacti that flaunt gorgeous, spiny flowers. In between are sandwiched little spots of bunch grass on which cattle fatten and sheep nibble as they blat their way over the flats and mesas from Utah eastward to the cool highlands of the White River plateau.

Southwestward the La Sal Mountains seem to stand clear-cut as cameos; or they recede, become almost unreal, as fairy mountains painted on some dazzling curtain. Then they are blue and distant. Again they are friendly mountains, colorful, beckoning and alluring.

On hot summer days tiny whirlwinds dance. Sage tang fills the air. It becomes a heady brew to be sniffed and sniffed until one's sense of smell is obliterated through the continuous odor of the desert perfume. Lizards sprawl in the sun, solemn owls come to the top of their burrows in abandoned prairie-dog towns and wait like lazy old men until the setting sun gives them a chance to see where they are journeying. Here is the home of that lonely brown bird, the road runner. Fleet of foot as any horse, he rarely takes to wing, but scoots away through the sage like a pixie of the wastelands.

Prairie-dog towns are everywhere. To intruders the inhabitants call menacing threats in prairie-dog language, barking in excitement and high dudgeon.

In winter fierce sharp blizzards race wildly over the sere countryside, mantling it with thin snows.

And when night comes there is a new land, winter or summer. Big black distances reach up into the heavens beyond the farthest blinking star. Night winds sigh through the sage or gallop in the dark with boisterous tumult. Wilderness night travelers pad-pad along the faint trails, keen eyes searching through the clear night darkness, alert ears listening for the first warning sound, noses sniffing the air for taint of the enemy. Then the queer rock forms on the sides of the arroyos and clinging to the fluted cliffs seem quite filled with the spirit of the unknown gods that brood over this lonely stronghold of frontiers.

On the northward the terrain breaks away in giant polychrome escarpments or in sloping, dun-colored plains. The drainage here is toward the Green and White rivers. Southward the waters flow toward the Colorado where it hurries toward the great cañon which is miles below.

Cutting the southward slope is the Great Salt Wash; a swirling torrent sweeping between sculptured cañon walls during freshet time, at others a trickle between water holes.

At many points the element-fretted cliffs along the wash are filled with holes that have leached in the rock. Here, in the rotten rock, was a great denning ground for wolves.

Spreading over wide acres of the divide between the Colorado and its northward tributaries, and embracing much of the Big Salt Wash lie the lands of the Flying W ranch. Its cattle winter in the open flats. In summer they find better picking in the high mountain pastures.

To this Salt Wash country, when it was still in the hands of the Utes came W. J. Nearing. He was a bit of a kid then. But he stayed, weathered the tough winters and baking summers. Cow-punching engaged him for many seasons. He cattle ranched on his own account with some success. Outdoors has always held him as her own.

Nearing was not tall; he was husky. No paunchy, flabby fat of cities hangs on his body. Hardened sinew built by miles of hiking, riding, days, months, years on the open range were the man materials that filled his clothes.

His joining the staff of the Biological Survey was as natural as had been Caywood's, Spangler's, or Hegewa's drift to this work. He had trapped independently for years before the Survey's predatory animal work was organized.

Spring was at hand when Nearing joined the Biological Survey in 1921. Little snow-water floods rushed down the arroyos. Anemones nodded on the upper slopes, sand lilies peeped forth from the low, spidery whorls of leaves that surround their virginal white blossoms. Springiness was in the air.

On a big, rangy gray horse Nearing rode the trails. It was wolf denning time. Riding along a ridge trail, he swept the green-gray slopes with keen eyes. The horse swung his head down to nip at a bit of fresh grass, stomped along the soft trail, stopped, filched another bit of forage, then ambled on.

Nearing's hands rested on the pommel, easing his swaying body in the stirrups. For a few moments he rode with one leg carrying his weight in one stirrup. It was trail relief from the constant saddle mauling.

They reached a hilltop. The horse stopped, looked with round eyes at the gigantic panorama. Nearing did not protest the pause. His gaze roved, swung southward, rested for a moment on what appeared to be a lake. It was the first mirage of the new season. It flashed through the atmosphere for a moment, faded, came back with new clearness, the trees on the shore line of the ghost lake standing in green stateliness; then it disappeared from the spot, only to leap into view in another.

Nearing smiled. Hundreds of these chimeras of the plains he had seen. Tenderfeet or the superstitious might find in them some fleeting vision of a far land. They stirred Nearing's imagination, twitted him a bit with their illusions, but held no grip on him.

Rocks rattled in the trail as they started again. The horse continued to swing low his head to bite at tempting grass. A magpie flapped away from the trail, found a perch in a tree, chattered and cawed.

Nearing's eyes, squinting, swept the horizon, then dropped their gaze on the trail below the horse's feet, fleetingly caught the vision of the mirage lake again, dancing, swelling, and waning as it hovered over the far mesas.

A mile passed. Suddenly he seemed to become taut without muscle motion. He stopped the horse, got off, peered at the trail. He had caught the print of a wolf foot. He walked for a few feet, found another track, then mounted and rode.

Evening found him still far from camp. A half-grown moon with the shadowed side showing clearly in the deep blue of the heavens, rode peacefully halfway up from the western horizon. The west sky line was edged with blue-green afterglow that follows the clear hours of western spring sun days. It faded, blended, shaded until it fanned out into the deep blue in which the silver of the moon seemed like a metal inlay in some inverted bowl of old blue pottery.

Dusk wrapped around the hills. A wind sighed in the trembling, half-nude sage. It whispered among the elfin-formed rocks along the side of the arroyo in which Nearing rode.

Faintly, filled with the weird, chanting music of the wild, there came the yapping call of a coyote at a kill. Nearer at hand an owl hooted in rhythmic monotony.

Man in the dusky, half-illumined night of the semidesert is not the man of the city. He is alert, sensitive to what is around him. He reverts to the keen free dweller of his ancestry. And if he is blessed or cursed with imagination and superstitions, the unknown night noises, the silent black shadows, strum his tightening nerves.

Nearing felt these things. No man living in the open does not. But he took them as everyday occurrences.

He reached the camp, loosened girth, lifted saddle, picked off the blanket, laid it over the saddle, spread it out so no folds would form during the night, then led the sweat-flecked horse to the corral. He dipped out a measure of grain for the tired pony, gave grain to the others, and with bridle clinking at his heels, went back to the shelter where his outfit was housed.

This cabin was like many in the western slope cow country. It was made of bleached, dried, weather-worn piñon poles, hewn on the exposed side to give the semblance of a straight rough wall. Between the logs there was adobe chinking. The roof was dirt; the floor was also earth.

Around the little shack rose shaly slopes. Being the one man-made thing in the gigantic sweep of surrounding country caused it to appear puny. But it was welcome shelter to those who rode the lonesome trails on the range of the Flying W. Nearing made it his regular headquarters during his many campaigns against the predatory beasts.

II: WRAITH OF THE DESERT

The next morning Nearing was on the trail again. An old slicker lashed to the back of his saddle and a can of baked beans for emergency lunch, rolled in its folds, were the only equipment he carried against hunger and storm. His first stop was at the headquarters of the Flying W, several miles up the wash.

Unlike the cow-camp cabin at which Nearing headquartered, the home ranch house of the Flying W was in the midst of flat alfalfa fields, watered by the erratic waters of the Big Salt Wash. It was an oasis in the gray hills. The buildings were long, low, with dirt roof and with walls made of piñon poles hewn on one side and then chinked with adobe. It was not the orthodox ranch house of the movies or stage. It was headquarters of a real cow outfit.

"Two more beef cattle killed night before last," reported one of the ranch hands. "Couple of long yearlings. Wolves did it."

"Where?" asked Nearing.

"Beyond the West Wash."

"How many wolves?"

"Maybe two. Didn't see sign of more. But they killed them two yearlin's just the same."

"I found a dead doe a couple of days ago," reported Nearing. "Wolf work, too."

"Got any line on 'em?"

"Last night just before dark, picked up a bunch of tracks leading away from a den. I'll find it in a couple of days."

Late one afternoon Nearing located the wolf den. Carefully he sneaked away. With a spade and a pick, and in company with two of the boys from the Flying W, he returned the next morning. The den was dug out by noon.

"Now for the old ones," said Nearing as he took one of the squirming whelps, slipped a collar on the little furry neck and staked the tiny wolf near the mouth of the den. "Old folks will come back."

Carefully he ringed the little wolf with traps.

"Can't get inside of those without lumbering into one or the other," observed Nearing, as they prepared to leave.

"Kinda looks impossible," agreed one of the cow hands.

But the next morning proved it had been done. The mother wolf had returned and left.

What had happened when she had reached the baby could only be guessed at.

The tender little body of the whelp had been ripped to shreds by the mother. Nearing shook his head when he viewed the strips of fur and flesh remaining in the collar he had so carefully fastened around the neck of the whelp.

"That beats the Dutch," he exploded. "My gosh, they can't content themselves with killing baby deer, little calves, beef stock. They commit murder on their own babies! Some wolves don't have no heart at all. But they have some brain! Look at the way she got by those traps."

"Luck or something," agreed one of the cow waddies.

For days Nearing scanned the trails for wolf tracks. The kills dropped off. The existing wolf tracks were wiped out by a quick shower. No new tracks appeared.

Fall came. The hunter made life a continual gamble for the coyotes that raided the white billows of sheep cascading down from the White River plateau. At a sheep camp he met Tom Kelly, sheepman.

To Kelly Nearing told the story of the wolf that had eluded his best trap sets, had slaughtered her own baby, and had seemed to melt into thin air.

"It's the Phantom wolf," declared Kelly with conviction.

Old Jesus Gonzales, wrinkled, stooped, brown-skinned sheep herder, had listened as Nearing talked to Kelly. The aged Mexican looked sharply at both men, crossed himself, and moved quietly away, muttering some charm or prayer.

"There you have it," said Kelly, jerking his thumb at Jesus. "All the herders around here know of that wolf. Haven't you heard of her before?"

Nearing nodded. "Oh, something," he admitted. "Didn't put much stock in the stories, though."

"Well, they all talk it—or don't—depending on how superstitious they are. You know how afraid of a bear a Mex sheep herder is. Well, they're just as leery of this wolf as any bear that ever came out of the White River section."

"What do they say about this wolf?" asked Nearing.

"Oh, it's some cock and bull story. They say it's a sort of werewolf—a wolf inhabited by the spirit of some bad man. It makes you creepy to hear these herders talk. Ask old Jesus about her; maybe he'll tell you.

"But don't let his ghost tales get your goat, Nearing. We want that wolf killed. She's a reality. Nope, don't exactly mean that." Kelly paused thoughtfully. "All same mirage, Nearing. Something like the spirit of this God forsaken country. Like a mirage, now you see her, now you don't. Kills one place one night, then hits another place miles away the next. Not a word for months. Then she'll come into a flock and play hell with the woollys. Just play hell!"

"And then disappear?"

"Like smoke."

Nearing rode away thoughtfully. From sheep herders of swarthy skin, quiet, uncommunicative fellows he had heard of this Phantom wolf. Giving little heed to what he considered fairy stories, it had not occurred to him that he had trailed this famous renegade.

The following day he guided his horse to where he knew Jesus Gonzales was herding his flock. As Nearing approached two furtive sheep dogs came racing out from the little pyramidal tent where Jesus slept. They barked, scurried away, crouched, tried to wag their tails, indicating friendliness, but then were over-come by shyness, stuck their tails between their legs and scurried back toward the tent.

Old Jesus himself came out of the tent as Nearing prepared to dismount. He seemed like the old man of the desert, another spirit of the place. Stooped by years, wrinkled, with scraggly grizzled beard masking part of his face, he was a patriarch of the sheep country.

"*Buenos dias*, Señor Nearing," he called. Nearing, the killer of coyotes, the protector of the flocks, was a friend of most of the herders, understood their vernacular. "*Como le va?* How goes it with you, Señor?"

"*Muy bien*," replied Nearing. "Quite good, Jesus. But the long trail sometimes gets me *mucho cansado*. Pretty doggone tired, too?"

"It is the desert life," replied the old man gravely. "We all are tired after days of it. But there is no escape. We are of it. "

"Was your season good?" asked Nearing.

"*Si*. But there was a bear, Señor. One hell of a big bear in the gulch just be-yond the edge of my forest allotment. He gave me worry, *mucho trabajo*."

"Any wolves this summer, Jesus?"

The old man looked sharply at Nearing, then turned to gaze far over the flats to the westward.

"No, no wolves this summer, Señor."

"I've come to talk of them to-day."

"But this was a big bear, a very big one!"

"He didn't molest you, did he?"

"No," reluctantly. "No, but he worried me."

"If he didn't bother you let's talk of this Phantom wolf. I want to know more about her."

Jesus shuffled uneasily. Nearing knew that he was going to have a hard time getting anything which might be information from the superstitious old Mexican.

"Do you know anything about this Phantom wolf, Jesus?"

"*Si*, a little."

"What sort of a wolf is she?"

Jesus' eyes were shifty, bright. "No wolf," he declared.

"Oh, I don't believe that. You're such a *muy sagas hombre* you don't really believe such a thing."

"But I do, Señor. This is no common wolf. It is a wolf with an evil spirit. There is the soul of a devil lives in that animal."

"That's all rot," declared the hunter, half angry. "You should know better than that."

"No common wolf could kill as this one. She kills, slaughters, drinks sheep blood, then flies away through the night without leaving a trail. She has been shot at. And who has shot at her has had trouble later. She whelps not wolves, but some form of devils. No one has ever found her den!"

"Well, I'll blow up that story right now. I dug out her den last spring and killed her whelps. They were common wolves."

Jesus looked sharply at Nearing, looked away, whipped back his glance, peering keenly at the hunter.

"You wear a charm," he remarked. "Or else they were not this Phantom wolf's whelps."

Further questioning, more evasion by the herder, little of anything which might be considered information filled another hour, while Nearing talked to the old man. As he rode away Nearing was convinced that he was on the trail of the famous Phantom wolf.

III: NEARING SCORES

Fall had flung her banners over the higher hills. Purples lurked in the cañons, crept under the shadowy edges of the colorful plateaus and bathed the hazy La

Sals. Winter had capped the higher peaks to the south and east with frosty top-knots of new snow. On hot fall days the lowlands still sweltered in heat.

Then frost rode on the night breeze, painted the oak and cottonwood, seered the range grass. Winter followed with skiffy wet snow that swept over the plains, made the trails greasy with adobe mud for a day, and then seemed to vanish.

The cow camp of the Flying W still was Nearing's headquarters. He was busy in his campaign against coyotes, lions, bobcats. Nearing was not wholly satisfied with killing these lesser renegades. A bad wolf was loose in that vast sweep of country north and west. She would come back, perhaps.

It was a clear fall night with frost nip in the air when Nearing got first warning. He had stepped to the door of the little cabin to look at the dark heavens to see if any flying clouds might have drifted into the unchartered seas of the night sky.

The little cookstove roared softly. A choppy, fragmentary wind whistled and sighed down the slopes.

High in the breaks back of the cow camp broke that eerie call to the pack. Wildly quavering, the breaks with blood-chilling echoes, the howl sped down from the cliff where the wolf perched. It was like a voice of a desert oracle, this challenging, threatening cry.

In spite of himself Nearing felt the lightest touch of awe. He closed the door and stepped from the cabin into the cold, clear darkness.

Pale night light from the star shine filled the big openness. Above, the blue-black sky was dotted with diamond points that flashed and waned. Across the bench lands and high in the open lanes of the air the full wind rushed.

Again came the call, now muted by the wind. It was thin as elfin music, as threatening as death. With powerful force came back all of the stories of the Phantom wolf. In the great black night, with the wind gods directing their streams of invisible force around him, with the land of fluted cliffs, of man-shaped rocks, of wilderness spirits on every side, Nearing, phlegmatic as he was, shivered a little, perhaps from the chill night air, then turned and went back to his magazine reading.

Wolf tracks appeared in the dusty parts of the trail. A new snow showed more. Poor, twisted steer bodies, the remains of a little fawn, slaughtered sheep on Kelly's range, all showed the work of the murderer of the Big Salt Wash.

Winter wore on. Nearing reached a stage where his stubborn determination was alone lashing him on in superefforts to find his wolf. No chance went by. He risked blizzard, cold, frostbite, just to keep on the trail.

At times he would not see a track for a week. Then he would find them in profusion. They would drop out of sight. A kill would again set him on the trail.

Whelping time came. The wolves howled no more. But killing broke out afresh. A half dozen long yearlings would fall in one night, would be stiff by morning. Only a few strips of flesh would be torn off. The rest would be left for the carrion-eaters—magpies, coyotes.

Half angry at being thwarted, Nearing set out on a systematic search of the old denning grounds. He checked trails, carefully avoided giving alarm, and finally was rewarded by narrowing the trails down to a point indicating that a den was near. Then he found it. With help he dug out the wolf pups.

"Goin' to set another little wolf for live bait?" asked one of the cow hands.

Nearing shook his head. "Nope, she'd kill the poor little devil," he said. "She's that kind."

With renewed vigilance Nearing followed the trails. The Phantom wolf was somewhere near. He placed blind sets, sets with scent, every conceivable sort of a trap. But suddenly the tracks appeared no more, the kills ceased.

Weeks passed. No more wolves were heard of in the whole watershed between the Colorado and the White rivers.

"I told you," declared Tom Kelly. "There's no question but that it's the Phantom. I don't believe any sort of a man trap will ever catch that lobo."

"Nor no man ever kill her," supplemented old Jesus Gonzales fervently. "It is a spirit wolf."

"Bunk!" exploded Nearing. "Just wait; I'll snag her."

"More power," said Kelly fervently.

But Jesus Gonzales looked long at his friend Nearing and shook his old tousled head. There would be trouble come yet if this man insisted on pursuing the devil wolf.

IV: NEARING SCARS A PHANTOM

The summer of 1922 passed much as the previous summer. It would have been a period of discouragement for less determined men than Nearing. His fellow hunters had succeeded, while he had not. Hegewa had trapped Bigfoot and Lefty. Caywood had "got his wolf" when he met Rags face to face on a lonely trail. Whitey, raider in the old buffalo haunts of the Bear Springs Mesa, had been brought to range justice. Three-Toes of the Apishapa had been trapped by Spangler, and her half-grown half-breed whelps had been tracked down and captured.

Nearing still trailed the Phantom.

Usually wolves keep to the same runways the year around. One killer wolf methodically crossed a certain point, almost at a fixed hour of the day, every nine days, each time traveling in a counterclockwise manner. Wolf habits of travel on their regular runways generally will vary somewhat more than this, but they follow certain runs. These habits make it possible for the hunters to lay plans for the capture of ordinary wolves.

But the Phantom was further proof that when one is trapping a renegade anything may happen. Usual wolf conduct, instinct, racial habit is thrown in the discard.

Now it was a question whether or not she would return to the Salt Wash.

Young came to visit Nearing, but could offer little to supplement the things Nearing had already done.

"Queer wolf," remarked Young at length.

"Spooky," agreed the hunter. "I think old Jesus Gonzales thinks she is no flesh and blood beast, but really a spirit."

"You don't believe that, do you, Nearing?"

"I've got darned good grounds to believe it. But while she kills cattle like she does, has real wolf whelps, leaves tracks in the trail, it'll take more than Mex herder's stories to make me change my mind. I'll get her sometime."

"That's the stuff."

They were silent a moment as both looked over the fall-touched landscape of grays, browns, soft-tinted purples and far haze. A mirage was shimmering over the flats.

"Kelly says she's just like that," said Nearing, pointing to the unreal scene that danced in the heat. "I swear, sometimes she does seem unreal. No one has ever seen her."

"I've been thinking," remarked Young after a moment, during which they had watched the mirage fade and a new one blossom at another point. "Maybe she comes here only to whelp. Maybe born here herself. And she comes back to the old home to have her babies. Now, if that's true, she'll be back again this coming mating season, or at least by whelping time."

Nearing nodded. "Just what I've thought."

"Well, Nearing, when you get her, I'll give you a boost in salary. Now go to it!"

Winter came again. Snows swirled over the flats, sheep found the low country and cattle were being fed alfalfa at the stack yards of the Flying W.

Early December found Nearing on the old trails, ready to act at the first sign of a wolf.

"She's back," he announced one day as he rode into the Flying W home ranch. "New wolf tracks over by the East Salt Wash. Slaughtered steer, too."

The foreman looked glumly out over the brown stubble of the meadows. "Guess that means we're in for a loss again," he gloomed. "Dang it, Nearing, isn't there anything we can do to help you?"

Nearing shook his head.

"You know I'm doin' my damndest. You've given me all the help I could ask for. Only thing is to stay on the job. Sometime we'll outsmart her."

The new year came. In the breaks, riding over slippery trails, working out from the kills made, Nearing stalked the elusive lobo. Fresh killing brought new tales of the Phantom from the men at sheep and cow camps. News of this wolf got to Fruita. It was a common street topic. Nearing was baffled, half angry.

The two previous years the Phantom had traveled alone. Now entered a new factor. A mate was with her. Nearing placed some new scent sets. The dog wolf charged around them.

Several days later Nearing caught the mate of the Phantom. Thus encouraged, he spread his traps everywhere. Days passed with no results. Finally he tore up those sets and placed them at new points.

Meanwhile, somewhere under the breaks, in the choppy cliffs of the Salt Wash, where wolves had denned since before white man's coming, the Phantom had her brood of killers.

Parent wolves start away from the den in a straight line. They go thus for several miles before they begin to scout. Returning they circle, sniff the wind, are suspicious. A circling track means a wolf is working back to the den. A straight trail means it is traveling away from the den. Back-tracking on the straight trails, Nearing finally narrowed the possible locations of the den to a limited section.

Then one day he spotted the den, lay watching it for an hour, hoping to see the whelps playing around it. He ventured closer. Quickly the intuition of those who live in the open came to help Nearing. He suddenly knew that the den had been abandoned.

Hurriedly he started circling. He verified his conjecture. Only some few hours before the Phantom had led her babies away. Perhaps the experience of previous years caused her to move, perhaps she had seen Nearing in spite of his care.

Back on his horse, Nearing started to follow the track of mother and whelps. For several hours he rode. He was north of Bookcliff Mountain, thirty-six miles north of Fruita. He was at a crucial point in his campaign against the Phantom. Hurrying, eager, Nearing urged his horse forward. Miles passed, evening approached.

The horse topped a little ridge, dropped down a shallow arroyo, came out on a broad dry wash.

A flash of gray on the hillside caught the hunter's eye.

It was a running wolf.

His hand dropped to his gun, yanked it out. The wolf dodged out of sight in the brush.

Nearing felt his muscles bunch, his eyes strain. He prepared for the next break in the grim game.

The sign in the trail, the faltering steps of the whelps, the frequent stops, had forecast that he was near a new den.

Again, fleetingly, he caught the movement on the hill; saw the leaping gray body.

Suddenly he realized that this was the Phantom, the ghost wolf of the Big Salt Wash!

Nearing jumped from his horse. He ran forward. His eye swept an open space across which the wolf would have to dash.

The fleeing wolf shot into view. Her rangy gray body swept along almost with the lightness of a flying bird.

Nearing threw the gun to his shoulder. He pulled the trigger.

The bullet whined of death, but spat harmlessly back of the fleeing renegade.

Nearing fired again. The bullet kicked up dust under the wolf. He hurriedly threw in a fresh cartridge.

Quick snap sights were taken.

The third lead pellet ripped through the air, found its mark. Like a furry fury the wolf stumbled, rolled, clawed, got up, fell again, dragged her stricken body a few feet and then lay still.

Exultation filled Nearing as he saw the Phantom wolf fall.

The long quest was ended; he had shot the Phantom!

He started forward on the run.

As though the ground had exploded there leaped from under his feet a scared little wolf. The whelp ran, dodged, huddled close to the ground, sought cover, and then suddenly ran to other shelter.

Nearing whirled from his run to the place where the dead Phantom lay. Rifle in hand, he dived after the scared little wolf. The whelp yapped a little, dodged, twisted, then in sheerest fright ran straight for the mouth of a newly dug den.

Nearing again started toward the Phantom, leaping over the low brush as he ran.

Another little wolf jumped up, ran, his little body a leaping, scurrying fluff ball.

Stumbling, running with all his might, Nearing turned and headed the little wolf. Down the hill they scrambled, back toward the den. A third wolf baby leaped from cover, circled, got in the way of Nearing, ran for his life, headed into the hole.

Three whelps were in the new den. Nearing scouted for more that might be outside. Usually the wolf litter is from five to eleven. He was certain that there were others.

Hurriedly searching, he kicked up another whelp. Nearing rushed her into the den. For several moments more he hunted for others, but found none.

He blocked the den. His heart pounded with the excitement and running. Anxiously he ran to find the dead Phantom.

His eyes searched the point where she fell. He looked at the rocks, the brush, the empty open space where she had fallen, stumbled, struggled up and then fallen to lie still.

Nearing was scowling as he completed the second searching look.

He brushed his eyes in perplexity. He would have wagered his worldly wealth that he had seen the wolf fall dead at the point where he stood.

Whatever had happened one thing was certain.

THE PHANTOM WOLF WAS GONE!

For a long moment Nearing stood looking at the point where he had seen the killer stumble and fall. There was blood on the ground.

But there was no dead wolf there with it.

A feeling of awe edged into Nearing's thoughts. The thing was uncanny. Fight as he might, there crept into his mind all the unreality, the almost supernatural qualities ascribed by the herders to this wolf.

Angry, disgusted, yet unwillingly admitting that there was something of witchery around this magical disappearance, Nearing hurried back to the den. He blocked it more securely. Then he flagged it with his coat so no wild thing would come to molest it while he was gone.

Night had come when he finished. He started for help at the Flying W. He needed aid—aid and shovels.

⟶⟵

Stars blinking, early summer winds whispering mysteriously in the brush, night life on the range, lowing of a distant cow, all filled the darkness around him as he followed the trail. He could not shake that tinge of awe that filled him following the curious, uncanny disappearance of the Phantom.

As he traveled the rough trail he wondered if he had actually seen the wolf that afternoon, seen her stumble and fall. Or had he really seen a vision?

He reached the ranch. He had traveled sixteen miles on foot since he left the den.

"Better stay until daylight," suggested one of the hands at the ranch.

"Can't," replied Nearing. "I'm not taking any chance of those whelps getting away. One wolf of that stripe on the range is enough!"

Back over the trail they plodded. Cowmen are some of the best coöperators the Survey hunter has, so one of the men of the Flying W accompanied him.

Footsore, tired—dog-tired—they reached that den. It was two o'clock in the morning.

They waited for sunup. Nearing did not sleep, for he was keyed to the slightest sound that might betray the return of the Phantom. Sitting quietly in the darkness, waiting, there seethed in his mind all of the old legends, the hearsay that had been woven around this wolf.

Rose, crimson, flame, burned in the heavens, and then came the sun. With hunger gnawing at his bowels Nearing took the brunt of the work. It was hard going. Rock, dirt, gravel were gouged out. By dint of digging and grunting labor the two men, by ten o'clock, finally reached the six baby wolves huddling in the far end of the new den. Snarling, struggling, they were thrust into a sack by the hunter.

Nearing threw the bag of whelps over his shoulder, trudged three miles over a mountain to his pack horse, where he had left it the day before. He loaded the whelps on the protesting horse. Leading the animal, he walked eight miles farther to his camp. Here he dumped the gunny sack full of young wolves into his automobile, grabbed a hasty lunch, and then started for Fruita.

Nearing had been on the job for thirty-six hours with little sleep and even less than a little to eat.

Behind him were hours of trailing, nerve-tense hunting, muscle-testing work. Even in this supreme effort he had partially failed.

Somewhere back there in the country where mirages shimmered, where wind elves had fashioned goblins out of rock, where the unknown mysteries of the semidesert brooded and throbbed, the Phantom wolf was hidden in the enchanted land of the Big Salt Wash.

V: THE DOGGED TRAIL

Back again at his camp with but a day's rest from his trial of the trail, Nearing started again to hunt the Phantom. Carefully he worked out from the point where he had seen her fall. Tracks had been obliterated—if there had been tracks when that gray apparition had melted into nothingness.

Contrary to his expectations, he found no dead wolf. Then he started to sniff the winds that blew from every quarter in that little area near the Phantom's last den. A dead wolf would taint the breeze until he could follow the smell to the dead, maggot-infested body.

But the winds did not stink with carrion.

The story of his encounter with the wolf spread. Nearing was questioned everywhere. Following his campaign against the coyotes as the sheep came up from the Utah border he met Tom Kelly.

"No common wolf; begins to look like the herders might be right," declared the sheep man. "This certainly lends some color to the contention of old Gonzales that she is no wolf at all, but just an evil spirit of the desert."

"If she's still alive our trail will cross again sometime," declared Nearing. "When it does I'll have better luck."

"Gosh, I hope so," declared Kelly. "No telling what damage she might do if these herders get any more hopped up about her. They're jumpy already, and you're not shootin' her has made 'em more so. They may quit their flocks."

Again and again Nearing searched intermittently for the dead wolf. Summer wore on, the mirages danced between the Salt Wash country and the La Sals, the sage got dusty, the ground parched and fall crept down mountain sides. The cow camp of the Flying W was stocked with supplies. From this base fortress Nearing made new war against the whole motley army of animal killers.

When blue purples had flooded into the shadows of the hills, when days of autumn haze were followed by the clearness brought by the first frost, Nearing rode the sage-land trails. On one of these one day he met the shepherd, Jesus Gonzales.

"It is good to see you again," said the old Mexican. "And to see you well, Señor."

Nearing laughed a little. He knew what was in the old man's mind.

"Never was in better health, Jesus. Can lick my weight twice over in wildcats."

"There is no other answer," declared the old man, half to himself and looking far away to the west. "You must carry the protection of some powerful saint— or a most powerful charm."

"Why?"

"Is it not true that you shot the Phantom wolf and knocked her down with a shot? And that you killed her cubs of this year?"

"Si," replied the hunter. "And if she comes back I'll do worse, or better, next time."

"Well, if your charm is so powerful, I hope it will protect the rest of us too, Señor. That is a bad wolf, an evil spirit, and if aroused may do great damage, most awful damage. I fear for my flocks, maybe for myself."

"Cheer up, Jesus. If that old sinner is alive she may be back. If she comes back it ain't goin' to be none too healthy for that lobo. And if I bring in her hide maybe it'll bust up your pipe dreams about her being a spirit wolf, a *lobo de las animas.*"

Nearing laughed at Jesus Gonzales and his superstitions—laughed and wondered a little in spite of himself. Then he shook the mood and plunged into his war against the beasts of slaughter.

On a clear morning early in December he rode a trail of sandy softness through a wash bordered by fretted and fluted walls where squat gnome shapes in rocks were scattered between dainty, colorful pagodas, temples, miniature castles, and hobgoblins of stone. His eyes swept the trail sign. For here was the story of the past few days written in the sand for those who might read it.

He reined in his horse, leaped to the ground, dropped to his knees, peered at the telltale track that had caught his eye.

It was the footprint of the Phantom!

Nearing could not have told how he recognized it. But he knew, with the first glimpse, that the old quest was renewed, that the Phantom still lived.

Back at the cabin he overhauled his wolf trap equipment. He buried it in the manure pile, waited two days for man scent to pass from the steel traps. Then with his other equipment wrapped in the descented setting cloth and the traps dangling against the horse, he set out to throw down a network of steel traps such as he had never built before.

His work in previous years had given him some knowledge of the erratic habits of the Phantom. This fragmentary data he now put to the best use. In one wide side wash that swung westward from the Big Salt Wash there was a trail over which the Phantom sometimes traveled. Here he put a gang of traps with great care.

"I'll get her," he declared with conviction to the men at the Flying W, as they all sat one night at supper. "She's my wolf. I branded her last spring and this fall I'll round her up."

Grins passed around. Nearing met them good-naturedly. "Oh, I know what you're thinkin'," he chaffed. "That this is a ghost lobo. Let me tell you this is a real wolf, and she's my meat!"

"You've been at it a long time," observed one of the men. "Nigh a couple of years, ain't it?"

There was a moment's pause filled with the clank of heavy ranch "silverware," the tinkle heavy porcelain dishes and cups and other sounds typical of any friendly board where folks come to get food and not as a social gesture.

"Yeh, guess more than that," replied Nearing slowly. "This is the fall of 1923. I started to trail her in the spring of 1921. Comin' on three year, ain't it? But I've taken twenty-one of her whelps in that time and that's nothin' to sneeze at."

"Nope, there's no kick on that," agreed the foreman soberly, for he knew what havoc each of those wolves might have caused if they had all lived. Roughly, they would have cost the stock industry around the Salt Wash in the neighborhood of forty thousand dollars if they had done the killing of stock accredited to average wolves. With the Phantom as their leader they might well have doubled that cost to the cattlemen.

The Pantom, still at large, drove Nearing into the field, early, late, everyday, rain, shine or snow. Beast, were-wolf, ghost—whatever this elusive killer might be—Nearing swore that he would meet her.

December twelfth came. He saddles his horse as usual. Thoughts of the three-year campaign against this miscreant filled his mind as he rode the sand-cushioned trail.

Wind whispered in the sage, late fall sun heat shimmered over the far plains. It soaked down into the arroyos until it routed the cold bite in the air.

The trail led by the side wash, the favorite route of the Phantom as she came in from the Uinta country in Utah.

The horse turned up this side wash. Some instinct flashed through Nearing, making his nerves tighten. The horse snorted.

Something called him to hurry on. He put spurs to the horse. The pony broke into a dogtrot. They passed the first wide stretch of the arroyo. They turned a corner, passed a twisty section, then rounded a bend. The horse dropped to a sharp walk.

Ahead was the trap set. Nearing shot a glance at the location of the trap. Big peace filled the wash.

Like the ripping of stout fabric the quiet shattered.

One instant Nearing was sitting relaxed in the saddle.

The next he was pulling leather, quieting the snorting, plunging horse.

Like a buff spirit, unreal as tawny fog, there sprang from the sage the rangy body of a big wolf.

IT WAS THE PHANTOM!

Nearing's hand laid quick grip on rifle stock. He jerked it out. He flung himself from the saddle, hurried forward.

Wildly the Phantom strained at the trap. Her tawny color, almost like that of a collie, indicated some dog ancestor. Perhaps it was this which had made her erratic, untrue to wolf tradition, and so knowing.

Her red jaws gaped wide. Gleaming teeth dared Nearing to come forward. She threw herself at him, snapping, then tried to tear away. Frantically she threatened; as frantically she strove to break to freedom.

Nearing raced forward heedlessly, stumbling in the sage thickets, slipping on loose rocks.

He reached a little open spot, stopped. The wolf, regal in tawny winter coat, quieted, slowly facing Nearing. Instantly Nearing had a feeling that he faced the supernatural; that here was the ghost of the very wolf he had killed months before.

His hand trembled as he lifted the gun, sighted it, pressed the trigger.

The Phantom leaped, fell, struggled, shuddered, and then lay still.

Nearing ran headlong. He wanted to reach her side, make sure, know that here indeed was a wolf. He reached the dying wild thing in the trap. He stopped.

The Phantom had passed. In her place was——

A dead wolf!

An hour later Nearing arose from his job of skinning. Like all good hunters he sought new facts. This had led him to dissect the body of the wolf. There he had found that she had already mated at a date unusually early, and that if she had been allowed to den she would have mothered seven whelps the next spring. Had this happened she would have given birth to twenty-eight whelps in four seasons.

"Ah, but Señor," protested Jesus Gonzales when he next met the hunter. "I have it all figured out. This is not the same wolf. You shot the Phantom last spring. That Phantom still roams the range. This is another wolf. You are still safe from witchery."

"Well, maybe," agreed Nearing. "But the scar of the bullet I shot through her eight months ago showed plainly on this wolf I trapped."

The old sheep herder looked up, belief and incredulity in mixed expression on his face.

"Perhaps it is the same," he said slowly. "And yet—I doubt it."

Nearing smiled indulgently. He knew his quest was ended. He had "got his wolf."

The Greenhorn Wolf

A big wind was sucking down the Huerfano valley. Some giant command sent the air pouring out of the hills and flats near the little towns of Malachite, Redwing and Gardner. Wind gusts were but points of high pressure in a steady, racing, powerful wind flood.

Gravel the size of big marbles rolled on the sandy benches, propelled by the sweeping wind. The air was filled with powdery dirt and sand that would cut and strangle any who tried to go through the dust-filled wind funnels.

The stinging sand clouds followed regular channels. For a strip a hundred yards wide the air would be saturated with dust. Then it would clear, but the hurricane would keep up. Then would come another chute in the air through which the solid dust clouds raced.

In the drab twilight there moved a gray form. Like an evil genius of the day and the country she skulked along. Plunging into a dust torrent, she staggered from the pelting force of the wind, then forged on doggedly.

She reached the clearer air on the opposite side, stopped, sneezed gustily. She looked back and growled at that inferno of misty earth. Then her inflamed eyes turned toward the squat, conical black little hill that pops up in symmetrical form out of the flat bottom lands of the Huerfano. It is the orphan butte which gives the Huerfano River its name, a landmark hill of the early Spanish adventurers.

Wind whipped the ragged pelt of the traveler. It drove the chill air of February into the marrow of the old she-wolf. It made her shiver and shake.

In bygone days she would have gloried in this wild, tempestuous day of the rowdy winds. It would have been a reflection of her own vicious nature.

But now she whined, hunched her shoulders, then turned and trotted past the solitary Huerfano butte. Hunger, loneliness, restlessness drove her to travel far; south to the Picketwire River, north to the outskirts of Pueblo, where the steel furnaces make the night skies warm and red.

Many seasons the Greenhorn wolf had traveled the wide open plains bordering mountains that thrust up from the bowels of the planet. And before her breed had ranged here while mighty changes occurred, changes that were of vast import, but at the same time had not moved a mountain nor made a mountain of a plain.

Years back, centuries even, gray wolves had trotted in the wake of the black herds of countless buffalo. Calves were plentiful. Old bison bulls would straggle or be driven out of the herds to die. Then wolves feasted. Running in powerful packs, they found plenty of food, plenty of shelter. No quadruped could stand against the attack of the pack. It was hey-a-day for the wolf tribe.

Then had come the first white man in shining armor. Many others followed. The red man fought with this foreign invader. But the newcomer was fired with the greed of conquest. The red man was swept before him, whipped, almost broken, but never shattered.

These were days of high feasting for the wolves. They would follow the hunters on the plains and glut themselves with the buffalo meat the two-legged killers left. Perhaps the hunter would take the liver and the loin only. Generally he did not take the whole carcass. There came a period in which the entire carcasses of the buffalo were left to the prairie beasts or to rot as the case might be. The hide of the big bison only was worth a price on the market—a price of ten cents each f.o.b. Pueblo!

Through all these changes the verdure-clad mountain north of the Huerfano stood like some brooding giant undisturbed by the happenings that moved swiftly around its base. It is one of the oldest geological formations in Colorado, this long ridge with its bare, high-lifted snout 12,530 feet above the level of the sea. This imposing mass of granite has seen other ranges born. A few centuries of dominance over the lands at its base by one race or another could not change the Greenhorn peak.

"Cuerno Verde," the Spanish conquerors had named it; the horn of green. For it resembles a horn in shape, and its sides carry timber as thick as can be found on the east slope of the Colorado Rockies. Men from eastward, translating the Spanish, had named it the Greenhorn.

It did not matter to the Cuerno Verde that these men in shining armor forecast thousands of others. Coronado was but one man to this mountain. Nor did it disturb the serenity of this mighty peak when other whites followed Lieutenant Pike across the snowy Greenhorn range in their desperate drive to find the Red River and a way to the Pacific.

When Spanish people came to settle at the base of this old peak, forming one of the first settlements by Europeans in Colorado, there was no change in the mountain. And when a runner from Taos, miles to the south, stumbled over the trail near Sierra Blanca, ran with heart pounding, hour after hour, until he reached this little settlement and there gasped out the news that Governor Bent had been murdered, the peak blushed rosy in the sunset, brooded in early morning hours, or wrapped a shroud of mist around its bald head, as though nothing of consequence had transpired.

Near the base of this mountain, just south of the cañon of the Saint Charles River, the San Carlos of the Spanish, the Greenhorn wolf was whelped. Throughout her life she had roamed among the breaks and choppy cañons of the limy plains, or the craggy cañons that break down from the ridge of the mountains.

She had feasted at kills in Grenaros cañon, and in the lovely aspen-decked cañon of the South Apache, where eight waterfalls leap and foam. She had traveled far of late into the cedar and sage country of the plains, out over the areas where the old buffalo herds had roamed.

Something of the mountain had entered the heart of the Greenhorn wolf. Some of the mysticism of the Cuerno Verde was hers.

Years back she had been one of a pack, a killer gang. At first they had raided ranches without molestation. Then their levy on the stock industry began to be felt. It was 1915, and the price of cattle would not allow a rancher to sacrifice a dozen or so beef cattle to the wolves each year. Traps, poison and guns had shattered the Greenhorn pack. But a few of the oldest, wisest, fiercest of the group survived this first attack.

Man had been unrelenting. His campaign had kept on. As the wolves became wary, man invented new death tricks. Whelps had come and been blotted out almost as soon as they began to travel. One by one the old wolves were outwitted by settlers or were forced to eat carrion because they had become so old they could not kill for themselves. And eating carrion eventually leads to eating poison.

Now, in 1923, the Greenhorn Wolf ranged alone. SHE WAS DESTINED TO BE THE LAST NATIVE RENEGADE GRAY WOLF IN COLORADO!

In other sections, after the ranchers had cleaned out some of the worst of the packs, the Biological Survey had mopped up. Civilization could not stand the vicious killing, the murderous slaughter of other wild life, the raiding on the livestock that is the very life of the gray wolf.

The Greenhorn wolf had had narrow escapes. She had been shot at often. An old bullet wound in her body ached on cold days. She had tasted poison and knew its bitter flavors. She could not know that there was a new poison lurking in the campaigns of the Biological Survey that was practically tasteless and odorless.

Twice the Greenhorn wolf had been in traps of private trappers. Steel jaws had nipped off a toe from each front foot. Both front paws left three-toed tracks.

These old scars must have ached as she battled through the ruck and roar of the windstorm of the Huerfano. Bitterness and hate, longing and hunger filled her.

She climbed out of the windy turmoil. She skirted Walsenburg in the nighttime, and swung westward to the lower buttresses of the conical Spanish Peaks, the Wa-ha-to-yah of the Indians. Here in these mountains, named "Breasts of the World" by the red man, slept old legend, lurked old tragedy, hid the fanciful, lurid romances of many frontier days.

The Greenhorn wolf slithered along through the dusk, seeking to appease that giant hunger that gnawed at her empty stomach. A calf on the Spoerleder ranch fell before her attack. She feasted. Then she found shelter near a rocky ledge and slept.

Eighteen years it is estimated she had lived in this country. Years of bitter battle for existence they were. And now she was facing the end. Days of starvation loomed duskily before her. Her teeth were worn. She could not kill as she had of old, slitting throats, snapping tendons with one quick dive. She was what Government wolfers call a "gummer," her cruncher teeth worn down close to red sockets, her wolf fangs blunted and broken.

Alone, hated by man, feared by the other animals on the range, with fear of the inevitable pulsing with her own heart beats, the Greenhorn wolf traveled the trail toward the happy hunting grounds.

It was sundown for the gray wolf murderers in Colorado.

Restlessly she hurried along the trail.

II: THE DESPERATE KILL

Spring had passed. The calf crop had been counted. The deer fawns in the mountain country were now almost as fleet as the doe mothers. The band of antelope, ranging the big 90,000-acre Butler pasture south of Pueblo, had seen the coming of antelope babies.

The Greenhorn wolf had followed this antelope herd through many years. The fawns were tender and while fleet of foot, were foolish and inquisitive. To this source of meat she now turned.

Dusk marched out from the dark pine timber on the eastern slope of Greenhorn Mountain. The purple and mauve of sunset tints arose in regular bands from the great level line of the eastern horizon. A summer breeze, bringing the cool of the high country snow, rustled through the thick scrub oak and rattled last year's leaves where they were stacked against yucca needles.

The wolf trotted slowly, alertly, along a dusty trail. It was high time that she killed. Her aging muscles needed young meat to give them strength.

The first stars winked. The wind of the night began to carry sounds of the dark hours. The wolf stopped, sniffed the breeze.

She trotted down a dry wash, by scraggly old cedars centuries old. Food should be somewhere ahead. She must have it, even if she ate of carrion.

She stopped at an old scent post, sniffed. Coyote scent only was there. Often she had sniffed here, each time with the tiniest shred of hope that she would find another wolf had been that way. Each time disappointment had followed.

The Greenhorn wolf stopped, walked a few steps, then lifted her keen nose and tested the breeze. Faintly, just as elusive as the echoes of a distant waterfall in spruce-filled cañon, there came a sound ahead. The wolf stopped stone still. The wind was toward her.

Then came the scent that made her mouth water, her jaw begin to chatter with excitement, expectancy. For on the night breeze had come the scent of antelope.

Slowly she moved forward. From sage clump to scrub cedar, from rock to little clump of soap weed she moved, like a ghost of the dusk.

For a long time the wolf stood in the shadow of a bit of lime rock, listening, sniffing. She could not afford to make mistakes.

She was hungry, frightfully hungry.

She edged up over a little rise in ground. She came to a well-defined trail that led toward a low saddle. She followed it, her feet eased by the cushion of sandy earth.

For many moments she worked up toward the high points on the trail. Just before she topped the saddle she deserted the trail, sought the shelter of dark shadows under a clump of scrub cedar.

She peered into the dark light of the night. Her muscles tensed. Instinctively she crouched. Her legs trembled. Her mouth slavered.

The antelope herd was resting easily, chewing the cud, drowsing, in a bit of an open park bordered by sage and cedar.

The wolf started to skirt the opening. Wind was favorable to her. It helped to mask the slight rustling sound of the wolf's feet.

Whipped by hunger, harried by the excitement of the kill, yet restrained by caution, she held her vicious drive in check until she reached a point back of a screening clump of cedar.

Then from this point she started edging out. She crouched, her legs doubled under her, her belly rubbing along through the short grass. Every fiber was tense, every nerve taut. Still she did not launch that plunging dive which would end in a leap at the throat of a victim.

A buck pronghorn snorted. It was the signal for the wolf to leap. Like a flying gray wraith she threw herself through the night.

With lightning swiftness the antelope were up on their feet. Those which had been on their springy legs when the attack came were away through the night with a flash of their white tails.

The wolf sprang at one, missed, scrambled to regain her balance, almost bumped into a half-grown little female antelope. In mid-spring the Greenhorn wolf threw her body in the path of that youngster. Her teeth closed on its windpipe. There was no chance of hamstringing. She had tried that before. Her teeth would not clip even the tender tendons of the little, frail antelope yearlings.

Her ragged teeth sank in to the tender flesh and cartilage in the throat of the little doe. The antelope stumbled, fell, got up. The wolf held desperately to the throat of her victim.

Vainly the antelope backed, shook its head, sank down, got up, then tried to stumble forward. A few sucking breaths got by the vise grip of the worn teeth of the Greenhorn wolf. The antelope rallied slightly. The wolf snapped for a new grip, got it, held on.

The doe tried to run again, stumbled, then tried to back and shake loose the grip of the wolf.

A minute passed. Some shadowy hand touched the poor little bewildered doe antelope. Far away in the dark her mates stopped in their mad race, looked back, wondered what tragedy might be hidden in the night.

Slowly the tiny, graceful legs of the antelope sagged. She fell, struggled, lay still, kicked feebly.

New life flowed in the veins of the Greenhorn wolf. Old wolf savagery throbbed in her heart. For a moment there came back into her time-worn old frame all the vicious murder mania of the young wolf at the kill. She jerked, worried the animal, braced her legs, clamped her jaws shut.

With a powerful, wrenching, twisting pull the wolf ripped the skin of the dying doe. Blood spurted. She tugged and tore with her old tooth snags, threw her weight into mangling that tender antelope baby.

The antelope doe lay still. From a leaping, joyous spirit of the plains, this poor little wildling had passed into wolf meat.

For many moments the wolf ripped and tore, growling hatefully, snarling, satisfying the murder hunger that dwells in every gray wolf.

In the morning a coyote slunk away from a rack of bones where the wolf had made the kill, and magpies came to fight over the shreds of flesh that had been left by the sharp teeth of the hairy scavenger.

The Greenhorn wolf trotted the trail or basked in the sun for three days. Then hunger came again. A kill of a rabbit merely whetted the killer's appetite.

Night came.

Down an arroyo, by cedars, near rocks and soap weed, the old she-wolf hunted for meat. Again she caught a scent on the breeze. It was from beef cattle.

In the old days, when the pack was by her side, they would have plunged over the trail without regard for concealment. But now there were no helpers to hamstring the kill, to head it, to throw it. The Greenhorn wolf stalked cautiously.

A little band of whitefaces lay resting in a little park. Again the rush, again the scattering, stumbling hurry of the herd.

The big, powerful jaws of the wolf clamped tight on another windpipe.

But this time she caught the throat of a long yearling steer, a steer that had seen nearly sixteen months of range life.

Somewhere in the ancestry of that steer there were purebred sires; and there were wiry, fighting, hardy range mothers, daughters of Texas longhorns.

As the wolf's teeth clamped the steer struck. A hoof grazed the ribs of the wolf. She threw her weight away from those stamping horn weapons. The steer fought madly. The wolf hung on, swung at the throat of the cow brute.

Down they went over a bank. The dust clouded up as they rolled in the dirt. The steer fought up to his feet. The wolf tugged and wrenched vainly, trying to shut off that last strip of breath that was whistling through the pinched windpipe of the steer.

Brute against brute, fighting spirit against fighting spirit, death against death, their bodies swirled through the dusty shadows of the little arroyo. The steer bellowed throatily, voicing his mad anger.

He shook himself like a great dog shakes free from a terrier. But the wolf hung on. Attached to that lever of bone and tooth that had clamped over his windpipe were muscles of unreal strength. In olden days those jaws had clipped through the bone and tendon of a steer's tail in one quick snip, had slashed many a windpipe in a single bite. Now every fiber in the jaw muscles of the wolf strained to hold to that tube of cartilage through which sifted and whistled the life breath of the fighting steer.

Through the sage, stumbling over rocks, down again, up again, the two eddied and hurtled. Tighter, tighter those wolf muscles pinched. One cartilage broke, another gave way.

The steer fought, desperately. His hoofs found the wolf body, slashed and pounded the gray killer.

Sick, battered, the wolf gave way, loosened her hold.

With legs sprawled, with-red foam on his lips, the steer faced the wolf, challenging, daring her to come back to the combat.

A stark, menacing specter arose before the wolf. It was hunger, hunger of the wilds.

She rushed at the steer.

But the fighting ancestors of the grade whiteface had willed him courage. He met the wolf's rush with lowered head, struck with his feet, counter-rushed her. The wolf dove at his windpipe, ripped the skin, brought blood, but lost her grip. Her old teeth would not hold.

In that instant the wolf knew she had lost the fight. The steer sensed that he had won.

But the brutal killer instinct of the wolf would not permit her to give way. She rushed in, ripped, lacerated the whiteface. She was met by thrashing hoofs, mad rushes.

Perhaps after hours the wolf would be able to wear down this steer until she could strangle him and thus get the food her old body must have.

Circling, diving, rush and counter-rush endured for an hour. The steer was tiring. But so also was the old wolf.

With desperate courage she threw herself at the one place she might get a hold that would kill the steer. Her teeth clicked as she missed his lacerated throat.

The whiteface was ready for that rush. He drove with his front feet. They found their mark. The Greenhorn wolf rolled away, bruised, dazed. The steer plunged after her.

Bones hurting, muscles sore, tired nigh to death, the wolf turned and found refuge in an oak thicket. The steer had won his fight for life.

Death had slipped a step nearer as it stalked the lonely lobo of the Cuerno Verde.

III: FOLLOWERS OF THE FRONTIERS

When big Bill Caywood stepped off the train at the old flood-stained Pueblo depot, he was met by an aggressive short man with cheery face and a happy-go-lucky air about him, W. H. Sawhill, county agent of Pueblo County.

With brief introductions they loaded into Sawhill's auto and were soon spinning toward the headquarters of the Butler pasture.

"Can't tell whether there's more than one or not," replied Sawhill in answer to a question of Caywood's. "I rather doubt it. May be an old lone wolf. Whatever it is, does a lot of killing and a slather of mutilating when it can't kill. Queer. It doesn't seem able to slaughter its victim like a wolf would, by cutting their throats. Rather seems to strangle them by hanging to their windpipes."

"Old wolf," remarked Bill. "Gummer. Teeth worn down to where they'll not cut any more."

After an hour's travel they reached the neat frame ranch house of the Butler ranch. It was often painted, but like all domiciles of the big plains, it soon weathered. Inside it was neat, well kept, maintained with businesslike foresight.

They were met by foreman Goss.

"How often does this wolf make a kill?" asked Caywood.

"Sometimes they're a month apart," answered Goss. "Other times they come several times in a week."

"Know anything about the range?"

"Not for sure. There's a wolf reported as far south as the Picketwire, and there is some wolf killing up nearly to the Beulah valley to the west. I'm sure she ranges east of here."

"You think it's an old she-wolf?"

Goss nodded. "Fact is, we think it is the last wolf of the old Greenhorn pack. Trappers got most of them, but we had to exclude the local trappers from the pasture."

Caywood looked questioningly. "How's that?" he asked.

"Poachers," replied Goss.

"Poachers?"

"The trappers are not the worst at that. Some of those young, high-powered sports from Pueblo that think they're some real men are the real crooks!" exploded Sawhill disgustedly. "They come out in a high-powered car, get through a gate or even cut the fence, find a few of the antelope band that is still left in the Butler pasture, run them down with the power that's in their gasoline motor, and then tear out of here with a dead antelope hidden in the back of their car." The county agent scowled.

"Some of the local men aren't so darned good either," continued Goss. "If we left trappers in the pasture we'd not have much of an antelope herd left."

"You're givin' 'em protection, then," suggested Caywood.

"You bet they are," said Sawhill emphatically. "If everyone else would do as much for them as the men of the Butler pasture, they might stand a chance. I've got a hunch that they want this wolf killer corralled as much for protection of the pronghorns as for the domestic stock. How about it, Goss?"

"Guess you're right. Rather lose a couple of yearlings than see any more of those antelope slaughtered. They're just about holdin' their own. I'd like to see some increase. But with two-legged lobos and a real wolf on the range they haven't a big chance."

Out of this conversation there grew in Bill Caywood's heart a determination that the fleet, shy antelope, this remnant hanging on long after the hordes of their predecessors had been slaughtered, should have another chance, and perhaps through protection they would bring back a race of wildlings that had been almost obliterated in the bloody march of progress.

Caywood found, upon questioning local citizens, that this wolf would leave the section for days at a time. She would not come back at any definite interval. Also he did not find here the usual hearty coöperation. Those local trappers who had campaigned against the Greenhorn wolf, who had helped wipe out the pack, were just a little miffed at the thought of an outside hunter trapping for the old wolf.

On the trails Caywood looked for wolf sign. He found none. Light snow came and then melted in the clear winter sunshine. Coyote tracks laced everywhere and Caywood spread a network of traps and offered the yip-yap chorus a fatal treat in the form of poison baits.

Magpies made his poison less effective. To obliterate this nuisance he spread the loose magpie poison everywhere. Dead black and white bird scavengers littered the ground near his poison stations. Their death is a gain to the range.

Stockmen have no use for them, for they often will keep a brand sore on the back of a beef steer or young calf open for weeks, ripping out bits of the live tissue, preventing the sore from healing.

"Even if you don't get that wolf you've done some whalin' bunch of good," remarked Goss to Caywood after he had been there a fortnight. "Magpies and coyotes cleaned out of the pasture will help some."

"But I'll get that wolf," assured the bronze-faced hunter, his old blue eyes flashing. "Some of these hombres around here are prayin' under their breath that I don't land her. I'll show 'em!"

One thought had come to stay with Caywood. He was a lone hunter in a great open sweep of country. Colorado spread away for miles on every side. In that great territory was left but one wolf. Just one last renegade. Millions and millions of acres she had to roam in. The whole state was hers. Any trail in mountain and plain beckoned to her. One man, one wolf—the last of her kind in the whole state!

Caywood was selected to write finis to the history of the renegades of the rangeland; would close the book against the gray raiders. In the pages of that book were written acts of bloody slaughter. The wolf account of stock killed could be written in the form of thousands of dollars. On the other pages there were months and years of silent trailing by dogged hunters.

It was fitting that big Bill Caywood, the craftiest, the most learned of all wolfers in the Rockies, should ring down the curtain on this tragedy of the gray wolf killers. No other man of modern days has ever equalled his knowledge of the big gray—knowledge wrung from days on snowy trails, nights in wet, chill camps, hours under baking suns, and weeks of stark, frosty winter.

Caywood's sympathies were against the wolf without the slightest hesitation. For he knew wolves.

Big loneliness, such as lived constantly with the old Greenhorn wolf came to Caywood as he rode alone over these trails that were in the country where much history of the frontier had been made. But a few miles to the south was the line of the old Santa Fe Trail. The old pack-horse trail from Pueblo to Santa Fe passed through one corner of the Butler pasture, swung around the symmetrical form of the Badito cone, threaded up the valley of the Huerfano, and then climbed over Sangre de Cristo pass, where many pioneer feet had traveled. Northward was the route traveled by the intrepid Pike. Pike's Peak stood clearcut in its snowy splendor to the north. The pasture itself was filled with old buffalo trails, the faint remnants of wallows, and even the old bedding grounds were marked by the growth of ranker vegetation.

The West was passing. It was falling before the march of the new West of finest auto roads, hydroelectric plants, industry and commerce. Even here in the big pasture there dwelt side by side the fading wild life, represented by the antelope, and that lonely old wolf, and the new order which demanded grade whitefaces in the place of the buffalo and the old longhorns.

Bill Caywood, big, bronzed, a bit of the Old West himself, was just a little sorry, perhaps just a little glad, at the change. To this very section he had come when a boy, riding with his parents across the unfenced prairies in an old oxcart. He had seen the florid life of the gold camps near Querida, that lay over the first ridge of mountains. Then he had carved his homestead out of the wilderness of the White River section, paying for his equipment out of the bounty money collected for the wolf pelts he had brought to the stockmen.

Now, following a last trail of the plains frontier, warring against the predatory killers, Caywood trailed the last wolf in his state. It meant the end of the trail of the wolf packs, sundown for the big gray!

Caywood had come to the Butler pasture the first of December. Christmas was but a few days distant. This Christmas of 1923 was to be memorable for two things to Bill Caywood. Stanley Young had approved his plan of leaving the trap and poison campaign a few days, and Caywood was going to spend Christmas with his aged mother, who still lived at Canon City. The other memorable event awaited his return to active duty.

IV: UNDER THE LASH OF FAMINE

Christmas cheer had penetrated into the ranch homes along the eastern base of the Wet Mountains. Greenhorn Peak, the highest point in this range, had donned a new cap of whiteness, as though in gala attire. Kiddies were thinking of Santa, older children were wondering what the holiday of gifts might bring, elderly folks checked over their treasure of reminiscences, took pleasure from associating with the children, and purest joy from watching the tots.

But to the animals of the range Christmas would be but another day of winter.

The little antelope herd shivered in raw winds that gathered on the top of Greenhorn Peak and then swept over the plains. Range cattle sought the shelter of stack yards or huddled in little arroyos.

Death walked daily with the lesser range animals. The rabbits were as still as lumps of snow or ran in panic when enemy appeared. Mice made inadequate meals for the kit foxes that hunted nervously in the brushy breaks. Occasionally a prairie dog would stick his blunt, inquisitive nose out of his burrow and then dive back to safety from the hunger-driven coyotes.

Alone, but forging on, led by the spirit of thousands of wolf ancestors, the Greenhorn wolf trotted the winter-marked trails.

Cold, frosty snow crystals, caught by a wind from the heights, swirled around the wolf as she trotted along, heart heavy, footsore, hungry. She had looked for food in the region of the South Apache Cañon. There was a ranch near the mouth of that red-walled gash in the granite. She had sniffed around the outskirts of its pastures and corrals. A door had opened and a dog had barked. Silently, swiftly, she ran away.

The wind lifted its tone a notch. It sighed in gusty breaths through the pine needles. The dead limbs of the frost-wrapped oak rattled noisily. A far bellow of a range bull was soft and musical among the sibilant voices of the night.

The wolf came to the McKinley ranch, passed so close to the old weather-grayed barn that she could scent the warm odor of the cattle and horses housed there. Inside the kitchen of the low rambling white house there was a light. A man laughed in good humor.

For many moments the old wolf stood in the cold white snow, listening, sniffing, hesitant. Her old outdoor home suddenly seemed not friendly as of old, but hostile, filled with penetrating cold, brimming with the great loneliness.

Wolves are companionable. They visit around in neighborly fashion. Mates stay true to each other for years. The Greenhorn wolf once had been a part of such a wolf community. To-night, Christmas Eve, for some unaccountable reason, there was a bitter pain in her heart, and a longing for just one friendly, kindly companion.

For others there might be the companionship of their kind. The towhees that fluttered like gray darts through the brown, leafless oak always seemed to travel in pairs. The coyotes hunted in twos. The stock gathered in whole colonies in their corrals and pasture shelters.

None on the range would accept her companionship. She was hated, shunned, or fought. The murderer instincts of all gray wolves had turned all range life against wolves. Even the coyotes, the nearest of kin of the wild things, ran from her when she approached.

The last native renegade wolf in Colorado was ALONE!

Then the memories of old days, the yearnings for some shred of comfort and friendliness, the great vacant hurt in her heart was crowded out by a much more urgent, physical, vital thing.

Hunger had traveled with the wolf for the past three days. Such a fast was not uncommon these days. But now the demand for food laid hold on the wolf.

Through the night, by other ranch houses, heading northeastward, toward the Butler pasture the lone wolf traveled. Her keen nose sniffed for any chance scent. Her keen eyes probed through the darkness, looking for enemy or food. Her ears were attuned to every slight night noise. For even a squeaking mouse might appease that torturing hunger.

Gray morning broke. The wolf had not found food. She would have eaten carrion if there had been any along the trail. No wolf will touch meat killed by others except for two reasons. Either he is a young, inexperienced wolf, unfamiliar with the death machines and poisons of man, or he is an old gummer with teeth so worn that he cannot make his own kills. Then only will the wolf turn to eating dead meat.

But not even that slight and questionable food supply was found by the Greenhorn wolf. The sun arose redly from the plains where Kansas blends into Colorado. Some bird life awoke and fluttered in the brush clamps. The wolf looked at them longingly. One tiny bird, feathers and all, would have been a welcome morsel to the Greenhorn wolf on this bright Christmas Day.

Under the shelter of an overhanging lime cliff where a tiny open cave reflected the sunlight from all angles, the wolf found shelter for the day. Through long sunny hours she dozed and rested her range-weary muscles. The bright, friendly sun seemed to caress her old sinewy body, warm it through, bring just a little of the strength into those old muscles that the lack of food had sapped out.

Occasionally a biting flea aroused her and she scratched vigorously. But like other wolves, she was not host to such quantities of fleas as live on coyotes.

The sun grew chill. It climbed down, hiding itself in a blaze of redness back of Greenhorn Peak.

The wolf stirred, got stiffly to her feet, prepared for another night on the famine trail.

For several hours she traveled, hunger driving her to forage in every possible place where food might be located.

The she struck a faint trail with meat taint!

Several days old, this meat-scented trail demanded her attention. She sniffed at it, started away, then came back to the thin line of meat taint and followed it.

Down a draw it ran, by several clumps of oak, then over a low ridge. Normally the old wolf would have known that at the end of such a trail there might be a trap set by man. But now anything which promised any sort of food must be investigated. All her learning, all her lore of the trails no longer dictated. Hunger only guided her movements. Caution was not in her.

At the top of a little rise she stopped, sniffed, lifted her head, howled. It was a thin, weak, quavering howl, a half-hearted, final challenge against the forces of wilderness that were closing in on her.

The meat-scented trail ended abruptly. Wired under a scrubby oak there was an old horsehead. It had been dragged there by Caywood.

There was still some meat lingering on those cold bones. The Greenhorn wolf scented it. Her first impulse was to dive in, get such nourishment as might be found.

But long habit of wariness for the moment routed hunger.

Mincing, with slow steps, the gaunt old wolf started around the poison station. She hunted for concealed traps. She came to a bit of flank fat square. She nosed it, sniffed at it. It smelled delicious, enticing. Her mouth watered. But she knew those chunks of fat held poison. She had tried one years back and had just barely escaped the effect of the raw strychnine poison it contained by disgorging it.

The Greenhorn wolf knew better than to approach that lure set by the trapper. She knew that it was encircled by some sort of tricky death. Her instinct warned her to run from it, shun it.

Yet she stayed. She moved away from the fat squares, sniffed at the head. The faint odor of the meat that had been ripped from those cold bones made her mouth water, tortured that demon of hunger that gnawed her vitals.

There may be some more powerful emotions, more dominant feelings than hunger. Mating call may blot out thought of food for a time. And fear may set aside a ravenous appetite. The Greenhorn wolf was almost beyond a point where any other emotion, no matter how strong, might interfere with hunger.

She trotted away, her eyes round, her tongue lolling, her stomach crying out against its long emptiness. Down a draw, then over a saddle, she lagged, and finally——

Back she came to that old horse head, where the deceitful beef and pork squares were scattered.

Perhaps she thought that Man had relented in his war on the range renegades. Perhaps she did not care what might come. More likely there was inside of the wolf the driving fury of that last and supreme law which demands food at all costs.

The Greenhorn wolf threw caution to the winds. She had lost her sense of fear. Stark, compelling hunger lashed her.

She trotted in to the little fatal circle where the poison baits were spread. She touched one. Then there came that warning intuition which had so often kept her from harm on the range. She nosed it, mouthed it a little, then dropped it.

In a few strides she was over to that old horse head. She tried to rip a tiny sliver of old dried tissue from the bone which had been plucked of almost its last shred of meat by the magpies.

She turned from that. It was but an aggravation. She nosed over toward a clump of oak, caught the odor of some other meat stuff, stopped.

In loose mass before her there was a different sort of a material than the little fatal fat squares. It was a pile of ground fat, as potent in its way as the squares. It was magpie poison.

In all her experiences the Greenhorn wolf had not before met this queer sort of shredded fat. She sniffed at it. She walked away, came back, drawn there irresistibly by the odor of the meat.

Carrion it was. Carrion charged with death.

But the Greenhorn wolf was no more a killer unchallenged. She had lost her ability to hunt for herself.

Slowly, yieldingly, the Greenhorn approached that pile of magpie poison. Slowly at first, then wolfishly, she gulped at the soft beef suet.

It was not a full meal. But it filled a part of that aching void that had been her stomach for hours. A new feeling of comfort momentarily came to the wolf.

But it passed. In its place there leaped new fire that started ripping and tearing at her bowels like nothing she had ever known. The processed strychnine is delayed in its action. It starts to spread, is absorbed a bit before its bitter death potion takes effect. There is no chance to spew it out.

The wolf staggered along the trail, ran for the top of a little ridge, fell, got up, struggled on, fell again, quivered.

Through the dusk her great tawny eyes looked up to the outline of where Greenhorn Peak was edged in the faint glow to the westward. They swept in dimming arc over the wintry landscape that spread toward the Butler pasture eastward. She tried again to get to her feet, clawed uselessly in that effort, sank with her scarred old nose between the trap-bitten paws of her front feet.

It was Christmas in the man world, filled with good cheer, good will, friendliness.

But on the range it was just another day of winter.

With the soft whispering winds of the plains in her old ears, with the shadowy bulk of old Greenhorn Peak lifting above her, with the brilliant, steely points of the stars luminous in the black sky, with the old range of her ancestors spreading for miles in every direction without one vestige of her kind in that whole vast empire, Greenhorn, the last renegade wolf, was conquered by the giant that she had taken within her.

Lonesome no more, living with the spirits of Whitey, Lefty, Unaweep, Gray Terror, Big Foot, Phantom, Rags, and of Three-Toes, with the myriads of those that had gone before, the cruel, wilderness soul of the wolf left the stiffening body and galloped away into that farther land where there are no traps, no guns, no poison, no enemies.

The big peace, the long sleep, the trail to that hunting ground of the red gods, had come to the poor, broken, hunger-driven old wolf of the Greenhorns.

Caywood returned from his short holiday. With mixed thoughts he rode over the trail to his trap lines. He passed trap sets, then swung to poison stations, then back to trap sets again. Winter winds nipped at his leathery cheek, made his old blue eyes water. He thwacked the horse under him.

The horse stopping at the poison station near the old horse head brought him back to the immediate moment. He looked around, saw several dead magpies. Then he discovered the wolf track. Instantly he was alert.

Through brush, over a little ravine, then up a tiny slope he hurried. His eye caught the cold gray form of the Greenhorn wolf.

In another moment Bill Caywood was standing beside the last known native wolf of Colorado.

For many moments he stood looking down at that poor old lanky wolf body that held in it much of defiance, so much of mute tragedy. No man in the world could have sensed so well as Caywood what this meant. Of the West, a kindred spirit, through the necessity of range law arrayed against the wolf, he yet admired—yes, even loved their good qualities while killing them mercilessly for the bad that was in them.

Here lay a big symbol. The West of the old days was passing. A new day was coming. In it there would be no naked red men riding in warring parties toward white settlements. There would be no big herds of bison that spread for acres over the open prairies. The Pony Express was but a memory, a tradition. The old stage coach was now crowded out by high-powered gas wagons. The longhorn cow had given away to grade and purebred whitefaces. Even the old type of man that trod the open spaces was giving way to a business man of the new West.

And in all this the gray wolf had no place.

In a moment more Caywood had stooped and had started to skin out the stiff carcass, taking the pelt and skull for the record and collection of the Biological Survey.

Appendix

Burns Hole, Colo.
Mar. 2nd, 1921.

To the
U. S. Biological Survey
212 Custom House
Denver, Colo.
Gentlemen:

Just a word of appreciation and to thank you for the
good work of U. S. Govt. Hunter Bert Hegewa in eradicating the wolves out of this section of Colorado.

It is a big relief to us to know that "Old Lefty" is a
thing of the past—for his track on the range meant he
was back and on the job of cattle killing once again. We
breathe a sigh of keen satisfaction, and fully realize
the capture of "Old Lefty" was truly a job for you
Government men who study out these things and apply
methods no ordinary amateur can touch. You are doing
a great work for us stockmen,—let us know when we
can be of any assistance in furthering your operations
on predatory animal control.

Very respectfully,
The Stockmen of the Castle Peak Ranges

PICEANCE, COLO.
TO U. S. BIOLOGICAL SURVEY
DENVER
COLO.
DEAR SIRS:

I am certainly pleased to learn that Bill Caywood last week caught and killed the old wolf called "Rags." I have tried to kill that wolf for a good many years,—and feel I know a little about wolf habits as I have trapped and killed forty-four of them in my time here, but I could never catch this fellow.

Good work, keep it up, your hunters are saving us many thousands of dollars in your successful campaign to-day against the remaining renegade wolves. They have all been trapped at, shot at, and poisoned at so long that they can darn near speak English.

Yours truly,
(SGD) BOB COATS.

R. R. 2,
GRAND JUNCTION, COLO.
MAY 11, 1922

MR. STANLEY P. YOUNG
DENVER, COLO.
DEAR SIR:

Your letter thanking us for helping Bert, Hunter H. A. Roberts, is at hand.

I have heard that "self preservation is nature's first law," and we were merely obeying that law when we did our best to coöperate with Roberts. We have used the range where that particular family of wolves were working only two years. The first year, something "happened" to about half of the calves. Last year, we put three hundred cattle out there,—with just about an even hundred little calves. Results, a forty per cent loss among the calves, besides a number of yearlings killed.

Lest you cry "black-leg," I tell you we vaccinate everything with the best serum obtainable.

We certainly appreciate the work done, and hope for more help in the future should the necessity arise.

Sincerely yours,
(SGD) E. J. CURRIER, JR.

P. S. I presume that the fact of the she-wolf having a hind foot gone, and the he-one's teeth being badly worn, accounts for their taste for calves more particularly than older stuff.

THATCHER, COLORADO
JUNE 30, 1923.

STANLEY P. YOUNG
DENVER, COLO.
DEAR SIR:

Enclosed please find pictures of the old gray wolf trapped by Roy Spangler, one of your men.

Old Three-Toes, as this particular wolf was called, was caught on June 11th in one of the Government traps especially constructed for wolves. Spangler later caught two of her pups.

Thousands of dollars worth of calves and sheep have been killed by Old Three-Toes and her pack. With her capture, this ends the pack of which she was leader. Just a few days prior to her capture, Old Three-Toes killed six calves for us here on our ranch on the Apishapa, eleven miles west of Thatcher. We hold a private grudge against this old gray wolf as she mated with our pet collie dog, even going so far as to dig him out of a pen. He heard the "Call of the Wild" and answered it, going off for days at a time. Sometimes coming home for a few days. At last went away for weeks. He was finally poisoned by one of your men which was a good thing as a collie hearing the "Call of the Wild" kills for his young too.

We extend our thanks to Mr. Stanley P. Young and his hunters for staying on the job and getting Old Three-Toes and her pack. Not only in getting her and other wolves, but trapping all predatory animals.

Other stockmen join us in our praise to you and your men as the loss from predatory animals has been reduced to almost nothing.

Thanking you, we remain

> Very truly,
> MONROE BROS. AND HENERSON

AVONDALE, COLO.
FEB. 14, 1924

MR. STANLEY P. YOUNG
DENVER, COLO.
DEAR MR. YOUNG:

As I did not get to see you when you left my place, I am taking this means to thank you for the services of Mr. Caywood in this neighborhood for the last two months. It is a great satisfaction to know that we are rid of probably the last wolf in this part of the country. Thank you for the interest you have shown.

Mr. Caywood has been a gentleman in every way and made himself entirely agreeable, assisted with chores but did not neglect his work. Assuring you that I will be glad to assist and coöperate with you at any time in this neighborhood, I am

> Yours very respectfully,
> (SGD) J. W. GOSS
> MANAGER OF BUTLER PASTURE.

Wolf Reintroduction
Historical and Current Issues

The Past and Future of Wolves in Colorado

ANDREW GULLIFORD

In its wariness of people, the wolf epitomizes our predominant contemporary image of nature: nature as separate from human beings
and human beings as divorced from nature. Where we are, there are
no wolves; where the wolf lives, there is wilderness.

> —Daniel B. Botkin, *Our Natural History:*
> *The Lessons of Lewis and Clark*

We have doomed the wolf not for what it is, but for what we deliberately and mistakenly perceive it to be—the mythologized epitome
of a savage ruthless killer—which is, in reality, no more than a
reflected image of ourselves.

> —Farley Mowat, *Never Cry Wolf: The Amazing*
> *True Story of Life among Arctic Wolves*

WOLVES BELONG [bumper sticker]

> —NMWild.org and gcwolfrecovery.org

In Colorado we have twelve streams named Wolf Creek. In
Mineral County on the Continental Divide, Wolf Creek Pass
crosses the San Juan Mountains at 10,857 feet. Three miles above
the pass is Lobo Overlook, yet we have no wolves in our state.

Arthur H. Carhart's book *The Last Stand of the Pack* describes in grim detail the struggle to pursue and kill the last
Colorado wolves still ranging in the wild in the 1920s.

Across America the same predator mania continued. The
frontier had officially ended in 1890, and the last vestiges of

DOI: 10.5876/9781607326939.c002

wilderness had to be cleansed of their large predators, especially the feared gray timber wolves, which once numbered in the thousands in Colorado.[1]

"In the span of less than fifty years man had systematically, consciously, intentionally killed every wolf in the West . . . Hundreds of thousands of wolves were killed—some in the name of protecting livestock, some for their pelts, some because we believed it was our inalienable right, and some just out of cold, hard vengeance and cruelty, a cruelty we so often attribute to the wolf," writes Renee Askins.[2]

In Colorado, stock growers associations paid bounties on wolves. On the eastern plains the minutes of the Bent-Prowers County Cattle and Horse Growers' Association on April 7, 1900, stated, "Motion made and carried that this association shall pay a reward of $5.00 for grown gray wolves, and $2.50 for cub wolves under 3 months old, killed upon the range of any member of this association."[3]

When the first federal forest reserves in the state became national forests in 1905, one of the duties of forest rangers was to hunt and kill predators. Ranger daybooks and diaries kept by forest rangers on the Pagosa Springs District of the San Juan National Forest include a variety of entries. Into one of the ranger stations a rancher named Parcell "brought in wolf this evening measuring 6 ft. 9 in. from tip to lip," wrote a ranger on May 6, 1920. Later that month he wrote, "Rec'd phone call from Reed asking me to join in a wolf hunt with all the men of the neighborhood. Left Sta. at 8:00 and met at big mail-box and went to Robbin's where we spread out and looked for dens. Keane and Reed found two dens but old ones were absent. Traps were set at the entrance of the dens."[4]

In June the forest ranger continued to dig out dens but found them empty. A year earlier, in 1919, US Forest Service staff had begun to spread poison pellets.

Even in Yellowstone National Park wolves were trapped, shot, and hunted to their dens so that wolf pups could be dragged out and clubbed to death or perhaps secured to a rope or chain so they could whine and howl and draw their parents back to the den to be dispatched first. Then the cubs were killed. National Park Service (NPS) rangers killed the last wolf in Yellowstone in 1926. In Colorado it took longer because of our vast mountainous terrain and the many plateaus, buttes, prairies, and canyons where wolves roamed.

The *Denver Post* states that the Bureau of Biological Survey (BBS) claimed to have killed Colorado's last wolf in 1935. Scholar Michael J. Robinson believed the date was 1945 in Conejos County, southwest of Alamosa.[5] Either way, decades have passed since Colorado's mountains have heard the full-throated

At the White River Museum in Meeker, Colorado, in a glass case against the back wall, is the hide and head of a snarling wolf—his pelt dusty, his teeth yellow—his glass eyes stare out at us. He was the last wolf killed in Rio Blanco County. Close to the pelt is a historic sheep wagon, a sarsaparilla machine, and other pioneer artifacts. Photo © Andrew Gulliford.

howls of a wolf pack on a moonlit night, but that may be changing. Single wolves are returning to their former habitat and a breeding pair may meet in the next decade if wolves in Wyoming remain on the Endangered Species List.[6]

In the town of New Castle, on Colorado's Western Slope, the old fire station is now the local museum and historical society. Amidst the usual pioneer bric-a-brac of black and white photographs, coffee grinders, knives, axes, and faded silk and cotton dresses, lies one unique artifact tacked on a wall in an inner room. More than most historic artifacts it represents the pioneer response to settling the American West in the late nineteenth and early twentieth centuries. It's a poorly done mount of a white wolf, hair in blotches, skull open, hide torn, teeth bared. The pelt stares glassy-eyed at the ceiling.

The wolf has small ears. Perhaps they were clipped for a state-sanctioned wolf bounty. I think the paws may also have been cut off. The hide is brittle, representing a deficient job of tanning. The wolf seems fragile, as if the hide had been improperly stretched and then too quickly dried.

Among the toys, dolls, medical equipment, newspapers, and guns, two mountain lions are displayed along with a stuffed bobcat and a golden eagle. The other mounts are also part of Colorado history, but New Castle's white wolf has his own unique story. The color of his pelt means he was quite old and probably lonely when he was shot in the winter of 1914–1915. In that Congressional session the US Congress decided to fund the Bureau of Biological Survey, whose goal would be to hire professional hunters to trap predators and varmints to make the world safe for sheep and cattle and to increase big game herds of deer and elk across the West.

That winter, about five miles north of New Castle on East Elk Creek, the John Wendell family worked to improve their homestead with two feet of snow on the ground and livestock requiring grass hay. With a hired hand, Wendell would load his sled and drive his horses to his pasture one-quarter mile from his house, slowly spreading the hay. His white fox terrier came along and began to play with an aging timber wolf that slipped out of the forest and down to the pasture.

Each time Wendell had a rifle the wolf failed to appear. Finally, one day the rancher shot and stunned the wolf and finished him off with a blow to the head from a wooden fence post. The Wendell Ranch became locally famous, and neighbors, hunters, and trappers all arrived to see the elusive gray timber wolf, so old its hair was white. The forlorn pelt of that lonely wolf now resides in the New Castle museum.

North of New Castle in Meeker, the White River Museum of the Rio Blanco County Historical Society has its own wolf pelt. This wolf is up against a wall, secure in an ornate oak and glass display case in the far back room of the museum. He's probably one of the best preserved of all of Colorado's historic wolves. The wolf's amber eyes stare straight ahead and its bared teeth almost emit a growl, but he's safe enough in the storage area among bear traps, a two-headed calf, a sarsaparilla bottling machine, and an ornate sheep wagon. George Wilber and Les Burns killed him on Oak Ridge. He was the last wolf to die on the White River Plateau in Rio Blanco County.

The wolf was shot in 1919, perhaps the same season when Arthur Carhart, the Forest Service's first landscape architect, surveyed Trappers Lake east of Meeker for summer cabins. Instead of recommending that private parties lease an acre each for cabins, Carhart urged his superiors to leave the pristine lakeshore alone. Thus, Trappers Lake became the "cradle for wilderness." Carhart was the first federal employee to advise that a landscape be left untouched and that vast expanses of federal lands should be protected from development.

In this photo by Ola Garrison, from the Garrison Photography Studio at Rifle, Colorado, a rancher and his wife pose with a dead wolf at their homestead, possibly near the Book Cliffs. Courtesy of Photo Collections, History Colorado, No. 20004085.

How ironic that in 1919, the same year Carhart had his vision about federal wilderness as an ideal, hunters killed the last wolf in Rio Blanco County. It took decades before Americans came to understand that wilderness without wildlife was just empty scenery.

→←

Across Colorado in the early twentieth century, wolf killing continued, as expertly detailed by Carhart in his thoughtful book *The Last Stand of the Pack*. He wrote it ten years after he'd been at Trappers Lake. Ranchers wanted wolves banished, and they sought the help of a new federal bureau.

By the 1900s, at the head of Parachute Creek, wolves chased yearling calves, chewing and damaging the legs of those they caught. Ivo Lindauer, from a long-standing Parachute ranch family, claims, "until the first of July, local ranchers would have as many as 25 yearlings in for doctoring with carbolic acid and tar until they healed up. Ranchers used every method they could think of in an attempt to eliminate the wolves," and that included contacting the Bureau of Biological Survey.[7]

Eventually the Survey sent them Bill Caywood, who lived along Piceance Creek in Rio Blanco County with Laura, his wife, and six children. A farmer, rancher, and independent trapper who followed trap lines in winter looking for thick fur, he joined the BBS the year Congress founded it in 1915. A few years earlier, during 1912 and 1913, "Big Bill" claimed to have killed 140 wolves, and local stockmen surrendered the $50 per head bounty. As a government trapper, he was now on salary and could take his time to fulfill the Survey's goals of killing every last Colorado wolf.

Funded by Congress a century ago, the Bureau of Biological Survey sought to trap, poison, and kill predators and "varmints." The result was an ecological holocaust of strychnine-ridden carcasses and indiscriminate destruction up the food chain. We tried to kill wolves and coyotes. Instead, we brought death to eagles.[8]

The initial goal was to eliminate predators to reduce losses by stockmen who raised sheep and cattle. A later goal was to increase game populations of deer and elk by destroying wolves as predators. In 1915 *ecology* and *environment* were not household words. Interrelationships among wildlife and habitat were not understood. Annual reports of the BBS and books like Michael J. Robinson's *Predatory Bureaucracy: The Extermination of Wolves and the Transformation of the West* (2005) reveal the massive onslaught of poisons and steel traps that permeated the West.[9]

Even a skilled naturalist and big game hunter like Theodore Roosevelt referred to wolves as "beasts of waste and desolation."[10] No one grasped the value of predator/prey relationships in maintaining healthy ecosystems. The West's remaining wolves became so famous they received nicknames.

Old Lobo and Blanca ranged in northern New Mexico. "Lobo's habit of permitting the pack to eat only that which they themselves had killed, was in numerous cases their salvation," wrote Ernest Thompson Seton. Everyone wanted Lobo's scalp: "The dread of this great wolf spread yearly among the ranchmen, and each year a larger price was set on his head, until at last it reached $1,000, an unparalleled wolf-bounty, surely; many a good man has been hunted down for less."[11]

Lobo could back up on his own path, "putting each paw exactly in its old track until he was off the dangerous ground," and then he would scratch rocks and dirt clods to spring hidden traps. Trappers caught Lobo's mate and tore her to pieces between two horses. "When he came to the spot where we had killed her, his heart-broken wailing was piteous to hear. It was sadder than I could possibly have believed," wrote Thompson Seton.[12] Yet the killing continued.

How odd that across Colorado and the West, hunters ruthlessly pursued wolves yet valued their power and presence enough to have them mounted, stuffed, and then photographed in the same mountain landscapes from which they had been extirpated. Ecologist Aldo Leopold wrote, "Man always kills the things he loves, and so we the pioneers have killed our wilderness." Courtesy of Photo Collections, History Colorado, No. 20030675.

In southeast Utah, trapper Roy Musselman from Moab caught Big Foot near Grand Gulch with a nine-pound steel leg trap and earned a $1,000 reward. He also killed Beef Basin Lobo.[13] To catch a wolf you have to live like one, and Musselman survived off the land, eating nuts and berries, taking short naps, and drinking from sandstone potholes.

Wolf hunters learned to think like wolves, wear moccasins instead of boots, bury #14 traps, and handle gear with gloves reeking of fresh manure to hide the man scent. They learned to leave no disturbed soil and to sift dust and earth on top of trap sets. Among Hispanic sheepherders, legends spoke of wolves that were not wolves at all but evil spirits of the desert—*diablos* or devils incarnate—who could not be caught, could not be killed, and whose howls in pinyon-juniper underbrush came from the dead. These were phantom wolves, spirit wolves, *a lobo de las animas*, ghost lobos.

Government trappers dismissed such folklore, but having spent days on horseback and months on the trails of these last gray wolves, perhaps the men wondered about those stories as they silently nodded in the saddle coming back to camp in a dark, windy rain or an early wet snow.

At cow camps the trappers ate biscuits, steaks, and fried potatoes cooked on a sheet metal stove. They devoured canned peaches and swallowed gallons of strong coffee, black as a thief's heart, laced with condensed milk. Wolf trappers left before dawn with a yellow slicker tied behind the saddle for rain and snow and a cold can of beans for lunch. All those details are here. Carhart described the cow camps and work routines of the government men. He believed in their mission—initially.

Carhart writes that trappers not hired by the Survey who sought state-based or grazing association rewards resented federal trappers. Both groups relentlessly pursued *Canis lupus*. One enterprising cowboy named Edgar Williams located an old female wolf that denned up every spring under Lavender Point in the Gypsum and Dry Creek Basin. Once she had pups, he'd dig out the cubs and sell them for $25 apiece, but he never bothered the female. He was outraged when a trapper killed her, and the cowboy lost an annual source of income.[14]

Wolf hunters, or wolfers, government trappers for the Biological Survey, became legendary on Colorado's Western Slope. "Wolf" Morgan trapped in the Disappointment Valley around 1915. Like other wolfers, he was a loner "not too well acquainted with a bathtub, he rarely changed his clothes. Dirty, bearded, and unkempt, he lived mostly to kill wolves," wrote rancher Howard E. Greager.[15]

"Beneath his admirable exterior he had the cruelest nature I have ever known," wrote David Lavender about trapper Slim Hawley. "His business was killing." Hawley placed steel traps in animal carcasses and waited for predators like coyotes, wolves, and bears to return.[16]

"I believe the grass which average coyotes save by putting a check on foraging rodents and insects far outweighs the value of the stock they harm," wrote Lavender, who ran his father's ranch in the Disappointment Valley.[17] Few stockmen had his insight. Instead, we poured poison onto public land. The BBS managed a special poison laboratory in Denver, experimenting with strychnine, arsenic, and cyanide.

In the 1918 Report of the Chief of the Bureau of Biological Survey, E. W. Nelson described the work of from "250 to 350 hunters under the direction of district supervisors" and how "predatory animals are destroyed by trapping, shooting, den hunting during the breeding season, and poisoning." He wrote that a "large area in southern Colorado was systematically poisoned with excellent effect."

Nelson proudly wrote that "predatory animals taken by hunters under the direction of this bureau" included "849 wolves, 20,241 coyotes, 85 mountain lions, 3,432 bobcats, 30 lynxes, and 41 bears."[18] That was only three years into the Survey's work. Wholesale slaughter across the West had just begun, and states, including Colorado, contributed thousands of dollars to augment the BBS's federal funding.

By 1931 the annual report claimed public lands had become "breeding reservoirs for predators and rodents," which "re-infested stocked and cultivated areas." That year, $35,752 was allocated for research on control methods and $404,062 was spent on poison, primarily strychnine laced in cubes of animal fat and placed in carcasses.[19] A horse carcass could be seeded with fifty or more poison pellets. Such random poisoning killed predators but also everything else, including eagles and other raptors.

Burt Hegewa trapped Old Lefty and captured Bigfoot. Bill Caywood killed Rags the Digger and Old Whitey. Roy Spangler found the female Three Toes. W. J. Nearing also killed wolves in Colorado. Wolves represented raw, untamed nature, and in the early twentieth century, during the Progressive Era, we practiced the gospel of efficiency—of order, rationality, punctuality, and production. The randomness of nature—the way wolves could make a fresh kill every night—required retribution and torture, including slipping a haywire muzzle over a wolf's jaws so it could starve to death. This was "range justice."

With raw words, sparing no blood, Arthur Carhart describes the last wolves killed in Colorado. This is nature writing at its best without anthropomorphizing. Carhart makes clear the economic losses suffered by ranchers and their visceral animosity toward wolves. Always on the run, harassing livestock because of the depletion in game, the last wolves had names like Old Lefty from Eagle County, the Phantom Wolf near Fruita, the Greenhorn Wolf south of Pueblo, the Unaweep Wolf from Unaweep Canyon, Bigfoot at De Beque, Old Whitey near Trinidad, and Rags the Digger at Cathedral Bluffs in Rio Blanco County.

Wolves harassed livestock because wild game populations had dramatically dropped. Most of Colorado's elk had been shot and killed by market hunters who were paid ten cents a pound for elk, deer, and antelope. Today's elk herds evolved from elk transplanted from Montana and Wyoming.[20]

❧❦

One of the major ideas in western history is the concept of the frontier, or the edge of civilization bumping up against wild lands as Americans moved across the Mississippi River and then west across the Great Plains. Historian Frederick Jackson Turner wrote about that. He claimed that, when the US superintendent of the census stated in 1890 that a line of frontier could no longer be discerned because there were on average five people per square mile across the United States, the frontier had ended. Turner argued that the first great era of American history had concluded with the passing of the frontier.

As the frontier came to a close by 1890 and homesteaders sought free land up every creek and drainage, they brought livestock that lured coyotes and wolves. No one questioned the value of "settling up the country." Killing a wolf became an act of heroism and notoriety for the hunter.

The location where these last wolves were killed also speaks to wildness and what were once wilderness settings—Burns Hole on the Colorado River in Eagle County; Greenhorn, or *Cuerno Verde*, near Huerfano Butte, where the Rockies meet the prairie in Pueblo County; up Piceance Creek and Cathedral Bluffs, now eviscerated by oil shale and shale gas roads, pumps, and compressor stations. A last wolf was trapped near Thatcher, out on the plains and "down on the Picketwire," which is the local pronunciation of the Purgatoire River in Bent and Las Animas Counties. The Unaweep Wolf was killed on the Uncompahgre Plateau and another died near the Ruby Canyon cow camp for the Flying W Ranch, up Big Salt Wash north of Fruita.

In Carhart's words, this was the last stand of the pack because "the West of the Old Days was passing."[21] These final Colorado wolves represented, in their living and by their dying, the real end of the frontier, not just the symbolic end in 1890 based on settlement patterns. Carhart gave standard western history an ecological twist. For him, the frontier ended not with Americans sprawled across the continent but with the death of wolves. Up to the early 1920s, these old wolves, male and female, had eluded capture. Carhart believed that with their passing the frontier truly ended, and the industrialized West of Ford Model A pickups, barbed wire, and repeating rifles triumphed. Or did it?

Dominance over the landscape by stockmen, with no wolves to trim herds, meant overgrazing, grass depletion, and arroyo cutting, which have left deep scars across the state and accelerated the replacement of native grasses with invasive species like cheatgrass that has no nutritional value. In many areas the end of the wolves coincided with the last of the vast stretches of grama grass, bluestem, and Indian ricegrass.

The last wolves that Carhart eloquently describes were not only the end of an era in Colorado history; their deaths also signified the end of a wild landscape that had attracted settlers in the first place. Some of the wolfers themselves had reservations about their brutal actions. "Then followed the inevitable tragedy [the loss of all wolves], the idea of which I shrank from afterward more than at the time," wrote Ernest Thompson Seton.[22]

"I've just got a lot of love and respect for the gray wolf. He's a real fellow, the big gray is. Lots of brains. I feel sorry for him. It's his way of livin.' He don't know better," opined wolfer Big Bill Caywood. "And I feel sorry every time I see one of those big fellows thrashin' around in a trap bellowin' bloody murder . . . Guess I'm too much a part of this outdoors to hold any grudge against animals," Caywood explained.[23] Yet most wolfers simply poisoned, shot, and trapped themselves out of business without any self-reflection. Deer hunters and forest rangers also shot wolves on sight without regret, with one notable exception: Aldo Leopold, whose life and career bridged nineteenth-century conservation and twentieth-century ecology.

→ ←

As a young forester in Arizona before statehood in 1912, Leopold shot a wolf without hesitation. Later in life he came to keenly regret that action, as his thinking evolved both as an ecologist and as an early proponent of wildlife or game management.

Wolves and grizzly bears were exterminated throughout the nineteenth and into the early twentieth centuries because of their impacts on domestic sheep and cattle that grazed public lands and because the top-tiered predators killed game animals like deer and elk. Leopold began his career as an ardent opponent of predators. In 1920 he argued, "It is going to take patience and money to catch the last wolf or lion in New Mexico. But the last one must be caught before the job can be called fully successful."[24]

"He had been a leader in a campaign by sportsmen and stockmen to eradicate wolves," writes Susan Flader, but his thinking evolved based on observing nature and the damage to Western watersheds. He came to see wolves differently. In Flader's words, "The wolf, as one of the large carnivores, belonged at the very apex of the biotic pyramid . . . it became Leopold's symbol of the pyramid itself, of land health."[25] It took until the 1930s when, as a far-seeing ecologist and public lands manager, Leopold began to understand that perhaps we should leave landscapes and habitat alone. Perhaps there were other more intrinsic values to the public domain besides grazing, mining, and lumbering.

In a famous ecological essay Leopold wrote about wolves, published posthumously in *A Sand County Almanac*, Leopold philosophized about our need to "think like a mountain" and not just consider animal life and habitat from a human-centered perspective. Having worked in the backcountry of Arizona and New Mexico in the 1920s, Leopold wrote about having shot a wolf and how he later came to question that decision. What he did was entirely commensurate with federal policy at the time. Later he would help to change that policy and become the father of wildlife management. He writes,

> A deep chesty bawl echoes from rimrock to rimrock, rolls down the mountain, and fades into the far blackness of the night. It is an outburst of wild defiant sorrow, and of contempt for all the adversities of the world. Every living thing (and perhaps many a dead one as well) pays heed to that call. To the deer it is a reminder of the way of all flesh, to the pine a forecast of midnight scuffles and blood upon the snow, to the coyote a promise of gleanings to come, to the cowman a threat of red ink at the bank, to the hunter a challenge of fang against bullet. Yet behind these obvious and immediate hopes and fears there lies a deeper meaning, known only to the mountain itself. Only the mountain has lived long enough to listen objectively to the howl of a wolf.

He explains about wolves and men and describes the death of the wolf he shot. He writes,

> We reached the old wolf in time to watch a fierce green fire dying in her eyes. I realized then, and have known ever since, that there was something new to me in those eyes—something known only to her and to the mountain. I was young then, and full of trigger-itch; I thought that because fewer wolves meant more deer, that no wolves would be a hunter's paradise. But after seeing the green fire die, I sensed that neither the wolf nor the mountain agreed with such a view.[26]

Though Leopold had a change of heart, it would be decades before federal policy evolved regarding killing predators, or varmints.

Leopold had come to understand "conservation as a state of land health," and he presented the image of land as a biotic pyramid—"a fountain of energy flowing through a circuit of soils, plants, and animals" in which predators had their place.[27]

The original conservation movement focused on utilizing landscapes for the greatest good for the greatest number for the longest time, to paraphrase Chief US Forester Gifford Pinchot. Everything revolved around the American utility of public land. The idea of ecological balance, that nature needed predators to keep game populations in check, had yet to evolve. The concept of food webs and food chains was not understood, so "bad" animals were routinely hunted and killed, with American wolves slaughtered almost to the point of extinction.

One intellectual who questioned that premise was Leopold. In the 1930s he had traveled to Germany to see a tame, utterly antiseptic forest managed for timber production only. In northern Mexico in the Sierra Madres, where Leopold explained, "It was here that I first clearly realized that land is an organism, that all my life I had seen only sick land, whereas here was a biota still in perfect aboriginal health."[28] Everything seemed to be in ecological balance with abundant deer and no coyotes. He wondered if wolves had kept them out.

But the American West's war on predators continued long after the initial publication of *The Last Stand of the Pack*. The M44 gun/trap, a "coyote getter," went off when a predator bit the bait. The gun propelled cyanide powder directly into a coyote's mouth. Government trappers also used Compound 1080, an odorless, tasteless poison toxic to mammals and outlawed in 1972 by an executive order signed by President Richard M. Nixon, the year before Congress passed the Endangered Species Act.

How ironic that the same government agency that sponsored decades of predator control—the Bureau of Biological Survey—evolved into the US Fish and Wildlife Service, mandated by Congress to protect endangered species, including some of the species that the Survey had spent years killing. Colorado Parks and Wildlife (CPW) even brought back lynx, which had previously been poisoned and trapped.

Beginning in 1915, across the West we waged war against predators. Now, a century later, we know more about ecological balance and land health. Hopefully, the decades of poison pellets are past.

Arthur Carhart met Aldo Leopold in Denver at the regional office of the Forest Service. Carhart voiced his opinion that Trappers Lake in northwest Colorado should be left pristine and void of tourist cabins. Leopold liked that idea and established the Gila Wilderness in the Gila National Forest of New Mexico in 1924. Thus began the evolution of American wilderness, "where man is a visitor who does not remain," as an idea, an ideal, and finally a law in 1964. Our thinking on wolves also changed.

Carhart left the Forest Service to pursue a career as a private conservationist and writer. Leopold left the Forest Service to become a professor of wildlife management at the University of Wisconsin. Both were avid hunters and out-

Taxidermist Edwin Carter, also termed a *naturist*, poses here in Breckenridge with a pelt from a large wolf taken in the Colorado Rockies. Courtesy of Photo Collections, History Colorado, No. 20031518.

doorsmen. Both men came to see wolves in a new way and to question "the bloody march of progress."

Leopold died in 1948 fighting a brush fire near his Wisconsin farm, but his son would write a famous report for the NPS recommending that in each unit of the park system all plants and animals should be restored to the full ecological complement that existed on park lands at the time of European contact, or approximately the year 1500. That meant wolves should be returned to their habitats in large western parks in the continental United States.

The younger Leopold's report was promptly shelved, but the idea gained currency. In 1973, with passage of the Endangered Species Act, Americans, through their representatives in the US Congress, requested the recovery of threatened or endangered animal and plant species. This revolutionary idea included the concept of reintroducing into the wild animals that had previously been extirpated—like wolves. Finally, in Yellowstone National Park, after sixty years without the howl of a wolf pack, wolves were brought back in 1994 and 1995.[29]

Conservation biology has not been the same since. Theories on the power of top-tier predators to order and stabilize entire landscapes have now been proven. To understand the potential for wolves in Colorado, it is vital to learn lessons from two decades of wolf recovery in Yellowstone National Park.

I teach my college students that wolves have brought beavers and songbirds back to Yellowstone. They are not sure what I'm saying. I explain the deep-seated changes that wolves have had on the Greater Yellowstone Ecosystem, beginning with cutting the coyote population in half, which has meant more young pronghorn living to maturity. With fewer coyotes, there are more small rodents and mammals aerating the soil and providing better grasses. But the largest and most dramatic effect has been the culling of the Yellowstone elk herd, which had grown too large even in Teddy Roosevelt's time. By 1995, the large ungulates had severely damaged the park. Wolves changed all that.

Elk had grown lazy and lived in the riparian zones and river corridors along the park eating fresh willow sprouts and young aspen trees that could not rejuvenate. As wolf packs began to hunt elk calves and old and infirm elk, the wapiti were frequently slowed and caught in downed timber along rivers and streams. There, wolves could move quickly and hamstring elk, wounding and then killing them. So the elk came to learn their safety was higher up on the sagebrush benches of the park, where they could see and smell better and have increased opportunities to outrun wolves.

With this return to a natural pattern, with fewer elk found in riparian zones, plants recovered. Willows sprouted. Aspen thrived.[30] And in this new thicker forest of riverine vegetation, beaver colonies established small pools of water, attracting other animals, insects, and, yes, butterflies. Wolves have brought new species of insects, including butterflies, back to Yellowstone. Leopold had speculated on the importance of wolves as an apex predator in a mountainous biotic pyramid. His ecological thinking has now been proven.

After twenty years of work by conservationists and environmentalists, dodging lawsuits from ranchers and the American Farm Bureau, the US Fish and Wildlife Service introduced fourteen wolves into Yellowstone National Park. Appropriately, scientists named the first naturally occurring pack the Leopold Pack. With wolves as a top-tier predator, an entire ecosystem has been rebalanced, the card deck shuffled, but not without howls—both from the wolf packs and also from ranchers, outfitters, and hunters bemoaning the decrease in elk and occasional forays by wolves into livestock.

"Wolves, when you get down to it, are a lot like us. They are powerful, aggressive, territorial, and predatory. They are smart, curious, cooperative, loyal and adaptable. They exert a profound influence on the ecosystems they inhabit," explains wildlife biologist Douglas Chadwick in "Wolf Wars, Once Protected, Now Hunted," published in *National Geographic*.[31] The thousands of wolf watchers at Yellowstone National Park add $35 million to the area's economy. So who's afraid of the big, bad wolf?

Hunters, who see fewer elk. Ranchers worried about their cattle and sheepmen forced to adopt new herding techniques and be more vigilant as sheep bed down for the night. The US Fish and Wildlife Service in 1995–1996 released wolves captured in Canada into 2.2 million acres of Yellowstone and Idaho wilderness areas. By 2008, 569 cattle and sheep had been confirmed dead by wolf attacks and 264 wolves were killed for attacking livestock in Wyoming, Idaho, and Montana.[32] For local ranchers, despite environmental or hunting regulations, the slogan is "Shoot, shovel, and shut-up."[33] Yet in Wyoming, wolf kills represent only 1 percent of sheep deaths, compared to 25 percent taken by coyotes.[34]

Wolves have their detractors as well as their champions, and a burgeoning new industry in Yellowstone—taking watchable wildlife to new heights—is wolf tourism, primarily in the Lamar Valley. "Not cuddly, anthropomorphic Disney nature, this, but nature red in tooth and claw. *Real* nature. To those who understand it, it is beautiful beyond description," writes David Petersen in his essay "Yellowstone Death Watch."[35]

Though tourists have always been thrilled sighting griz and vast herds of elk, Petersen explains, "With the return of the wolves, the spectator sport of predator-watching extends year-round. In winter—when the weakest ungulates are starving and deep snow slows their escape and even adult moose and bison can be vulnerable to snowshoe-pawed canids—sightings of wolves giving chase and making kills are frequent and poignant."[36]

Echoing Leopold, legendary bow-hunting elk hunter Petersen argues, "Life feeds on life: It's hard, but it works. And it's absolutely essential. Without predation, life on earth would spiral rapidly into oblivion. Where big predators exist in viable numbers atop a sturdy food pyramid, wild nature remains most nearly in balance."[37] Chadwick explains that in Yellowstone, "From a single new predatory force on the landscape, a rebalancing effect ripples all the way to microbes in the soil. Biologists define the series of top-down changes as a trophic cascade."[38]

So how would wolves change Colorado ecosystems? We have yet to find out, but just as wolves have reshaped Yellowstone's ecology, Colorado's Rocky Mountain National Park is sorely in need of wolves to cut its excessive elk numbers, which is why I tell my students that whenever the first wolf shows up in Estes Park, I'll buy it an ice cream cone.

We need more wolves in Colorado, and certainly in Rocky Mountain National Park, but they "clearly wouldn't stay in RMNP."[39] If they worked in RMNP, we know *Canis lupus* would be effective in culling elk, improving vegetation, and creating watchable wildlife with sharp teeth. But no one will introduce them there—it's too close to the Front Range cities of Fort Collins, Greeley, Boulder, Loveland, and Denver and all the asphalt and sprawling suburbs in between. Instead, wolves at RMNP will just have to wander down from Wyoming on their own. Which they will do. They're coming. Double chocolate dip or plain vanilla?

In 2006 Defenders of Wildlife wrote checks totaling $154,000 for probable kills of livestock by wolves.[40] A year later, in *Outside Magazine*, Douglas Gantenbein wrote, "Fire Away—Hunting Wolves Will Soon Be Legal—Exactly What the Species Needs." He explained, "Wolves were extirpated in the Rockies only with an aggressive combination of poisoning, pup clubbing, and bounties—none of which would be tolerated today. More important, state game officials know the feds might step back in if they push things too far."[41]

At the end of 2008, hunting seasons had been reopened for wolves and the Northern Rockies held more than 1,645 wolves living across a dispersed terrain in 217 packs, with more than 1,500 wolves outside national park boundaries. A federal court ruling put wolves back on the endangered list for a few years, but since 2011, wolf hunting has continued in two western states. Yellowstone

Bureau of Biological Survey hunter Bill Smith poses with a chained wolf pup at the entrance to a wolf den. The pup was chained to attract its parents so they could be killed. Courtesy Western History Collection, Denver Public Library, No. Z-1565.

National Park includes thousands of acres in Wyoming and Montana, and as the wolves thrive, additional packs form because at age three, wolves seek a mate and new territory. They are coming south. Will they make it to Colorado's national forests and national parks?

First they have to cross the Red Desert of Wyoming and Rio Blanco and Moffat Counties in Colorado, where most sheep and cattle ranchers carry .30-06 hunting rifles on gun racks in their pickup trucks. They'll have to halt cars as they cross Interstate 70. They must learn to dodge hunters and hikers and guardian dogs surrounding sheep. Will wolves make it? A USFS wildlife biologist told me, wolves are coming, but "there's all those guns between us and the

Wyoming wolf packs."[42] The problem is not just with illegal hunters; it has also been with the Department of Justice.

—>€—

In Montana, after biologists had reintroduced wolves into the Yellowstone ecosystem in 1995, Chad McKittrick, out bear hunting but with his truck stuck on a road, saw a large animal on the horizon 140 yards away. He said to his companion, "That's a wolf. I'm going to shoot it," and he focused the scope on his Ruger M77, a 7mm magnum rifle.

McKittrick dropped the wolf and then saw the radio collar clearly marked "Yellowstone National Park." He cut the head off the animal, hacked at the hide, but left the paws. His accomplice, Dusty Steinmasel, kept the radio collar after using a special wrench to remove it and later threw it in a creek, where the collar continued to send a fast series of beeps to wolf biologists signaling that the wolf was dead. Investigators soon found the collar, and Steinmasel provided a written confession and enough evidence for a search warrant.

McKittrick claimed he shot at a feral dog. If so, why keep the head and hide? "Even in Montana they rarely mount dogs as game trophies," wryly commented author Renee Askins, who chronicles this event in her book *Shadow Mountain*.[43]

On October 10, 1996, a jury of eight men and four women convicted McKittrick of three misdemeanor counts—killing an endangered species, possessing it, and transporting it. His sentence included three months in jail, three months in a halfway house, and $10,000 in restitution. At trial he testified that he thought the animal he killed was a rabid dog and, based on a "mistaken identity" argument, appealed to the US Supreme Court. McKittrick lost, but then he won, because the Department of Justice back-paddled, as if in a rowboat approaching a waterfall.

The DOJ named its new legal position the McKittrick Policy, giving lasting fame to someone who pulled a trigger on a Yellowstone wolf. The policy basically states that US attorneys will only prosecute for the illegal killing of Endangered Species Act–protected species when they can prove that the killer specifically intended to kill an endangered species. Thus, wolves are shot by hunters who "thought" the animals were coyotes—even though coyotes rarely wear radio collars.

WildEarth Guardians and the New Mexico Wilderness Alliance sued the US Department of Justice in federal court, stating, "Since the Mexican gray wolf reintroduction program began in 1998, the Fish & Wildlife Service (FWS) has catalogued 48 wolves that have been the victims of illegal killings." The policy "has the practical effect of removing the threat of criminal prosecution for would-be wolf killers who are opposed to the reintroduction of the Mexican gray wolf."[44]

Impacts of the McKittrick Policy reverberated across the country. "Suspects in the killing of some of the nation's most imperiled animals are escaping prosecution under the federal Endangered Species Act because of a Justice Department policy that some federal wildlife officials call a significant loophole in the law," stated Deborah Schoch in the *Los Angeles Times*. She explained, "When the [McKittrick] case reached the US Supreme Court, Justice Department lawyers reexamined the issue. They decided that the jury instructions prosecutors had argued for were wrong . . . They decided a person could not be convicted of 'knowingly' killing an endangered animal unless prosecutors could prove that the person actually knew what kind of animal he or she had shot."[45]

Former Oregon US Attorney Kris Olson laments, "The issue was the standard of intent. I am ashamed to say that it was my colleagues in the Clinton Administration who created the mess that followed—the new McKittrick Policy of requiring the prosecution to prove that the defendant knew it was an animal on the ESA list. Finally, in June 2017 the WildEarth Guardians won in court and the McKittrick policy is now invalid, but the federal government has appealed.[46]

What does that contentious policy mean for Colorado? It means wolves have a long way to go to arrive in a Colorado national forest or national park. But there's hope. Wolves are wily and fast. They travel in packs. They travel in pairs. They travel alone.

In Colorado—in the Flattops, Mount Zirkel, Maroon Bells, the Raggeds, the Weminuche, or South San Juan Wildernesses—we only need a breeding pair. Just two young wolves with amorous intent. Unlike in Yellowstone, they will probably not be introduced by the US Fish and Wildlife Service. There'll be no free ride down from Canada in an aluminum cage. Instead, they'll have to walk and lope and run. Wolves are coming back to Colorado. They'll get here. In fact, they are moving across the West.[47]

In 2011 the Montana Fish and Wildlife Commission authorized a limit of 220 wolves to be killed in a fall hunt because, according to Chairman Rob Ream, "We are making the best, science-based decision that we can . . . Wolves are here to stay."[48] With recommendations from top biologists, the Secretary of the Interior removed gray wolves in the Northern Rockies from the endangered species list. Environmentalists howled, and a temporary court order made Oregon a wolf-safe zone.

Idaho issued state licenses to kill wolves. Over 18,000 were sold, including the first license requested by the Idaho governor, but hunters only got a handful of wolves in their rifle sights. The killing was minimal.[49] Just as wolf tourism has impacted Yellowstone National Park, wolf hunting may also bring radical changes and wolf-friendly support groups. One of the great ironies of conservation and wolf recovery is that all the groups work to maintain animal species and habitats—the Rocky Mountain Elk Foundation, the National Wild Turkey Federation, Ducks Unlimited—just to shoot them. The same may happen with wolves.[50] Meanwhile, individual wolves keep moving.

After a seventy-year absence, biologists tracked a collared female wolf known as 914F that appeared in November 2014 on the North Rim of the Grand Canyon on the Kaibab Plateau, having come 450 miles into Arizona. She was later shot near Beaver, Utah. The US Fish and Wildlife Service did not charge the coyote hunter with a crime.[51] A wolf named OR-7 has bounced between Oregon and Northern California, and in August 2015 a confirmed wolf pack with cubs appeared in Northern California near Mount Shasta. Other Idaho wolves have established homes in northeastern Oregon.

In Colorado, in June 2004, a wolf died along Interstate 70 after being hit by a car. Five years later, a GPS-collared wolf traveled 3,000 miles in seven months before being killed by banned Compound 1080 poison in Rio Blanco County. The female died 400 miles from her home pack. In April 2015 a coyote hunter killed a gray wolf near Kremmling and later claimed he did not know it was a wolf. [52] Gray wolves are listed as endangered under state and federal law. Those are the confirmed deaths.

As for sightings across Colorado—and especially the Western Slope—wolf stories abound. In small rural cafes there's no better way to draw a crowd then to talk about having seen a wolf and where.

"It was 1 a.m. at Ironton Park, just beyond Ouray. We were headed south and stopped in the road where the wolf was standing. Our son-in-law and daughter were in front of us in their vehicle with their dog inside. The wolf actually sniffed at the door and window. Their dog was barking madly. The wolf's back was the height of a car door handle," relates Terri Brokering from Silverton.[53]

In the 4th Street Diner & Bakery in Saguache, two transplanted Canadians who know wolves swear to seeing a pair of gray wolves in Antora Meadows, near Findley Gulch west of town. In the Weminuche Wilderness, backpackers west of Bear Town saw an animal larger than a coyote bring down an elk calf. And one of my students, a Wyoming elk hunter, swore he saw wolves playing near a wilderness boundary north of Lemon Reservoir in the San Juan National Forest. I asked him if he had collected any hair or scat. No, he was elk hunting, but he knew wolves, and he was adamant about what he had seen.

"I saw a jet black wolf in the middle of the day on Red Mountain Pass between Mineral Creek and an old mine. No doubt what it was. It was big and black. We could not have gotten a more clear look," states Durango hunter and outfitter Mike Murphy. "It came down from above the road, crossed in front of us, and kept going down the other slope. It was big. There's no mistaking a jet black wolf like that. Ears, tail, head. It was a wolf," he recalls.[54]

High Lonesome Ranch north of Grand Junction thought it had a gray wolf—traveling in the wildlife corridor defined in the Wildlands Network Spine of the Continent conservation initiative—but, alas, it was just scat from that ol' trickster, the coyote. Wolves could be at home in the area, perfectly poised near Douglas Pass and deeply isolated in Garfield and Mesa Counties. The headline in *High Country News* read: "Prodigal Dogs—Have gray wolves found a home in Colorado?" Not yet, but rancher Paul Vahldiek stated, "If they help the land be healthier, I'm for that."[55]

Wolves are coming back to Colorado. Probably to the Western Slope. Then what? Colorado Parks and Wildlife already has a plan. It's over a decade old, but "Findings and Recommendations for Managing Wolves that Migrate into Colorado" by the Colorado Wolf Management Working Group offers interesting scenarios.

→←

The working group begins with the premise that "there would be positive and negative impacts from wolf presence in Colorado" and that management strategies would include adaptive or flexible management, monitoring of wolves to understand wolf populations, and damage payments for any livestock killed. Key ideas in the report include "[m]igrating wolves should be allowed to live with no boundaries where they find habitat" and "[w]olf distribution in Colorado will ultimately be defined by the interplay between ecological needs and social tolerance."[56] Any negative impacts would be addressed on a case-by-case basis.

"Opportunities should be available to livestock producers to implement non-lethal management tools and other proactive measures to reduce the potential for wolf-livestock conflict," states the report.[57] The negative impacts would be on livestock. Wolves would decrease elk numbers but ultimately strengthen elk, their favorite food, by weeding out the sick and decreasing disease transmission.

I like the potential monitoring methods, including aerial tracking, snow tracking, scent marking, radio collaring, remote photography, genetic profiling, and howling surveys. I'd love to participate in a howling survey because the clear, crisp sound of a wolf howl connotes wildness and wilderness better than any auditory clue I know. To have wolves back in Colorado and listen to packs howl would provide an unforgettable sensory experience. The report mentions positive economic impacts that could come from gray wolf tourism.

Meanwhile, the Mexican wolf, which could eventually find a home in southern Colorado, is not recovering well in Arizona and New Mexico. It keeps getting shot and killed, and genetic variability and viability continue to diminish.[58]

The report argues persuasively that "wolves in Colorado should be managed flexibly with an impact-based 'live and let live' approach. Wolves that cause no problems will be left alone."[59] The animals cover extensive ground. In Greater Yellowstone, wolf territories average 344 square miles but have ranged from 33 to 934 square miles.

What can we look forward to? Pelt colors of grizzled gray and black. Pack size averages of around nine wolves, which would include a dominant breeding pair, offspring from the previous year, new pups, and perhaps an uncle or two to keep the pups in line. Because wolves act like a keystone species, they could dramatically alter Colorado ecosystems, resulting in an increase in aspen and willow trees, healthier streamside riparian areas, more vigilance on behalf of elk, and lower coyote populations.

Once here, CPW staff "will implement programs to make sure that wolves are included as a part of its wildlife heritage," but *Canis lupus* will certainly be an eco–wild card because "one of the most fundamental challenges of wolves returning to Colorado is the uncertainty of the outcome, as a large carnivore that has been missing for decades resumes its functional role in the ecosystem."[60]

No one knows how wolves will fit into the Colorado landscape, but many of us are waiting to find out. A survey conducted by Colorado State University found that 73 percent of Coloradans, most living on the Front Range, support wolves in Colorado, and 20 percent do not.[61] Obviously, that 20 percent includes ranchers who have a different perspective, but that's all the more reason to begin a dialogue on wolves. "Many urban residents want to have a sustainable wolf population in Colorado; while many livestock producers and some rural communities do not want any wolves in the state," the working group wrote.[62]

The report makes clear that ranchers will be compensated for any loss of livestock either from a Colorado fund or the Defenders of Wildlife Bailey Wildlife Foundation Wolf Compensation Trust, which has paid $400,000 in compensation in the Northern Rockies and invested over $200,000 in wolf mitigation and prevention techniques.[63] But what about Colorado hunting guides and outfitters?

"Wolves. We've progressed passed them. We have too much industry and agriculture to ever go back to wolves," states Dan Schwartz, owner of Ripple Creek Lodge, east of Meeker near Trappers Lake. "But they're coming. Wolves are here. You hear about them all the time. I don't think they'll decimate the elk population, but they'll change elk habitat. It'll be a completely different hunt. If they move down [from Yellowstone] the ecosystem will allow it, but to introduce them is insanity. We need to get ahead of the game on wolf management before the feds get involved."[64]

The working group correctly states, "Wolf management will probably remain complicated, expensive, political and controversial."[65] To its credit, the Colorado Wolf Management Working Group listed educational goals and public outreach as a key component of any on-the-ground wolf recovery.[66]

So if wolves are coming back to Colorado, why not help them out? Why not reintroduce them? Three times Colorado Parks and Wildlife has passed resolutions opposing the reintroduction of wolves to the state—in 1982, 1989, and early in 2016.[67] Perhaps it's time to revisit that important decision. If wolves arrive on their own, we'll have to live with where they appear. If wolves are introduced, there can be more flexibility on where they live and certainly more planning.

Wolf reintroduction would first require a positive vote from the CPW. A second affirmative vote must come from the Colorado State Legislature because the legislature voted itself authority over the introduction of any threatened or endangered species. Legislators have approved reintroducing black-footed ferrets and a few endangered fish. Prior to the legislation, CPW brought back lynx.

Colorado Parks and Wildlife reintroduced the forty-five pound Canada lynx into the Weminuche Wilderness of both the Rio Grande and San Juan National Forests despite fears from ranchers and hunting outfitters. After a rocky start because of a "hard release," in which the furry cats were not acclimated to the area, the lynx seem to be settling in, though there have been a few years with no litters of kittens at all. A slow start to wolf recovery in Colorado could be managed in a similar fashion. What are the reasons not to? They are both practical and philosophical.

Renee Askins knows. She helped with wolf recovery into Yellowstone National Park. "Without Renee Askins these wolves wouldn't be here today," comments former Secretary of the Interior Bruce Babbitt. In her book *Shadow Mountain*, she writes,

> *For many people in the West a value system is at stake, the way they view themselves, their relationship to wildlife and the land is being challenged because national attitudes toward wilderness and wild animals have been shifting. When I began working on wolf recovery I believed it was wolves we were arguing about; I thought conservationists could win the debates if we just assimilated enough solid biological information, filed enough successful lawsuits, or marshaled enough political support. I no longer believe that. These confrontations did not center on biological facts or abstract laws. These were moral questions, and moral questions are resolved on a cultural level, within the context of personal emotion: love, passion, and anger. Our value systems are called into question by issues like wolf reintroduction, and we're asked to examine what we believe and feel on a profound and intimate level.*[68]

She's right. Wolf reintroduction into Colorado, just like wolves being welcomed into Yellowstone National Park, will take time and patience. Folks who would never normally speak to each other—because they wear different hats, different footwear, drive different vehicles, support different causes—will have to sit at the same table and share their values, their thoughts, their hopes for their families, as well as their future.

With 5.5 million people, Colorado is essentially an urban state, with suburban sprawl on the Front Range and less than a quarter-million people on the Western Slope, where wolves would be introduced. Askins knows the pitfalls and the opportunities. She believes correctly, "We also need to listen—listen to the stories, come to understand the rhythm and reason of these lives we think of as antithetical to our own."

She adds, "We need to come to understand their arguments and their fears, and be able to articulate these fears and threats as well as or better than they can. Help them hear their own voices. It is a very powerful thing for people who view you as an outsider to hear you name their concerns."[69]

A howling wolf has a front paw caught in a leg trap. Currently, the legal status of these traps varies across the west, but they can be used by federal trappers working for the US Department of Agriculture's Wildlife Services Department. Courtesy Western History Collections, Denver Public Library, No. Z-1574.

A twenty-five-year veteran of the Colorado Division of Wildlife (now Colorado Parks and Wildlife), Gary Skiba succinctly states that wolf reintroduction is not yet feasible. He feels, "In our current environment, it's not going to happen. There are extremes on both sides. Wolves have this mythical status as a symbol of wilderness, but they're just an animal." He explains, "Currently we have an incomplete ecosystem without wolves, but many people are satisfied with that. There are people who view them as the devil and there are others who view them as the heart of an ecosystem."[70]

CPW should revisit the idea of introducing wolves to Colorado. They're coming anyway. Why not restore our full complement of wildlife sooner rather than later? We'll probably never have grizzly bears back in Colorado. They take too much territory and live at the same elevations that we do, but wolves . . . I think we could adjust. I think we could learn to accommodate ourselves to another top-tier predator beside ourselves. But I admit, as a Colorado wildlife biologist told me, "More hearts have to be won."

Lewis and Clark wrote about wolves two hundred years ago as the explorers journeyed up the Missouri River. As the Corps of Discovery entered the heart of the West and began to traverse the Great Plains along the Missouri River, they repeatedly saw wolves among the vast bison herds blanketing the prairies. Objective in their writing and journal entries, the captains reported what they saw without emotion.

Among great quantities of buffalo on September 15, 1804, Capt. William Clark saw "their companions the wolves." Excellent observers, Lewis and Clark came to realize what modern science knows. They wrote, "Wolves follow their [prey's] movements and feed upon those which die by accident or which are too poor to keep pace with the herd." Wolves were the "usual attendants" of the big game that flourished across the American West before livestock and barbed wire fences. The two explained, "Whatever is left out at night falls to the share of the wolves who are the constant and numerous attendants of the buffalo."[71]

On April 29, 1805, the expedition found itself "surrounded with deer, elk, buffalo, antelopes and their companions the wolves, which have become more numerous and make great ravages among them."[72] Lewis and Clark intuitively knew the value of wolves among large game herds, and though the men of the expedition routinely shot grizzly bears, they rarely shot wolves—unlike the next several generations of westerners who persecuted American wolves almost to extinction.

Forest ranger, game management specialist, and prescient ecologist Aldo Leopold did shoot a wolf. He lived to regret it. In his pivotal essay in *A Sand County Almanac* Leopold wrote,

> *I now suspect that just as a deer herd lives in mortal fear of its wolves, so does a mountain live in mortal fear of its deer. And perhaps with better cause, for while a buck pulled down by wolves can be replaced in two or three years, a range pulled down by too many deer may fail of replacement in as many decades. So also with cows. The cowman who cleans his range of wolves does not realize that he is taking over the wolf's job of trimming the herd to fit the range. He has not learned to think like a mountain. Hence we have dustbowls, and rivers washing the future into the sea.*

Leopold wrote in the 1930s during the Dust Bowl that swept the plains states and decimated southeastern Colorado. He knew we had erred with our dryland farming techniques, and he sought a metaphor for ecological balance and land health. He found it in the throat of a wolf. He concludes his powerful essay with these haunting words:

We all strive for safety, prosperity, comfort, long life, and dullness. A measure of success in this is well enough, and perhaps is a requisite to objective thinking, but too much safety seems to yield only danger in the long run. Perhaps this is behind Thoreau's dictum: In wildness is the salvation of the world. Perhaps this is the hidden meaning in the howl of the wolf, long known among mountains, but seldom perceived among men.

→ ←

Wolves are part of our western heritage. Learning to live with them again in the Rocky Mountains may be one of our most important twenty-first-century lessons in ecology and humility. We killed wolves with poisons, traps, and guns. Arthur Carhart came to realize the pervasive power of industrialized death.

A year after publishing *The Last Stand of the Pack*, Carhart questioned co-author Stanley P. Young whether exterminating wolves "to please squawking stockmen" could be justified. "Isn't it a just consideration that the cats and wolves and coyotes have a damn sight better basic right to live in the hills and have use of that part of the world as their own than the domestic livestock of the stockmen?" he asserted.[73] Carhart, father of the wilderness idea, wanted wild creatures in wild places.

Decades later, Carhart wrote "Poisons—The Creeping Killer" for the November 1959 issue of *Sports Afield*. The Bureau of Biological Survey had become the Bureau of Sport Fisheries and Wildlife and was still disseminating poisons. At the beginning of the environmental movement, conservationist Carhart raised the alarm about poisons just as Rachel Carson would become famous for doing the same with pesticides in her 1962 book *Silent Spring*.[74]

In *The Last Stand of the Pack*, Carhart wrote in great detail about experienced trappers in the 1920s using a variety of methods to trap and poison Colorado's last wolves. Compound 1080 and M-44 sodium cyanide bombs are still utilized by the USDA Wildlife Services, death-dealing descendant of the BBS, which continues to use leg traps.

In 1996 voters approved Colorado Revised Statute (CRS) 33-6-203, also known as Amendment 14, prohibiting poisons, snares, or leghold traps, though special traps may be used for "bona fide scientific research." How ironic to think that such research, performed under the federal Animal Welfare Act, might include a better understanding of wolf habits and patterns if wolves must be trapped in order to be radio collared or relocated.

James Shaw poses with a dead wolf killed near Thatcher in Las Animas County. This was one of the last wolves killed on Colorado's eastern plains. Courtesy Western History Collection, Denver Public Library, No. Z-1580.

What would Carhart think of wolves returning to Colorado? As a wilderness advocate—a "wilderness prophet" in the words of Tom Wolf—Carhart surely would have seen the connection between wild landscapes and *Canis lupus*.[75] As a hunter and a sportsman interested in healthy big game populations, he probably could have come to learn what Lewis and Clark understood and what Aldo Leopold tried to teach: that wolves have their place.

Until wolves are delisted from the Endangered Species Act, the US Fish and Wildlife Service has management authority. Once wolves become delisted, then Colorado Parks and Wildlife will utilize the Wolf Management Working Group guidelines. Because wolves are also state listed as a special species, there is no legal shooting or "take" of them. The wolves that we get will probably arrive on their own from Wyoming or Utah.

I tell my college students that wolves are coming home to Colorado—hopefully in my lifetime, certainly in theirs. We need them back. We need to hear their howls on moonlit nights deep in the Weminuche Wilderness or high on the Flattops. Gray shadows should leave paw prints in snow beneath dark trees. Maybe wolves will even return to their old haunts where Carhart wrote about them in Unaweep Canyon, on the Book Cliffs, along Huerfano Creek, beside the Purgatoire.

Wolf recovery in Colorado will be a grand experiment. I wish Arthur Carhart were alive to write about it. He'd love to record the cycle of ecological change and humans foregoing hubris for humility. *The Last Stand of the Pack* is a valuable historical account of Colorado conservation at the beginning of the twentieth century. Now in the twenty-first century, we should turn a new page and allow a top-tier predator to bring balance back to our ecosystems.

—⟫⟪—

NOTES

1. Gary Wockner, Gregory McNamee, and SueEllen Campbell, eds., *Comeback Wolves: Western Writers Welcome the Wolf Home* (Boulder, CO: Johnson Books, 2005), estimate 30,000 wolves on p. xii. A better approximation of wolf numbers in Colorado, based on research by Michael J. Robinson, would be 5,000–10,000 wolves. For a powerful treatise on wolves, see the classic by Barry Holstun Lopez, *Of Wolves and Men* (New York: Charles Scribner's Sons, 1978).

2. Renee Askins, *Shadow Mountain: A Memoir of Wolves, a Woman, and the Wild* (New York: Anchor, 2002), 29. For a general history, see Bruce Hampton, *The Great American Wolf* (New York: Henry Holt, 1997). For a fictional account of a cruel wolf hunter, or wolfer, on the northern plains, read about Brose Turley in Ivan Doig's *The Whistling Season* (New York: Harcourt Brace, 2006).

3. Cited in Kim Long, *Wolves: A Wildlife Handbook* (Boulder, CO: Johnson Books, 1996), 155.

4. San Juan National Forest Pagosa Ranger District, Rangers' Logbooks, 1921–1925, Collection M 080, Series 1.4, Center of Southwest Studies, Fort Lewis College, Durango, CO. By 1920 the US Forest Service encouraged killing wolves, but it had become the official duty of the Bureau of Biological Survey.

5. Tom Wolf, "World Champion Wolfer," *Inside/Outside Southwest*, March 2009, 20, and Susan J. Tweit, "Wolf," in *Comeback Wolves: Western Writers Welcome the Wolf Home*, ed. Gary Wockner, Gregory McNamee, and SueEllen Campbell (Boulder, CO: Johnson Books, 2005), 14. Robinson is not quoted in Tweit's essay, but Tweit confirms "the last known wild gray wolf in this part of Colorado was killed in the Conejos Valley in 1945." Glen A. Hinshaw, in *Crusaders for Wildlife: A History of Wildlife Stewardship in Southwestern Colorado* (Ouray, CO: Western Reflections, 2000), 22, states that the last wolf was killed in the South San Juans in the Navajo drainage south of Pagosa Springs in 1938.

6. Michael J. Robinson assisted with corrections and clarifications to this essay. He thinks that leaving wolves on the endangered species list in Wyoming is "a dicey proposition."

7. Ivo E. Lindauer, *Up the Creek: Parachute Creek's Pioneer Families and Energy Development 1875–2015* (Parachute, CO: Double F., 2016), 135–36. For another pioneer account

in which western wolves killed horses, see "Sacrifices Horses to Ravenous Wolves," about Utah cattleman Victor Corn, *Grand Junction Daily Sentinel*, December 27, 1912.

8. Michael J. Robinson also argues that in these early decades of the twentieth century, "Eagles were also intentionally targeted."

9. Michael J. Robinson, *Predatory Bureaucracy: The Extermination of Wolves and the Transformation of the West* (Boulder: University Press of Colorado, 2005).

10. Jeremy Johnston, "Preserving the Beasts of Waste and Desolation: Theodore Roosevelt and Predator Control in Yellowstone," *Yellowstone Science* 10, no. 2 (Spring 2002): 14–21. For wolves' impact on deer, see Richard Nelson, *Heart and Blood: Living with Deer in America* (New York: Alfred A. Knopf, 1997).

11. Ernest Thompson Seton, *Lobo, Rag and Vixen: Being the Personal Histories of Lobo, Redruff, Raggylug and Vixen* (New York: Charles Scribner's Sons, 1908).

12. Ibid., 17.

13. Robert S. McPherson, *Life in a Corner: Cultural Episodes in Southeastern Utah, 1880–1950* (Norman: University of Oklahoma Press, 2015). See the chapter "Preying Predators: Wolf and Coyote Control in Southeastern Utah, 1900–1950," 141–65.

14. Howard E. Greager, *In the Company of Cowboys* (privately printed, 1990), 135.

15. Ibid., 137.

16. David Lavender, *One Man's West* (Lincoln: University of Nebraska Press, 1977), 250.

17. Ibid., 251.

18. E. W. Nelson, "Report of the Chief of the Bureau of Biological Survey" (Washington, DC: USDA, August 29, 1918).

19. Paul G. Redington, "Report of the Chief of the Bureau of Biological Survey" (Washington, DC: USDA, August 31, 1931).

20. The Colorado Division of Wildlife reintroduced elk into the state from Wyoming elk in 1916. In that year Pueblo businessmen and the Pueblo Elks Lodge bought fifty elk from the surplus at the National Elk Refuge in Jackson. Those transplants have thrived, and the current population is about 260,000. Colorado's first hunting licenses were issued in 1903, but because of the scarcity of elk, no elk hunting was allowed until 1929.

21. Arthur H. Carhart and Stanley P. Young, *The Last Stand of the Pack* (New York: J. H. Sears, 1929), 288.

22. Thompson Seton, *Lobo, Rag and Vixen*.

23. Wolf, "World Champion Wolfer."

24. Susan L. Flader, *Thinking Like a Mountain: Aldo Leopold and the Evolution of an Ecological Attitude toward Deer, Wolves and Forests* (Madison: University of Wisconsin Press, 1974), 93.

25. Ibid., 2. At one point, Leopold was asked to take over as chief of the BBS. He declined. See ibid., 27.

26. Aldo Leopold, "Thinking Like a Mountain," in *A Sand County Almanac: With Essays on Conservation from Round River* (New York: Ballantine, 1970), 137–41.

27. Flader, *Thinking Like a Mountain*, 30. To further understand Leopold's thinking, see Marybeth Lorbiecki, *Aldo Leopold: A Fierce Green Fire* (Guilford, CT: Falcon, 2005); David E. Brown, ed., *The Wolf in the Southwest: The Making of an Endangered Species* (Tucson: University of Arizona Press, 1984); and David E. Brown and Neil B. Carmony, eds., *Aldo Leopold's Wilderness: Selected Early Writings by the Author of "A Sand County Almanac"* (Harrisburg, PA: Stackpole Books, 1990).

28. Flader, *Thinking Like a Mountain*, 153. What Leopold thought about wolves is also in Curt Meine, *Aldo Leopold: His Life and Work* (Madison: University of Wisconsin Press, 1988).

29. Though the reintroduction of wolves and wolf packs occurred in 1995, two wolves managed to make it into the park and were documented three years earlier, in 1992.

30. See Robert L. Beschta, "Cottonwoods, Elk and Wolves in the Lamar Valley of Yellowstone National Park," *Ecological Applications* 13, no. 5 (2003): 1295–1309. For dramatic film footage of his conclusions, see *Lords of Nature: Life in a Land of Great Predators*, directed by Karen Meyer and Ralf Meyer (La Grande, OR: Green Fire Productions, 2009).

31. Douglas H. Chadwick, "Wolf Wars: Once Protected, Now Hunted," *National Geographic*, March 2010, 38. Also see Jon R. Luoma, "New Federation and the Wolf," *Audubon*, March 1983; Sherry Devlin, "Wolf Provokes Inadvertent Howlers," *High Country News*, September 19, 1994; Rocky Barker, "Imported Wolves Lope Off into Idaho Wilderness," *High Country News*, January 23, 1995; Michael Milstein, "The Wolves Are Back, Big Time," *High Country News*, February 6, 1995; and Scott McMillion, "In Surprising Ways, Wolves Will Restore Natural Balance," *High Country News*, February 6, 1995.

32. Chadwick, "Wolf Wars," 38. Also see Tim Findley, "The Wolves of Gooseberry Creek: Tall Tales, Tangled Webs, Folks and Feds," *Range Magazine*, Summer 2004; Daniel Glick, "Still Howling Wolf: Will Westerners Finally Learn How to Live with *Canis lupus*?," *High Country News*, November 10, 2008; and Hal Herring, "Wolf Whiplash," *High Country News*, May 30, 2011.

33. Since 2011, in Idaho and Montana, wolf hunters no longer need to shovel or shut up. They can legally pursue their elusive quarry.

34. Chadwick, "Wolf Wars," 42. For book-length accounts of returning wolves to Yellowstone, see Hank Fischer, *Wolf Wars: The Remarkable Inside Story of the Restoration of Wolves to Yellowstone* (Helena, MT: Falcon, 1995); Thomas McNamee, *The Return of the Wolf to Yellowstone* (New York: Henry Holt, 1997); and, by wildlife biologists Michael K. Phillips and Douglas W. Smith, *The Wolves of Yellowstone* (Stillwater, MN: Voyageur Press, 1996).

35. David Petersen, *The Nearby Faraway: A Personal Journey through the Heart of the West* (Boulder, CO: Johnson Books, 1997), 161.

36. Petersen, *Nearby Faraway*, 162. To understand wolves and ravens and the possibility that ravens "evolved with wolves in a mutualism that is millions of years old," see the chapter "Ravens and Wolves in Yellowstone," in Bernd Heinrich, *Mind of the Raven: Investigations and Adventures with Wolf-Birds* (New York: HarperCollins, 1999), 226–35.

37. Petersen, *Nearby Faraway*, 162.

38. Chadwick, "Wolf Wars," 54. For a more recent look at Yellowstone's wolves and their impacts, see Warren Cornwall, "Have Returning Wolves Really Saved Yellowstone?," *High Country News*, December 8, 2014.

39. In Yellowstone, wolves of each pack average an elk kill every 1.5 days. For too many elk and not enough wolves at Rocky Mountain National Park, see Karl Hess Jr., *Rocky Times in Rocky Mountain National Park: An Unnatural History* (Boulder: University Press of Colorado, 1993) and Scott Kirkwood, "Too Much of a Good Thing? Elk Overpopulation in Rocky Mountain National Park Is Taking a Toll on the Ecosystem, and the Results Can't Be Ignored Any Longer," *National Parks*, Fall 2006. Eric Odell, Colorado Department of Natural Resources, in an e-mail to the author, stated, "Wolves in RMNP clearly wouldn't stay in RMNP."

40. "Depredation Payouts from Wolves Hit Record," sidebar by the Associated Press in Jesse Harlan Alderman, "Idaho Governor Wants Wolf Hunting," *Durango Herald*, January 19, 2007.

41. Douglas Gantenbein, "Fire Away: Hunting Wolves Will Soon Be Legal—Exactly What the Species Needs," *Outside Magazine*, December 2007. Also see Hal Herring, "One Way to Save the Wolf? Hunt It," *High Country News*, October 24, 2010. Michael J. Robinson argues, "Bounties were not capable of extirpating wolves in the Rockies, hence the federal program described in *The Last Stand of the Pack*."

42. Elizabeth Miller, "Who's Afraid? Wyoming's Open Hunting Season on Wolves Could Kill Colorado's Chances of Getting a Pack of Its Own," *Boulder Weekly*, May 24, 2012.

43. Askins, *Shadow Mountain*, 242.

44. Jamie Ross, "Groups Fight Pass Given to Rare Species Killers," Courthouse News Service, June 3, 2013.

45. Deborah Schoch, "Policy Limits Endangered Species Act Prosecutions," *Los Angeles Times*, June 22, 2013. Also see Edward A. Fitzgerald, *Wolves, Courts, and Public Policy: The Children of the Night Return to the Northern Rocky Mountains* (Lanham, MD: Lexington Books, 2015).

46. Kris Olson, e-mail to author, August 31, 2015.

47. Wolf specialists Michael K. Phillips and Michael J. Robinson feel this is too optimistic. Without specific, scientific wolf reintroduction, gray wolves returning to Colorado will never succeed to be genetically viable.

48. Matthew Brown, "Western Lawmakers Turn Sights on Gray Wolves," *Durango Herald*, October 4, 2010 and Matthew Brown, "Montana Sets Quota of 220 Wolves for Fall Hunt," *Cortez Journal*, July 16, 2011.

49. According to Michael J. Robinson, Idaho wolf numbers are dropping due to a wolf hunting season by the public and federal culling, or killing.

50. See a variety of published research, including Adrian Treves, "Hunting for Large Carnivore Conservation," *Journal of Applied Ecology* 46, no. 6 (December 2009): 1350–56; Adrian Treves et al., "Predators and the Public Trust," *Biological Reviews* (November 3, 2015); and Jamie Hogberg, Adrian Treves, Bret Shaw, and Lisa Naughton-Treves, "Changes in Attitudes toward Wolves before and after an Inaugural Public Hunting and Trapping Season: Early Evidence from Wisconsin's Wolf Range," *Environmental Conservation* (May 21, 2015).

51. US Fish and Wildlife Service, "Investigation Complete for Wolf Killed in Utah," news release, July 9, 2015. Also see Maximilian Werner, "Op-ed: Hunter's Story of Wolf Killing is Highly Dubious," *Salt Lake Tribune*, September 5, 2015.

52. Allen Best, "Hunter Who Killed Wolf Not Charged," *Durango Telegraph*, December 3, 2015.

53. Terri Brokering, interview with and e-mail to author, July 16, 2015.

54. Mike Murphy, interview with author, August 31, 2015. Other wolves have been sighted in the South San Juan Mountains, on Kebler Pass outside Crested Butte, and on the Pine River near Granite Peaks Ranch. Some Colorado ranchers want wolves to return. See Jim Patterson, "Crying Wolf: Apex Predator Makes Its Way Back into Colorado," *Steamboat Pilot*, May 16, 2016; and Allen Best, "Re-establishing Wolves in Colorado," *Durango Telegraph*, June 23, 2016.

55. Michelle Nijhuis, "Prodigal Dogs: Have Gray Wolves Found a Home in Colorado?," *High Country News*, February 5, 2010.

56. Colorado Parks and Wildlife (CPW) and Colorado Wolf Management Working Group (Wolf Working Group), "Findings and Recommendations for Managing Wolves that Migrate into Colorado," December 28, 2004, 1 (hereafter "Findings"). Twelve years later, CPW admits wolf sightings are on the increase. See the CPW news release published in the *Leadville Herald Democrat*, "Wolf Sightings, Confirmed and Unconfirmed, on the Increase," July 21, 2016.

57. "Findings," 2. Dr. Michael Soulé spoke about wolves in Colorado in Durango in his lecture "Courageous Carnivores and Compromised Conservationists," on September 3, 2015. See Jonathan Romeo, "Should Colorado Reintroduce Wolves?," *Durango Herald*, September 3, 2015. Also see Jim Carlton, "Wolf's Return to California Stirs Debate," *Wall Street Journal*, September 21, 2015.

58. For information on the beleaguered Mexican wolf, see Joshua Zaffos, "An Ecosystem Wanting for Wolves," *High Country News*, January 23, 2006; John Dougherty, "Last Chance for the Lobo: How Politics, Poaching and Inbreeding Have Turned the Mexican Wolf Program into a Bloody Mess," *High Country News*, December 24, 2007; WildEarth Guardians, "Building on Leopold's Legacy: Protecting Wolves and Wilderness in the Southwest," *Wild at Heart*, no. 20 (Fall 2014); Judy Calman, "Campaign Update: Mexican Gray Wolves," *New Mexico Wild: Newsletter of the New Mexico Wilderness*

Alliance 12, no. 1 (Spring/Summer 2015). For an intriguing novel about bringing Mexican wolves into the Gila Wilderness without government sanctions, see M. H. Salmon, *Home Is the River: A Novel of the Wild* (Silver City, NM: High-Lonesome Books, 1989). For the most recent information on Mexican wolves, see Dan Elliott, "Feds' Wolf Plan Eyed Warily," *Durango Herald*, January 18, 2016; Leslie Vreeland, "Lost Lobos: Could the Mexican Wolf Survive in Southern Colorado?," *The Watch*, March 9, 2016; CPW and Wolf Working Group, "Mexican Wolves in Colorado, More than Political," news release, May 23, 2016; and Cally Carswell, "Line of Descent: How Poor Management Left Mexican Wolves Dangerously Inbred," *High Country News*, August 8, 2016.

59. "Findings," 17. New research indicates that coyotes and wolves howl in dialects. One author suggests, "The study has implications for conservation. In Montana, where the predatory habits of wolves and coyotes put them in conflict with livestock, certain howl types could be played back in order to discourage canids from inhabiting areas used by livestock." Allen Best, "Coyotes and Wolves Howl in Dialects," *Durango Telegraph*, March 17, 2016.

60. "Findings," 22.

61. Information on the survey completed in 1993 by CSU is from Eric Odell, Colorado Department of Natural Resources, in an e-mail to author. For a more recent assessment of values and attitudes on Colorado wolf reintroduction, see Richard P. Reading, ed., *Awakening Spirits: Wolves in the Southern Rockies* (Golden, CO: Fulcrum, 2010).

62. To learn about wolves and cattle ranches, read *Badluck Way*. It is a well-written memoir of a ranch hand working on a $27 million conservation-based ranch in the Madison Valley of Montana, which has a new and powerful wolf pack called the Wedge Pack that threatens the summer's bovine herds. Bryce Andrews, *Badluck Way: A Year on the Ragged Edge of the West* (New York: Atria, 2014). He writes, "That was the great and damning thing about wolf biology—given an ample prey base and enough room to roam, they spread easily across the landscape. With an average litter size between four and seven pups, two wolves became a dozen in very short order. This didn't bode well in a valley like the Madison, with thousands of cattle wandering the foothills" (95).

63. "Findings," 43.

64. Dan Schwartz, interview on horseback with author, September 18, 2015.

65. "Findings," 23. For modern wolf recovery issues, also see Askins, *Shadow Mountain*; Cristina Eisenberg, *The Carnivore Way: Coexisting with and Conserving North America's Predators* (Washington, DC: Island Press, 2014); and John Shivik, *The Predator Paradox: Ending the War with Wolves, Bears, Cougars, and Coyotes* (New York: Beacon, 2014).

66. "Findings," 9, 10.

67. Perhaps the CPW opposes wolf reintroduction because it will mean fewer elk in Colorado to hunt, and maybe fewer hunters will buy elk licenses. The CPW needs the revenue from hunting licenses. On the other hand, how much does the

state pay out each year for damage to farmland and hayfields from oversized elk herds? That is also a significant expense.

68. Askins, *Shadow Mountain*, 173.

69. Ibid., 176.

70. Gary Skiba, interview with author, August 31, 2015. For a good book for children about wolves, see Sylvia A. Johnson and Alice Aamodt, *Wolf Pack: Tracking Wolves in the Wild* (Minneapolis: Lerner Publications, 1985).

71. See Daniel B. Botkin, "Wolves, People, and Biodiversity," chap. 7 in *Our Natural History: The Lessons of Lewis and Clark* (New York: Berkley, 1995).

72. Lewis and Clark journal entry cited in Botkin, "Wolves, People, and Biodiversity," 137.

73. Carhart letter cited in Robinson, *Predatory Bureaucracy*, 222–23.

74. Ibid., 305.

75. For the definitive biography on Arthur Carhart, written with attention to detail, compassion, and insight, see Tom Wolf, *Arthur Carhart: Wilderness Prophet* (Boulder: University Press of Colorado, 2008).

BIBLIOGRAPHY

Alderman, Jesse Harlan. "Idaho Governor Wants Wolf Hunting." *Durango Herald*, January 19, 2007.

Andrews, Bryce. *Badluck Way: A Year on the Ragged Edge of the West*. New York: Atria, 2014.

Askins, Renee. *Shadow Mountain: A Memoir of Wolves, a Woman, and the Wild*. New York: Anchor, 2002.

Barker, Rocky. "Imported Wolves Lope Off into Idaho Wilderness." *High Country News*, January 23, 1995.

Barnard, Jeff. "No-Kill Wolf Ban Spurs Non-Lethal Options." *Durango Herald*, March 3, 2013.

Beschta, R. L. "Cottonwoods, Elk and Wolves in the Lamar Valley of Yellowstone National Park." *Ecological Applications* 13, no. 5 (2003): 1295–1309.

Best, Allen. "Coyotes and Wolves Howl in Dialects." *Durango Telegraph*, March 17, 2016.

Best, Allen. "Re-establishing Wolves in Colorado." *Durango Telegraph*, June 23, 2016.

"Bill Addresses Losses from Wolves." *Durango Herald*, June 28, 2015.

Botkin, Daniel B. *Our Natural History: The Lessons of Lewis and Clark*. New York: Berkley, 1995.

Brown, David E., ed. *The Wolf in the Southwest: The Making of an Endangered Species*. Tucson: University of Arizona Press, 1984.

Brown, David E., and Neil B. Carmony, eds. *Aldo Leopold's Wilderness: Selected Early Writings by the Author of "A Sand County Almanac."* Harrisburg, PA: Stackpole Books, 1990.

Brown, Matthew. "Montana Sets Quota of 220 Wolves for Fall Hunt." *Cortez Journal*, July 16, 2011.

Brown, Matthew. "Western Lawmakers Turn Sights on Gray Wolves." *Durango Herald*, October 4, 2010.

Bryan, Susan Montoya. "Wolves Released South of Border." *Durango Herald*, October 23, 2011.

Calman, Judy. "Campaign Update: Mexican Gray Wolves." *New Mexico Wild: Newsletter of the New Mexico Wilderness Alliance* 12, no. 1 (Spring/Summer 2015).

Carhart, Arthur H., and Stanley P. Young. *The Last Stand of the Pack*. New York: J. H. Sears, 1929.

Carlton, Jim. "Wolf's Return to California Stirs Debate." *Wall Street Journal*, September 21, 2015.

Carswell, Cally. "Line of Descent: How Poor Management Left Mexican Wolves Dangerously Inbred." *High Country News*, August 8, 2016.

Chadwick, Douglas H. "Wolf Wars: Once Protected, Now Hunted." *National Geographic*, March 2010.

Colorado Parks and Wildlife, Colorado Wolf Management Working Group. "Findings and Recommendations for Managing Wolves that Migrate into Colorado." December 28, 2004.

Colorado Parks and Wildlife, Colorado Wolf Management Working Group. "Mexican Wolves in Colorado, More than Political." News release. May 23, 2016.

Colorado Parks and Wildlife, Colorado Wolf Management Working Group. "Wolf Sightings, Confirmed and Unconfirmed on the Increase." News release. *Leadville Herald Democrat*, July 21, 2016.

Cook, Tricia M. "Sun Setting on Wolf Recovery?" *Durango Herald*, November 21, 2013.

Cornwall, Warren. "Have Returning Wolves Really Saved Yellowstone?" *High Country News*, December 8, 2014.

"Depredations from Wolves Hit Record." Sidebar by the Associated Press in Jesse Harlan Alderman, "Idaho Governor Wants Wolf Hunting," *Durango Herald*, January 19, 2007.

Devlin, Sherry. "Wolf Provokes Inadvertent Howlers." *High Country News*, September 19, 1994.

Doig, Ivan. *The Whistling Season*. New York: Harcourt Brace, 2006.

Dougherty, John. "Last Chance for the Lobo: How Politics, Poaching and Inbreeding Have Turned the Mexican Wolf Program into a Bloody Mess." *High Country News*, December 24, 2007.

Eisenberg, Cristina. *The Carnivore Way: Coexisting with and Conserving North America's Predators*. Washington, DC: Island Press, 2014.

Elliott, Dan. "Feds' Wolf Plan Eyed Warily." *Durango Herald*, January 18, 2016.

Findley, Tim. "The Wolves of Gooseberry Creek: Tall Tales, Tangled Webs, Folks and Feds." *Range Magazine*, Summer 2004.

Fischer, Hank. *Wolf Wars: The Remarkable Inside Story of the Restoration of Wolves to Yellowsone.* Helena, MT: Falcon, 1995.

Fitzgerald, Edward A. *Wolves, Courts, and Public Policy: The Children of the Night Return to the Northern Rocky Mountains.* Lanham, MD: Lexington Books, 2015.

Flader, Susan L. *Thinking Like a Mountain: Aldo Leopold and the Evolution of an Ecological Attitude toward Deer, Wolves and Forests.* Madison: University of Wisconsin Press, 1974.

Fonseca, Felicia. "After 70 Years, Wolf Returns." *Durango Herald*, November 27, 2014.

Gantenbein, Douglas. "Fire Away: Hunting Wolves Will Soon Be Legal—Exactly What the Species Needs." *Outside Magazine*, December 2007.

Gathright, Alan. "DNA Confirms Coyote Hunter Killed Gray Wolf in Kremmling Last Month." 7News. May 28, 2015.

Glick, Daniel. "Still Howling Wolf: Will Westerners Finally Learn to Live with *Canis lupus?*" *High Country News*, November 10, 2008.

"Gray Wolves Going Back into Wild at Yellowstone." *Tennessean*, January 8, 1995.

Greager, Howard E. *In the Company of Cowboys.* Privately printed, 1990.

Hampton, Bruce. *The Great American Wolf.* New York: Henry Holt, 1997.

Heinrich, Bernd. *Mind of the Raven: Investigations and Adventures with Wolf-Birds.* New York: HarperCollins, 1999.

Herring, Hal. "One Way to Save the Wolf? Hunt It." *High Country News*, October 24, 2010.

Herring, Hal. "Wolf Whiplash." *High Country News*, May 30, 2011.

Hess, Karl, Jr. *Rocky Times in Rocky Mountain National Park: An Unnatural History.* Boulder: University Press of Colorado, 1993.

Hinshaw, Glen A. *Crusaders for Wildlife: A History of Wildlife Stewardship in Southwestern Colorado.* Ouray, CO: Western Reflections, 2000.

Hogberg, Jamie, Adrian Treves, Bret Shaw, and Lisa Naughton-Treves. "Changes in Attitudes toward Wolves before and after an Inaugural Public Hunting and Trapping Season: Early Evidence from Wisconsin's Wolf Range." *Environmental Conservation* (May 21, 2015).

Holmes, Sue Major. "Feds Delay Arizona Release of Wolves." *Durango Herald*, October 9, 2010.

Johnson, Sylvia A., and Alice Aamodt. *Wolf Pack: Tracking Wolves in the Wild.* Minneapolis: Lerner Publications, 1985.

Johnston, Jeremy, "Preserving the Beasts of Waste and Desolation: Theodore Roosevelt and Predator Control in Yellowstone." *Yellowstone Science* 10, no. 2 (Spring 2002): 14–21.

Ketcham, Christopher. "How to Kill a Wolf: An Undercover Report from the Idaho Coyote and Wolf Derby." March 13, 2014, www.vice.com/en_us/article/how-to-kill-a-wolf-0000259-v21n3.

Kirkwood, Scott. "Too Much of a Good Thing? Elk Overpopulation in Rocky Mountain National Park Is Taking a Toll on the Ecosystem, and the Results Can't Be Ignored Any Longer." *National Parks*, Fall 2006.

Knickerbocker, Brad. "The Dance to Coexist with Wolves." *Christian Science Monitor*, December 6, 1994.

Lavender, David. *One Man's West*. Lincoln: University of Nebraska Press, 1977.

Leopold, Aldo. *A Sand County Almanac: With Essays on Conservation from Round River*. New York: Ballantine, 1970.

Lindauer, Ivo E. *Up the Creek: Parachute Creek's Pioneer Families and Energy Development 1875–2015*. Parachute, CO: Double F., 2016.

Long, Kim. *Wolves: A Wildlife Handbook*. Boulder, CO: Johnson Books, 1996.

Lopez, Barry Holstun. *Of Wolves and Men*. New York: Charles Scribner's Sons, 1978.

Lorbiecki, Marybeth. *Aldo Leopold: A Fierce Green Fire*. Guilford, CT: Falcon, 2005.

Lords of Nature: Life in a Land of Great Predators. Directed by Karen Meyer and Ralf Meyer. La Grande, OR: Green Fire Productions, 2009. DVD, 60 min.

Luoma, Jon R. "New Federation and the Wolf." *Audubon*, March 1983.

Mann, Jim. "The Canis Lupus Olympics: Wolf Recovery Doesn't Come Easy but the Northern Rockies Experience Proves It's Possible for the Southwest Too." *Santa Fe Reporter*, June 10, 2015.

McMillion, Scott. "In Surprising Ways, Wolves Will Restore Natural Balance." *High Country News*, February 6, 1995.

McNamee, Thomas. *The Return of the Wolf to Yellowstone*. New York: Henry Holt, 1997.

McPherson, Robert S. *Life in a Corner: Cultural Episodes in Southeastern Utah, 1880–1950*. Norman: University of Oklahoma Press, 2015.

Mech, David. "At Home with the Arctic Wolf." *National Geographic*, May 1987.

Meine, Curt. *Aldo Leopold: His Life and Work*. Madison: University of Wisconsin Press, 1988.

Mertens, Richard. "Midwest Wolves Stir Protest Howls." *Christian Science Monitor*, July 26, 2010.

Miller, Elizabeth. "Who's Afraid? Wyoming's Open Hunting Season on Wolves Could Kill Colorado's Chances of Getting a Pack of Its Own." *Boulder Weekly*, May 24, 2012.

Milstein, Michael. "The Wolves Are Back, Big Time." *High Country News*, February 6, 1995.

Most, Stephen. *Green Fire: Aldo Leopold and a Land Ethic for Our Time*. Directed by David Steinke and Steve Dunsky, produced by the Aldo Leopold Foundation, the Center for Humans and Nature, and the US Forest Service, 2011. DVD, 73 min.

Nelson, E. W. "Report of the Chief of the Bureau of Biological Survey." Washington, DC: USDA, August 29, 1918.

Nelson, Richard. *Heart and Blood: Living with Deer in America*. New York: Alfred A. Knopf, 1997.

Nijhuis, Michelle. "Prodigal Dogs: Have Gray Wolves Found a Home in Colorado?" *High Country News*, February 15, 2010.

Niskanen, Chris. "Dancing with Wolves." *St. Paul Pioneer Press-Dispatch*, October 10, 1994.

O'Driscoll, Patrick. "Wolf Shot." *USA Today*, November 27, 1998.

Patterson, Jim. "Crying Wolf: Apex Predator Makes Its Way Back into Colorado." *Steamboat Pilot*, May 16, 2016.

Petersen, David. *The Nearby Faraway*. Boulder, CO: Johnson Books, 1997.

Phillips, Michael K., and Douglas W. Smith. *The Wolves of Yellowstone*. Stillwater, MN: Voyageur Press, 1996.

Redington, Paul G. "Report of the Chief of the Bureau of Biological Survey." Washington, DC: USDA, August 31, 1931.

Robinson, Michael J. *Predatory Bureaucracy: The Extermination of Wolves and the Transformation of the West*. Boulder: University Press of Colorado, 2005.

Romeo, Jonathan. "Should Colorado Reintroduce Wolves?" *Durango Herald*, September 3, 2015.

Ross, Jamie. "Groups Fight Pass Given to Rare Species Killers." Courthouse News Service, June 3, 2013.

"Sacrifices Horses to Ravenous Wolves." *Grand Junction Daily Sentinel*, December 27, 1912.

Salmon, M. H. *Home Is the River: A Novel of the Wild*. Silver City, NM: High-Lonesome Books, 1989.

Sands, Will. "Back on the Road to Recovery: Settlement Boosts Mexican Wolf Recovery Efforts." *Durango Telegraph*, December 10, 2009.

Sands, Will. "Mexican Wolf Goes Back in Crosshairs." *Durango Telegraph*, November 18, 2010.

San Juan National Forest Pagosa Ranger District, Rangers' Logbooks. 1921–1925. Collection M 080, Series 1.4. Center of Southwest Studies, Fort Lewis College, Durango, CO.

Schoch, Deborah. "Policy Limits Endangered Species Act Prosecutions." *Los Angeles Times*, June 22, 2013.

Shivik, John. *The Predator Paradox: Ending the War with Wolves, Bears, Cougars, and Coyotes*. New York: Beacon, 2014.

Thompson Seton, Ernest. *Lobo, Rag and Vixen: Being the Personal Histories of Lobo, Redruff, Raggylug and Vixen*. New York: Charles Scribner's Sons, 1908.

Treves, Adrian. "Hunting for Large Carnivore Conservation." *Journal of Applied Ecology* 46, no. 6 (December 2009): 1350–56.

Treves, Adrian, Guillaume Chapron, Jose V. López-Bao, Chase Shoemaker, Apollonia R. Goeckner, and Jeremy T. Bruskotter. "Predators and the Public Trust." *Biological Reviews* (November 3, 2015).

Tweit, Susan J. "Wolf." In *Comeback Wolves: Western Writers Welcome the Wolf Home*, ed. Gary Wockner, Gregory McNamee, and SueEllen Campbell, 13–17. Boulder, CO: Johnson Books, 2005.

US Fish and Wildlife Service. "Investigation Complete for Wolf Killed in Utah." News release. July 9, 2015.

"U.S. to Wolves: Come Back. All Is Forgiven." *New York Times*, January 8, 1995.

Vreeland, Leslie. "Lost Lobos: Could the Mexican Wolf Survive in Southern Colorado?" *The Watch*, March 9, 2016.

Werner, Maximilian. "Op-ed: Hunter's Story of Wolf Killing Is Highly Dubious." *Salt Lake Tribune*, September 9, 2015.

WildEarth Guardians, "Building on Leopold's Legacy: Protecting Wolves and Wilderness in the Southwest." *Wild at Heart*, no. 20 (Fall 2014).

Wockner, Gary, Gregory McNamee, and SueEllen Campbell, eds. *Comeback Wolves: Western Writers Welcome the Wolf Home*. Boulder, CO: Johnson Books, 2005.

Wolf, Tom. *Arthur Carhart: Wilderness Prophet*. Boulder: University Press of Colorado, 2008.

Wolf, Tom. "World Champion Wolfer." *Inside/Outside Southwest*, March 2009.

Zaffos, Joshua. "An Ecosystem Wanting for Wolves." *High Country News*, January 23, 2006.

Reasons Not to Reintroduce Wolves into Colorado

A Rancher and Biologist Responds

TOM COMPTON

The development of sound public policy requires a thorough examination of all sides of an issue, paying particular attention to the potential for unintended consequences. I believe there are some sound reasons to support Colorado Parks and Wildlife's recent resolution opposing wolf reintroduction into Colorado's landscapes.[1] A primary justification for wolf reintroduction is based on a well-reasoned argument that any ecosystem cannot be fully functional without all of its component parts in place. Strong evidence to support this argument exists in the results of the reintroduction of the gray wolf into the Yellowstone National Park ecosystem. That ecosystem was functioning poorly, causing environmental damage throughout due to the lack of natural checks and balances. The wolves brought the overpopulation of elk back into balance with the rest of the system.

The success of this experiment was due in large part to the relatively unique environment in which it was conducted—vast areas of land that are relatively self-contained and have minimal competing interests. I believe a great deal of caution must be exercised when considering the application of this successful experiment into other areas that may not possess the same characteristics as the Yellowstone ecosystem.

Western Colorado does not present a situation sufficiently similar to the Yellowstone ecosystem. For one thing, our rela-

DOI: 10.5876/9781607326939.c003

tively high human population adds a competing interest that exists only minimally in Yellowstone due to the management of the national park. This higher human population density in Colorado elevates concerns with the potential for increased human/wolf interaction.

In Yellowstone these human/wolf interactions have been managed by strict safety regulations. For example, the park website lists such regulations as "you must stay 100 yards away from wolves at all times, keep dogs leashed at all times and never leave small children unattended." The website goes on to say, "wolves can quickly learn to associate campgrounds, picnic areas, and roads with food. This can lead to aggressive behavior toward humans."[2] The idea that these precautions are necessary for safety when wolves are in an area is concerning for those who live in and around potential sites for reintroduction. Changes to laws necessary to enforce these types of safety regulations outside of a national park will likely be difficult to enforce and likely to meet resistance from the general public. This is just one example of how the success of the Yellowstone experiment was contingent on various factors, including social factors that would be difficult to replicate outside an intensively managed national park.

With respect to the health of an ecosystem, I do not believe the presence of the wolf is necessary for a healthy, functional system over all landscapes. Ecosystems are never static. Their only real constant is change. In fact, perturbation is the norm for an ecological system. Ecosystems have evolved with the ability to react to change. Whether fire, disease, or the constant ebb and flow of predator/prey populations, these systems have the inherent capacity to evolve with environmental fluctuations. As one component of the system wanes, others fill the gap.

I believe the current suite of large predators (mountain lions, black bear, coyote, lynx, and including humans) can be effectively managed to appropriately balance prey populations within the carrying capacities of their environment. I would certainly stipulate this may require some shift in our current sport hunting philosophy, but it is within our capabilities. Proponents of wolf reintroduction had indicated that the major prey species for wolves currently have population densities that are too high.

A 2016 bulletin from Colorado Parks and Wildlife states that their decades of monitoring deer and elk populations across southern management units indicate populations that are far below management objectives and are exhibiting low productivity. It goes on to say that these populations have declined precipitously in the southeast and southwest regions of the state.[3]

As a cattleman, I am concerned about the potential impact of wolves on domestic livestock production. Ranching in western Colorado is typically a low-margin business. Anything that elevates expenses reduces the profit even more, and—make no mistake—management changes necessitated by the presence of wolves would elevate the rancher's expenses. Most of western Colorado's ranches are family operations, and excessive costs could result in business failure.

Why should you care if my business fails? Our family ranch provides a significant number of environmental attributes to society. In addition to clean air, clean water, open space, and viewsheds, we provide habitat for at least part of each year for mule deer, elk, bears, coyotes, lynx, foxes, mountain lions, and many other creatures. We have recorded the presence of about sixty-seven avian species, including hawks, owls, eagles, and wild turkeys. Our ranch is considered to be a carbon sink, trapping more carbon than we create, thus helping to control this important greenhouse gas. If we are forced out of business due to excessive cost, our land would likely have to be sold for development, and our thousand acres would become thirty homesites with no, or limited, environmental attributes.

Now multiply that by several thousand additional ranches, and you will experience a serious decline in your quality of life. It is certainly our desire to pass this ranch along to our children and grandchildren so they can continue to provide these environmental attributes, but we can only accomplish that desire if the business is sustainable.

Finally, it is an established fact that human death as a result of interaction with wolves is a rare event. Rare means it doesn't happen very often. Rare does not mean it never happens. It would seem that placing these predators in closer association with humans might well increase the probability of this rare event occurring. Even without the tragedy of human death, the increase in human/wolf interactions will cause society's tolerance to wear thin, especially in the towns and villages of western Colorado, where increasing populations of deer, bears, and mountain lions already cause a great deal of concern.

Of course, those of us on the front lines dealing with wolves on a day-to-day basis would be at a higher risk. It makes me nervous to consider placing my grandchildren in a situation such as this. Ranching families are already familiar with the management adjustments necessary to successfully deal with predators. Adding the wolf to this mix may be a bit too much to ask.

While I have been discussing the reintroduction of the gray wolf, I am aware of the proposal to reintroduce the Mexican wolf into southern Colorado. I believe the science offers two obstacles. There is little historical evidence to suggest the Mexican wolf ever established successful populations in southern Colorado. Also, Colorado would provide a very valuable buffer between populations of the gray wolf and the Mexican wolf to protect the genetic integrity of these two subspecies.

I do hope those who advocate for wolf reintroduction into Colorado will occasionally remind themselves who it is they are asking to bear the brunt of having these new neighbors next door. Wolf management is a costly endeavor. We are asking farmers, ranchers, and sportsmen to deal with the increased workload, the increased financial cost, and, perhaps the most onerous of all, the increased emotional cost.

NOTES

1. Colorado Parks and Wildlife Bulletin, "Explanation of Wolf Resolution Considered by Parks and Wildlife Commission," January 8, 2016 (hereafter CPW Bulletin).

2. Yellowstone National Park Service website, https://www.nps.gov/yell/index.htm.

3. CPW Bulletin.

The Great Divide

Wolves in Colorado?

BONNIE BROWN

At the January 2016 Colorado Parks and Wildlife Commission meeting, I testified on behalf of the Colorado Wool Growers Association opposing wolf reintroduction in Colorado. As the saying goes, "This ain't my first rodeo." Over a decade ago, I was one of the four representatives for the livestock industry that helped write "Findings and Recommendations for Managing Wolves That Migrate into Colorado."[1]

To me, the Wildlife Commission meeting was nothing short of a circus, complete with warm, fuzzy wolf pictures, including one pro-wolf sign done in beautiful pastel rainbow colors, featuring a serene and friendly looking wolf. Good grief, I thought! Why don't wolf advocates make posters, coffee cups, and T-shirts with a mama cow with her hind end eaten away by wolves as she was giving birth and has her partially eaten dead calf hanging out of her? She doesn't have the strength to get up or away, and the only kindness she receives is when the rancher finds her and shoots her to end her suffering. Try using that image for a fund-raising campaign for wolves! Don't even get me started about the damage wolves do to sheep, sometimes killing dozens in a single attack. Distraught, forlorn shepherds kneeling in the torn and bloody earth, tears streaming down their sunburned cheeks, cradle their working dogs in their arms, watching them draw their last ragged breath. They find little solace in knowing that their courageous canine companions died trying to protect the flock from wolves.

DOI: 10.5876/9781607326939.c004

At the Wildlife Commission meeting, an impassioned grandmother held up a stuffed toy wolf and tearfully told the commissioners that she gives each grandchild a stuffed wolf to sleep with. She implored the commissioners to restore wolves to Colorado for the sake of her grandchildren. I desperately want to shout out, "What about little nine-year-old Stacy Miller in New Mexico who lost her horse, Six? A pack of wolves killed Six in its corral, the only 'safe' place the horse had to go." It's not a fairy tale or bedtime story with a happy ending. It was a bloody, horrific mess. It's a devastating tragedy and an irreplaceable loss they will never forget. What about that family?

So after over a decade of being involved in the wolf debate, feelings still run deep and emotions high on both sides of the divide.

Do wolves belong in Colorado? This isn't Yellowstone National Park, and the wildlife commissioners' current resolution opposing wolf reintroduction was adopted after thoughtful analysis of several key issues: appropriate and available habitat, impacts on other wildlife species, impacts on the livestock industry, and management resources.

From a livestock producers' perspective, depredation by wolves and other carnivores represents a significant cost to ranching operations. I have worked for the livestock industry for sixteen years and work on predator issues across the West. Farmers and ranchers with wolves in proximity of their land and livestock continue to experience significant problems because of wolves.

Colorado Parks and Wildlife (CPW) has long recognized the importance of landowners in the partnership of managing our state's wildlife. Farmers and ranchers own a substantial portion of the critical winter habitat that enables big game to survive our harsh winters. While much of the summer high country is managed by the US Forest Service, it is not viable winter habitat, and big game herds and livestock migrate into the valleys to survive the winter. Since wolves can't live on snow and pinecones, they will follow the food source.

The primary revenue source for managing predators and big game comes from sportsmen's dollars, and those dollars are already stretched thin to meet a variety of demands. Millions of sportsmen's dollars have been spent to improve habitat and increase populations for a variety of wildlife species. Moose transplanted on the Grand Mesa is one recent success story. As shown in Wyoming, Idaho, and Montana, reintroducing wolves has a negative impact on prey species, including large ungulate herds. Colorado already has its share of large carnivore problems.

The following statements were published in the 2016 CPW "Human-Bear Conflicts" report submitted to the Colorado State Legislature:

- "Between 1980 and 2010, the human population in Colorado grew from 2.9 million to over 5 million, one of the highest growth rates in the country."
- "State forecasters project that Colorado's population will exceed 7.1 million by 2040."
- "For a growing number of Area and District Wildlife Managers, bear management activities are consuming an inordinate amount of staff time during spring, summer and fall, resulting in the near total exclusion of other critical responsibilities. Despite these efforts, the number of human-bear interactions and conflicts continue to rise."[2]

The CPW is already experiencing significant problems managing bears. We do not need to introduce another large predatory carnivore into the state.

Despite what you hear from wolf advocates, the Wildlife Commission did not capitulate to the demands of the livestock industry and sportsmen. Passage of the resolution opposing wolf reintroduction was a commonsense acknowledgement of the overall impact of wolves, the contributions that landowners and sportsmen make in maintaining thriving and diverse wildlife species, and the complexities of managing large carnivores in a highly populated state with limited habitat.

NOTES

1. Colorado Parks and Wildlife and Colorado Wolf Management Working Group. "Findings and Recommendations for Managing Wolves that Migrate into Colorado." December 28, 2004.

2. Colorado Parks and Wildlife, "Human-Bear Conflicts" (December 31, 2015), 6, 6, 5.

The Wolf in Colorado

Destruction to Restoration

MIKE PHILLIPS, NORM BISHOP, AND CHENEY GARDNER

The future cannot be denied, and so it is with consideration of restoring the gray wolf (*Canis lupus*) to western Colorado. After completing decades of wolf recovery work elsewhere in the United States, conservationists can now focus on the last great remaining expanse of wolfless wildlands in the lower forty-eight states—the public lands of the Southern Rockies Ecoregion of western Colorado. It is altogether fitting that such a focus should begin by looking back, by reviewing the history of the last wolves in Colorado and their purposeful, hateful, and needless destruction. As described in vivid detail by Arthur H. Carhart in his important book *The Last Stand of the Pack*, wolf extermination in Colorado involved brutish means applied by zealots. While the species was rendered all but ecologically extinct by the 1930s, the last wolf hung on until 1945, when it was killed near the Colorado-New Mexico border. With that death, the clarion call of Colorado's wildlands was silenced.

HISTORY OF EXTERMINATION

As recently as 150 years ago, the gray wolf was distributed throughout the contiguous United States, except from central Texas to the Atlantic coast, where the red wolf (*Canis rufus*) roamed. Historically, the gray wolf was the most widely distributed large mammal in North America. Tolerant of

DOI: 10.5876/9781607326939.c005

environmental extremes, wolves inhabited areas from central Mexico to the North Pole. This expansive distribution was greatly reduced as a result of long-term extermination efforts that began as Europeans settled in North America. Conflict with agricultural interests resulted in government-supported eradication campaigns, beginning in colonial Massachusetts in 1630. Eventually wolf extermination became the policy of the federal government and was applied relentlessly, including in the western United States.

For millions of years the western United States had been wolf and bison (*Bison bison*) country. As the cardinal features of the region, these two species greatly shaped its ecology. Of the two, the wolf had an overseer role, with authority provided by predation. Through that authority wolves were the shepherds of the buffalo and other big game.

The settling of the region to make it suitable for ranching exotic cattle and sheep imported from Europe brought about profound reductions in the wolf's native prey. Even the mighty bison was slaughtered to the brink of extinction. In desperation, wolves turned to sheep and cattle. The response by livestock men was certain, swift, and furious.

As Barry Lopez wrote, "The wolf was not the cattlemen's only problem. There was weather to contend with, disease, rustling, fluctuating beef prices, the hazards of the trail drives, the cost of running such enormous operations. But more and more the cattlemen blamed any economic shortfall on the wolf . . . The wolf became an object of pathological hatred."[1]

At the behest of ranchers pursuing their anger-fueled sense of Manifest Destiny, bounty hunters and government field agents shot, roped, trapped, gassed, stomped, and strangled wolves.[2] By the 1930s the ranchers' hatred had rendered wolves uncommon. Some of the last to survive were given names and a permanent place in western folklore. Montana's last wolf was called Snowdrift. South Dakota's sole survivor was the Custer Wolf. Wolves named Rags, Whitey, and Lefty were among Colorado's last, and one final story from the state involves a female wolf named Three-Toes. Wandering alone, driven by an urge she could not control, she mated with a dog, which sealed her fate. Pinned down by motherhood, her habits were discovered by federal agents. They used that knowledge to kill her, the dog, and their puppies.

In the early 1950s government trappers turned to northern Mexico and the few wolves there that dispersed to the United States. This influx was eliminated by the end of that decade when wolf numbers reached an all-time low. At that time less than one thousand persisted in the remote Superior National Forest of northeastern Minnesota. Additionally, probably less than twenty wolves inhabited Isle Royale National Park, a small island located in Lake Superior about twenty miles from the northeast Minnesota mainland.

STATE PROTECTION

Given the extermination of the wolf in Colorado, it is altogether fitting that the species is listed as endangered under Colorado's Nongame, Endangered, or Threatened Species Conservation Act. The act states that "species or subspecies of wildlife indigenous to this state which may be found to be endangered or threatened . . . should be accorded protection in order to maintain and enhance their numbers to the extent possible . . . this state should assist in the protection of species or subspecies of wildlife which are deemed to be endangered or threatened."[3]

Despite the clear intent of Colorado law, it is unlikely that any proactive state-led recovery effort will surface. Why? The state's law is best suited for management actions that promote the persistence of imperiled but extant species. For extirpated species like the gray wolf, the law specifies that reintroductions must be authorized by the Colorado legislature. Given the influence of the livestock industry, and to a lesser extent the big game hunting industry, it seems unlikely that the legislature would ever willingly authorize wolf reintroductions. Some people continue to harbor a pathological hatred of wolves.

FEDERAL PROTECTION

The federal Endangered Species Act (ESA) passed in 1973, and by 1978 it provided protection to the gray wolf throughout the continental United States, including Colorado. Starting with about one thousand wolves in Minnesota in the early 1970s, by 2016 ESA-related recovery actions had led to the establishment of about six thousand wolves in Minnesota, Michigan, Wisconsin, Montana, Idaho, Wyoming, Oregon, and Washington spread across about 15 percent of the species' historical range. Recovery actions also led to a population of about one hundred Mexican gray wolves in southwestern New Mexico and southeastern Arizona.

Since the gray wolf is listed as endangered in Colorado under the ESA, recovery should be inevitable. After all, the ESA mandates the secretary of the interior to use all methods and procedures necessary to recover a listed species, including reintroductions, to restore viable populations to unoccupied habitat. For more than twenty years, however, the US Fish and Wildlife Service has shown no interest in restoring the wolf to western Colorado. In 2013 the agency made it clear that disinterest was its official policy, when it released a draft proposed rule for the species to be removed (delisted) from the federal list of endangered and threatened species for most of the country, including Colorado.[4] Delisting would absolve the Service from any future obligations to advance wolf recovery beyond the range currently occupied. This would, of course, eliminate the potential for a federally led restoration effort in Colorado. Curiously though, as of November 2017, the proposed rule had not been advanced beyond the draft stage.

Many believe that if finalized as drafted, the proposed rule would be flawed and probably unable to withstand judicial review, which is inevitable given the certainty of litigation. This belief is based on many things, including the fact that reintroducing wolves to western Colorado would ensure the establishment of a population, thereby advancing recovery of the species throughout a significant portion of its historical range, which is the cardinal mandate of the ESA.

While the ESA of 1973 was the third in a series of laws aimed at protecting imperiled species, it was the first to offer protection to species in danger of extinction throughout only a portion of its historic range. Previous federal laws—the Endangered Species Preservation Act of 1966 and the Endangered Species Conservation Act of 1969—only considered species facing total extinction. In contrast, the 1973 ESA defined an endangered species to be any species in danger of extinction throughout all or a significant portion of its range; a threatened species was any species that is likely to become an endangered species within the foreseeable future throughout all or a significant portion of its range. By including the phrase, "significant portion of its range," Congress elevated the threshold for recovery by establishing the expectation that a recovered species would be well distributed within its historical range.[5]

This expectation was buttressed when Congress included in the important but often overlooked "Findings, Purposes, and Policy" section of the ESA the recognition that imperiled species "are of esthetic, ecological, educational, historical, recreational, and scientific value to the Nation and its people."[6] It would be impossible for many of these values to be realized if a recovered species occupied only an insignificant portion of its historical range. There is, for example, no way for a species' ecological values to be manifest if it is absent from the vast majority of different ecological settings reasonably available to it.

The expectation that a recovered species would be reasonably well distributed within its historical range, at least where suitable habitat exists, was further buttressed when Congress defined the term *species* to include "any subspecies of fish or wildlife or plants, and any distinct population segment of any species of vertebrate fish or wildlife which interbreeds when mature."[7] Thus, ESA protections and recovery activities can be applied to a population segment of an otherwise common species as long as the population segment in question is discrete, significant, and threatened or endangered.

For all these reasons, it seems clear that Congress intended that the ESA's recovery mandate would have wide geographic application. Not surprisingly, previous delisting actions and case law upheld this intent. To emphasize this point, when considering recovery of the flat-tailed horned lizard (*Phrynosoma mcallii*), the Ninth Circuit Court of Appeals concluded that the text of the ESA and its subsequent application have been guided by Aldo Leopold's maxim: "There seems to be a tacit assumption that if grizzlies survive in Canada and Alaska, that is good enough. It is not good enough for me . . . Relegating grizzlies to Alaska is about like relegating happiness to heaven; one may never get there."[8]

Relegating the gray wolf to about 15 percent of its historical range and at population levels that are but a shadow of historical abundance fails to honor the spirit and intent of the ESA.[9] As long as the gray wolf remains extirpated in Colorado, the western half of the state will represent a significant gap in the species' range. That is exactly the problem that the ESA aims to correct.

HABITAT SUITABILITY—BIOLOGICAL AND SOCIAL ASPECTS

In addition to state and federal endangered species laws, wolf restoration to Colorado is strongly indicated by the presence of extensive and highly suitable habitat. In short, western Colorado contains more public land and prey for wolves than anywhere else in the United States.

As the heart of the Southern Rockies Ecoregion, western Colorado is a mother lode of biological opportunity for the gray wolf. The ecoregion stretches from north-central Wyoming, through western Colorado, into north-central New Mexico and includes nearly 25 million acres of public land (figure 6.1).

The vast majority of the ecoregion lies in western Colorado in the form of public land that stretches across about 18 million acres that are managed for conservation purposes and support robust populations of native ungulates (hoofed mammals like elk [*Cervus elaphus*] and deer [*Odocoileus* spp.]), the gray wolf's preferred prey.

Although wolves sometimes occur outside core protected areas of public land, it is clear that the beachheads of security offered by public land are essential for their long-term persistence. It is not coincidental that by the late

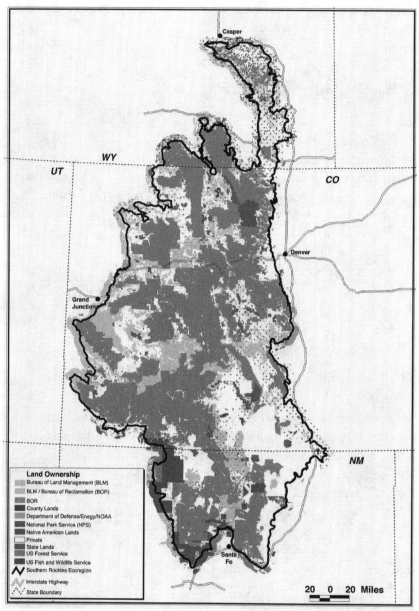

The Southern Rockies Ecoregion is centered on western Colorado and includes millions of acres of public land that is highly suitable for the gray wolf (from Shinneman, McClellan, and Smith, *The State of the Southern Rockies Ecoregion*).

1950s, when wolves had been exterminated throughout most of the continental United States, only several hundred survived in the Superior National Forest in northeastern Minnesota. And it is not coincidental that all wolf recovery projects have been centered on public lands.

Across the vast assemblage of public land in western Colorado, prey populations are more than sufficient for wolves. From 2004 through 2015, Colorado's combined post-hunt population (i.e., after recreational hunters killed a combined number of elk and deer that averaged 85,279 animals annually) of elk and deer averaged 758,314 animals.[10] This probably represents the largest and densest population of ungulates for wolves anywhere in the world.

The persistent commonness of elk and deer in western Colorado is noteworthy since prey abundance is the best predictor of habitat quality for wolves in areas where human-caused mortality of wolves is low.[11] Not surprisingly, a 1994 congressionally mandated study conducted by the US Fish and Wildlife Service concluded that Colorado could support over one thousand wolves.[12] Three additional studies, using increasingly reliable techniques, concluded that Colorado could easily support a self-sustaining population of wolves.[13]

In addition to extensive suitable habitat, as defined by large tracts of public land and robust prey populations, there is significant public support for the wolf's return to Colorado. Regional public opinion surveys conducted across a span of twenty years reveal strong and durable support for restoring the wolf to Colorado. In a public opinion survey conducted in 1996, 66 percent of the respondents said they would vote yes on a referendum to restore wolves.[14] This level of support persisted through the early 2000s, and a February 2014 survey affirmed that the vast majority (64 percent) of Coloradans want to see the wolf restored.[15]

RESTORATION: NATURAL RECOLONIZATION
VERSUS REINTRODUCTIONS

Even though western Colorado is ideally suited for the gray wolf, the area is a considerable distance from wolf populations elsewhere. It is highly unlikely that a viable population will inhabit the area through natural recolonization.[16] Conventional wisdom, based on decades of reliable research and wolf recovery actions, indicates that reintroductions provide the best guarantee for reestablishing a wolf population in western Colorado. It is simply too far, and there are too many mortality hazards along the way, for a sufficient number of wolves from the Northern Rockies or the Great Lakes states to wander to Colorado, find one another, and survive long enough to give birth to the countless litters of pups required to give rise to a viable population.

The limits of natural recolonization are apparent elsewhere. A viable population of wolves does not exist in western Minnesota and the Dakotas, despite over two thousand wolves in the northeastern quarter of Minnesota. It is quite likely that without reintroductions a viable population of wolves would not exist in Yellowstone National Park and the surrounding national forests despite about one thousand wolves nearby in Idaho and Montana.

When considering natural recolonization versus reintroductions as the mode of restoration, it is important to note that naturally recolonizing wolves (and any offspring) in Colorado would be fully protected as endangered under the federal ESA. Such protection significantly restricts management options. In contrast, reintroduced wolves (and any offspring) could be managed in a much more accommodating manner to address the needs and concerns of Coloradans.

The tremendous success of wolf reintroductions in Yellowstone National Park has relevance to western Colorado. While the park and surrounding national forests were certainly suitable for wolves, western Colorado's vast tracts of public land and unusually large populations of deer and elk make it even more so. What was done safely and cost-effectively in Yellowstone Park can more easily be done in the Rocky Mountains of western Colorado.

Given that the wolf was purposefully, but needlessly, exterminated from the area during the first half of the 1900s, reintroductions represent a responsible and practical way of restoring Colorado's natural balance. Claiming that it is likely that wolves will naturally recolonize the state is a red herring and detracts from a central fact: carefully planned and implemented reintroductions are the most certain way of restoring the gray wolf to the snow-capped peaks, rimrock canyons, and primeval forests of the Rocky Mountains of western Colorado. In contrast, counting on wolves to naturally recolonize Colorado is nothing more than an exercise in futility and one that has scant chance of restoring the wolf's howl, the cardinal voice of Colorado's wildlands.

The importance of restoring the wolf to western Colorado is especially significant when considered against a continental perspective. Because western Colorado is nearly equidistant from wolf populations in the Northern Rockies and southwestern New Mexico/southeastern Arizona)—a population that includes several hundred animals, through the movement of many wolves dispersing both north and south—would serve as the arch stone for a metapopulation of wolves (a population of populations) extending from the High Arctic to Mexico.

Reestablishing the gray wolf in western Colorado represents the last step for restoring the species from the High Arctic to the Mexican border. Credit R. P. Reading, B. Miller, A. L. Masching, R. Edward, and M. K. Phillips (eds), *Awakening Spirits: Wolves in the Southern Rockies* (Golden, CO: Fulcrum Publishing, 2010).

Why does this matter? There is no other region in the world where one can imagine the restoration of a large carnivore species across such a sweeping continental landscape (figure 6.2). On this, the dean of wolf biologists, Dr. L. D. Mech, observed, "Ultimately then restoration to western Colorado could connect the entire North American wolf population from Minnesota, Wisconsin, and Michigan through Canada and Alaska, down the Rocky Mountains and into Mexico. It would be difficult to overestimate the biological and conservation value of this achievement."[17]

CONSEQUENCES OF RESTORATION

If wolves were restored to western Colorado, some people would be anxious about the consequences. Why? There is the persistent notion, based nearly exclusively on myths, that wolves are a threat to human safety, livestock, and big game hunting. Indeed, if we have learned anything from the last fifty years of wolf conservation it is that the species affirms the power of myths. But the real wolf is a mere shadow of what people conjure it to be. The following summary aims to set the record straight on the basics of the interactions between wolves and humans, big game, and livestock. For those interested, M. K. Phillips et al. (2010) offer a more detailed assessment.[18]

Wolves and Human Safety

Despite overwhelming evidence that wolves do not pose an acknowledgeable threat to humans, many find this fact hard to accept. Perhaps this is because wolves are large predators and in superficial respects are doglike; probably nearly everyone has had at least one, if not several, negative, nerve-rattling encounters with dogs. In reality, though, wolves represent an infinitesimal threat to human safety.

The Alaska Department of Fish and Game considered this issue extensively and documented only twenty-eight cases of humans being injured by wolf attacks since 1890, even though more than sixty thousand wolves exist in Alaska and Canada. In North America, from 1900 to 2000, no healthy wolf killed a human being.[19] However, it is worth noting that wolves may have killed a Canadian man in northern Saskatchewan in 2005, although some experts concluded that the actual culprit was a black bear. More clearly, in 2010 wolves killed a woman jogging alone in a very remote part of Alaska. The final report from the investigation of that tragedy concluded, "Jogging alone and other solo activities in remote parts of Alaska entail inherent risk, but an attack by wolves is not considered to be a risk commensurate with bear attacks, inclement weather or personal injury."[20] These two cases notwithstanding, M. E. McNay concluded that wolves represent very little threat to human safety.[21]

It is useful to note the absence of dangerous interactions between humans and wolves in Minnesota, Michigan, and Wisconsin even though approximately 22 million people live in those states alongside about four thousand wolves. It is useful to note that about 19 million visitor days have been recorded in the Superior National Forest—always a stronghold for wolves—without any wolf attacks. Additionally, millions of visitor days have been recorded without incident at national parks and wilderness areas in Canada, Alaska, and the northern Rocky Mountains. Consider camping in Yellowstone Park. From 1995 to 2014, there were nearly 2.6 million tent-camper overnight stays in the park's developed campgrounds and backcountry sites. During this period, no camper was injured by a wolf despite the fact that an average of 115 wolves were distributed in eleven packs throughout the park.

Nearly all wolves are shy and avoid humans. Encounters between the two are rare, and those that do occur typically have been a result of mistaken identities, defensive reactions, habituation, or a person getting between wolves and a dog they were attacking.

Lightning strikes, bee stings, car collisions with deer, inclement weather, or random shootings all represent a much greater threat to human safety than wolves. Nonetheless, wolves—like bears, cougars, and coyotes—are wild animals and should be respected as such. If wolves were ever restored to western Colorado, a big part of such respect would involve following simple guidelines (e.g., see www.wolf.org/wolf-info/basic-wolf-info/wolves-and-humans) for reducing the potential for conflicts between humans and wolves.[22]

Wolves and Big Game

When considering the wolf as a predator of big game, it is important to acknowledge that it is not a wanton killer able to exercise its will on a whim. Indeed, life for a wolf is a nearly constant struggle to survive.

On average, a wolf needs to consume seven to ten pounds of sustenance (meat, fat, minerals, vitamins) on a daily basis to maintain itself in good condition. Typically this is hard to do. Wolves often go for days with no food. Feast or famine is the wolf's modus operandi. Starvation is a common cause of death.

Not surprisingly, reliable studies have revealed that hunting by wolves is an endeavor overwhelmingly characterized by failure. Typically 80 percent or more of hunting attempts end unsuccessfully.[23] In the constant battle between predator and prey, wolves typically lose. They survive, despite long odds, because they refuse to give up. They are doggedly determined.

It is fair to conclude that a wolf is kept fed by its feet. They are willing and able and often must travel considerable distances to find prey that is somehow predisposed to predation. (Wolf pack territories commonly extend across hundreds of square miles or more.) Yet they do find such prey and by doing so, remove the young and old; the weak, sick, and infirm; and the unlucky. Wolves relentlessly shepherd their prey.

Hunting is a dangerous endeavor, and injuries are common. In a study of 225 skulls from wolves shot by the Alaska Department of Fish and Game and examined by Phillips, 25 percent revealed injuries (e.g., broken jaw, nose, skull) from blunt force trauma caused by escaping prey animals. Rolf Peterson has studied wolves on Isle Royale National Park since the early 1970s; nearly every wolf he has examined has shown similar traumatic injuries, many of which were caused by a moose in defense of its life.

It is important to acknowledge the wolf's difficulty in using just its teeth to kill a prey animal that is typically much larger than itself. It may be surprising given wolves' reliance on predation, but they are not particularly well designed physically for the task. D. R. MacNulty, D. R. Stahler, and D. W. Smith considered this lack of specialization and wrote, "In general, wolves lack a specialized skeleton for killing."[24] Its front-most teeth—the incisors and canines—are their only tools for grabbing and subduing prey, and these wear out with age.[25] Also, its skull is not mechanically configured to deliver a killing bite like other mammalian carnivores such as cats and hyenas. Specifically, a relatively long snout reduces the force of jaw-closing muscles that is extended at the canine tips during the bite.[26] In addition, the joint where the jaw connects to the skull does not allow the jaw to be locked or heavily stabilized when biting prey.[27] Wolves also lack retractile claws and supinating, muscular forelimbs, which precludes them from grabbing prey as other large carnivores (e.g., cougars and grizzly bears) do.

Despite the difficulties and dangers of hunting and the lack of specialized physical traits to overcome them, wolf predation still has the potential to sharply influence the population dynamics of prey species. Often this potential, even with no reliable evidence that it has been realized, prompts cries to reduce wolf numbers to allow game populations to increase in size. In this regard, Alaska has a long history of killing wolves specifically to address concern over ungulate populations, with mixed success.[28] Notably, few such conflicts have arisen in wolf range in the continental United States. In the western Great Lake states, for example, where white-tailed deer (*Odocoileus viginianus*) are the primary prey, wolf predation does not usually negatively affect hunter harvest.

In the Northern Rockies, where elk and deer are also important prey and wolf recovery has occurred in areas that support cougars (*Puma concolor*), bears (*Ursus* spp.), and coyotes (*Canis latrans*), wolf predation, as one of many mortality factors affecting elk and deer survival, may negatively affect hunter harvests.[29] On this possibility for western Montana, which is a reasonable analog for western Colorado, S. Hazen wrote, "Using the current data available wolves are not having a significant effect on elk harvest in Montana. On the other hand, they are shifting demand in the southwest region from areas in close proximity to the border of Yellowstone National Park to areas farther away."[30]

There remain outstanding opportunities to hunt elk and deer in Montana, Wyoming, and Idaho even though the region supports about 1,500 wolves. In Montana, for example, a state that supports about five hundred wolves, the majority of the elk management units are at or over the population objective established by the state game department; many of these units support wolves. In 2016 Montana took the unprecedented step of adding shoulder seasons to the regulations for nearly a third of the state's hunting districts (many of which support wolves) because of an overabundance of elk.

Despite claims to the contrary, wolves have not brought about a reduction in or an end to big game hunting in the northern Rocky Mountains.

What could Colorado big game hunters expect if several hundred wolves occupied the western half of the state? While it is notoriously difficult to reliably predict the specific effects of wolf predation on any localized elk or deer herd, it would be reasonable to expect some reduction in their numbers in specific areas where many native carnivores (e.g., wolves, bears, cougars, and coyotes) and humans vied for the same prey, winter weather was severe, or the herd was small and isolated. It is important to note that in a setting that supports many native carnivores, adding one more does not necessarily mean a direct increase in predation pressure on local ungulates. Recent meta-analyses of more than two thousand elk calves across the northwestern United States reveal compensatory mortality between predator species in calf survival.[31]

For all these factors, and as is the case in the Northern Rockies, it is most reasonable to expect that the persistently large numbers of deer and elk in Colorado could support gray wolves and recreational hunters.

Despite being a concern to some hunters, wolf predation has the potential to generate ecological benefits. By tending to kill prey that are somehow predisposed to predation, wolves help to cleanse big game herds of the maladies that inevitably affect them.[32] Take old age, for example. By differentially selecting older prey, many of which are past their reproductive prime, wolf predation can help minimize competition within members of a game herd for nutritious forage. Chronic wasting disease (CWD), a fatal neurological disorder that has no cure, can kill large numbers of deer and elk and curb enthusiasm among hunters. For obvious reasons, chronic wasting disease is a great concern to big game managers and hunters. That the disease is becoming more widespread geographically—and now includes Colorado—and its prevalence is increasing among ungulate populations adds to everyone's angst.

The presence of the disease has precipitated draconian control efforts. For example, after finding chronic wasting disease in white-tailed deer in 2002, the Wisconsin Department of Natural Resources killed thousands of deer through 2006 and spent $27 million to control the disease. The report from a chronic wasting disease workshop identified predators (wolves and coyotes) as one additional element that could limit the disease. The absence of predators may allow sick animals a longer period in which to spread chronic wasting disease. M. A.

Wild et al. concluded "that as CWD distribution and wolf range overlap in the future, wolf predation may suppress disease emergence or limit prevalence."[33] Notably, it is live infected elk, deer, and moose (*Alces alces*) that replicate and spread the malformed protein responsible for the disease; dead animals do not.

Because wolves are coursing predators that typically chase prey over some distance, they would be especially adept at detecting and killing animals in poor health from chronic wasting disease. M. A. Wild et al. concluded "that as CWD distribution and wolf range overlap in the future, wolf predation may suppress disease emergence or limit prevalence."[34] Studies suggest that wolf predation of overcrowded elk in Rocky Mountain National Park, where an estimated 10 to 13 percent of the elk are infected with chronic wasting disease, could eliminate or greatly reduce the incidence of the disease.[35]

It has been said that wolves are ecological engineers because of predatory habits that can cause a ripple of effects—a trophic cascade—that give shape and functionality to an ecosystem that would not exist otherwise. How? The classic view of a trophic cascade is one in which predators reduce the density of their herbivore prey with repercussions on plant production and important consequences for many species. How does it work? Simply put, more wolves can mean fewer prey with altered behavior, which can lead to more plant biomass and, in turn, greater biological diversity. It has been known for decades that a reduction in prey numbers due to wolves can facilitate a release of vegetation that the prey feed on.[36] This was the essence of Leopold's seminal essay "Thinking Like a Mountain":

> Since then I have lived to see state after state extirpate its wolves. I have watched the face of many a newly wolfless mountain, and seen the south-facing slopes wrinkle with a maze of many new deer trails. I have seen every edible bush and seedling browsed, first to anemic desuetude, and then to death. I have seen every edible tree defoliated to the height of a saddle-horn. Such a mountain looks as if someone had given God new pruning shears, and forbidden Him all other activities. In the end the starved bones of the hoped-for deer herd, dead of its own too-much, bleach with the bones of the dead sage, or molder under the high-lined junipers. I suspect just as a deer herd lives in mortal fear of its wolves, so does a mountain live in fear of its deer.[37]

While the existence of trophic cascades is well documented,[38] identifying the presence and architecture of any specific one can be exceedingly difficult and typically requires assessing the importance of predation and herbivory on the population dynamics of many interacting species. As R. O. Peterson et al.

pointed out, "This, in turn, requires data that are difficult to collect and infer-
ences about cause-and-effect that are difficult to make and easy to get wrong."[39]

In the well-studied wolf-elk system in the northern portion of Yellowstone,
it has been postulated that the reduction in elk numbers and changes in their
behavior due to wolf predation have led to renewed growth in willow and aspen,
which has led to an increase in beavers, songbirds, and other species, as well as
changes in waterways. In a summary of twenty-four studies in Yellowstone in-
volving wolves, elk, and plant species such as aspen, cottonwoods, and willows,
Beschta and Ripple wrote:

> The multi-decadal absence of wolves allowed native ungulates, principally elk,
> to assume a dominant role in altering the composition, structure, and func-
> tion of riparian plant communities ... in which native species biodiversity
> and ecosystem services decline. ... [R]esearch results following wolf reintro-
> duction are generally supportive of the concept that the contemporary large
> carnivore guild is increasingly, via a trophic cascade, mediating the effects of
> elk herbivory on riparian plant communities. The reduction in elk herbivory
> has thus been helping to recover and sustain riparian plant communities in
> northern Yellowstone, thereby improving important food-web [sic] and habi-
> tat support for numerous terrestrial and aquatic organisms.[40]

The potential for wolf predation to cause or contribute to a trophic cascade
is a function of wolf density, distribution, and persistence. To serve as ecological engineers, wolves must be common enough for a long enough period of
time to sufficiently change the demographics and behavior of prey to cause
the changes in patterns of herbivory necessary for a trophic cascade. As L. D.
Mech observed, this probably is why the trophic cascades attributed to wolves
come from studies conducted in national parks, areas where wolf densities can
achieve levels necessary for inducing trophic cascades. In a cautionary warning
about overextending understanding of wolf ecology, Mech concluded, "Thus
to whatever extent the findings [of wolf-induced trophic cascades] are valid,
they apply to National Parks and not necessarily elsewhere ... To the extent
that wolves in National Parks do influence lower trophic levels, for them to do
so outside of parks, their population would have to reach natural densities for
long periods. Because wolf populations will almost always be managed outside
of National Parks ... their densities will probably never consistently reach the
densities of wolves in National Parks."[41]

Because of insufficient density of wolves across much of their occupied
range and myriad other factors, trophic cascades do not follow wolves wherever

they go. It is nonetheless important to note that the conclusions reached by researchers in Yellowstone and Isle Royale National Parks are consistent with those reached by researchers working in northern Wisconsin as well as Banff and Olympic National Parks.[42] It is not unreasonable to expect that wolves could have a similar effect on the ecology of Rocky Mountain National Park, an area the supports an elk population in need of chronic and aggressive management to minimize the continued degradation of aspen and willow communities and consequent biodiversity.

When considering the ecological consequences of wolf restoration, a few words about wolf-coyote interactions are in order. Wolves regularly kill coyotes, and this sometimes can precipitate a population reduction. This is not part of a trophic cascade per se, since coyotes are not an important prey item even though wolves will sometimes consume them. (The word *trophic* specifically relates to feeding and nutrition.) Nonetheless, killing coyotes is another way that wolves can engineer ecosystem changes. With fewer coyotes, predation pressure on the medium- and small-sized mammals on which they subsist is reduced. This has the potential to alter the trophic system by bringing about increases in the distribution and abundance of small herbivores like rodents and rabbits with concomitant benefits to predators, from red foxes and badgers to raptors. But as with trophic cascades, the magnitude of the consequence of wolves killing coyotes depends on wolf population density and persistence. The resilience and resourcefulness of coyotes is also worth mentioning; their populations are notoriously difficult to control. Even in Yellowstone National Park, where shortly after the wolf's return the species had caused a noticeable reduction in the number of coyote packs, that number has returned to pre-wolf levels.[43]

Wolf predation can be a powerful ecological force capable of affecting the interactions of numerous animals and plants and the consequent structure and function of ecosystems. Thus, the preservation or restoration of gray wolves can be important actions for helping to maintain the diversity and resiliency of wildland ecosystems. From a purely biological diversity perspective, which is increasingly important as the sixth great extinction crisis to confront the planet tightens its hold, a laudable goal of conservation could be to establish ecologically effective populations of wolves wherever possible.[44] On this, Beschta and Ripple wrote, "Results from Yellowstone, other areas in western North America, and around the world increasingly point to a need for recovering ecologically effective populations of large predators to help recover or maintain biodiversity in ungulate populated landscapes."[45] Other important scientific investigations favorably view large carnivores, like wolves, as essential to the integrity of ecosystems.[46]

While the potential for wolves to promote the ecological health of landscapes favors their return to Colorado, any ecosystem response to the wolf's return would take decades to unfold and be greatly influenced by the number of wolves involved and their persistence in specific areas.

Wolves and Livestock

Conflicts between wolves and livestock and their resolution are typically controversial. Even though wolf depredations are relatively uncommon—it is the atypical wolf that kills livestock—the public expects immediate and certain action to resolve problems when they do arise, especially those that occur on private land. For example, as the wolf population in the Northern Rockies increased over the last twenty-nine years, the number of wolves killed to resolve conflicts with livestock increased from 4 animals in 1987 to 168 animals in 2015.[47]

Such frequent control, however, belies the actual magnitude of the wolf-livestock problem. Over the last twenty-nine years in the Northern Rockies, the average annual number of confirmed livestock losses to wolves included 78 cattle and 156 sheep.[48] In response, eighty-four wolves on average were killed. To put the magnitude of these livestock losses in perspective, using 2010 as a typical year, cattle producers in Montana, Wyoming, and Idaho reported losses of 198,800 cattle to non-predator causes like digestive problems, respiratory problems, metabolic problems, mastitis, lameness or injury, and diseases.[49] In other words, average wolf-caused cattle losses amounted to 0.03 percent of the cattle lost to other causes in 2010.

Or take 2014, another typical year for wolf-livestock interactions in the Northern Rockies.[50] During that year, Montana, Idaho, and Wyoming collectively supported nearly 6.9 million cattle and sheep and 1,657 wolves. Confirmed wolf depredations for the year included 136 cattle and 114 sheep, or a minuscule fraction of the total populations (cattle [0.0023 percent] and sheep [0.0208 percent]) (table 6.1). In response, 161 wolves were killed, or about 10 percent of the population. Additionally, ranchers were paid nearly $275,000 in compensation for their losses.

It is important to acknowledge that more livestock are lost to wolves than are verified.[51] To promote fairness, livestock-compensation programs should include an upward adjustment if payments are solely based on confirmed wolf-killed cattle.

Table 6.1. Cattle and sheep in Montana, Wyoming, and Idaho in 2014 and confirmed depredations by wolves.

Year 2014	Cattle	Sheep
Montana	2,550,000	220,000
Idaho	2,240,000	260,000
Wyoming	1,270,000	335,000
Total population	6,060,000	815,000
Total confirmed wolf depredations	136	114

A proper assessment of the interaction between wolves and livestock goes beyond a simple accounting of livestock deaths. For example, a persistent concern exists in the Northern Rockies that wolves can affect the weight gain of domestic calves because wolves can routinely encounter and stress, but not kill, domestic livestock.[52] However, a reliable study of this issue for eighteen ranches in Montana found no evidence that wolf packs with territories that overlapped them had any detrimental effects on calf weight.[53] But just as importantly, they found that for ranches that experienced a confirmed depredation by wolves, the average calf weight declined by 3.5 percent (about twenty-two pounds) across the herd, possibly due to inefficient foraging behavior or stress to mother cows. (They also concluded that ranch-specific husbandry and climatological factors were much more important for determining calf weight than wolves.) J. P. Ramler et al. concluded, "Although this may not seem like a large loss, it is not economically insignificant. Given that the average compensation for a wolf depredation is $900 per cow, the uncompensated estimated indirect loss for the average ranch was approximately 7.5 times the compensated loss."[54] As with unconfirmed livestock losses by wolves, compensation payments should be adjusted upward to account for a reduction in weight gain of calves when depredations are confirmed.

It has always been a challenge for ranchers to reduce the death of livestock (from a variety of causes) and ensure sufficient weight gain before animals are slaughtered for profit. But for the vast majority, wolves do not influence that challenge.

Because of the infrequent nature of wolf depredations, the impact from those that do occur is too small to be of consequence to the economics of the livestock industry. Nonetheless, if not addressed quickly, wolf depredations and related problems can cause significant problems for individual producers and create great animosity toward wolf recovery.

Many livestock producers have cooperated with recovery because they believe that wolf-induced problems will be resolved quickly and equitably.

Monetary compensation for livestock losses has proven useful in this regard and for minimizing animosity toward wolves. Lethal control of wolves has also proven useful in attenuating opposition to wolf recovery, even though legalized killing of carnivores to prevent livestock loss does not have a strong record of effectiveness and in some cases can have a counterproductive effect.[55]

Besides compensation and killing wolves, other tools and approaches can be useful for preventing and minimizing encounters between wolves and livestock, including releasing older and larger calves to pasture (small calves are most vulnerable to wolves), keeping vulnerable calves in lighted yards or close to human buildings, altering grazing regimes, and deploying ranger riders, guard dogs, sound devices, and fladry (flagging). A number of conservation organizations are willing to provide assistance to promote coexistence between livestock and wolves.

THE FUTURE

Gray wolf restoration remains a controversial and divisive issue. Consequently, the species continues to be restricted to about 15 percent of its historical range despite an abundance of suitable but unoccupied habitat, most notably in western Colorado. The best conservation science instructs that the widespread absence of this important species creates a problem of simplification for nature. The big, bold idea of restoring the wolf remains a viable solution to this problem. In one fell swoop, wolf restoration could help to revitalize biologically compromised landscapes and move the world forward by reminding humanity of the wondrous diversity of life on earth and our undeniable capacity to restore it.

The legal backdrop that strongly favors restoration and the knowledge gained from previous reintroduction projects affirm that western Colorado is an ideal area to restore the species to its rightful place as an essential and fascinating part of our nation's ecological past and future.

To advance this future, the Rocky Mountain Wolf Project (RMWP) (figure 6.3) was launched in March 2016 to improve public understanding of gray wolf behavior, ecology, and restoration options of relevance to western Colorado. The RMWP intends to

- Disseminate science-based information about wolves and dispel existing myths.
- Engage Coloradans about the reality of coexisting with wolves, including ways to mitigate the effects on hunters, ranchers, and others concerned about wolves.
- Cultivate enthusiasm among Coloradans about returning wolves to the western half of the state.

ROCKY MOUNTAIN WOLF PROJECT

RESTORING COLORADO'S NATURAL BALANCE

The Rocky Mountain Wolf Project (www.rockymountainwolfproject.org) is an outreach effort based on the belief that education advances the restoration of the gray wolf to western Colorado.

The RMWP recognizes that wolf restoration is framed by several key elements:

- Wolves were native to Colorado, having once existed across the state, but were rendered extinct by the 1940s.
- Wolves were, and could be again, an integral part of the ecology of western Colorado, helping to restore the state's natural balance.
- Successful wolf projects in places like Yellowstone National Park demonstrate that a gradual reintroduction of wolves can be done safely, effectively, and humanely and with great certainty lead to the restoration of a viable population.
- Reliable science has shown that wolves do not represent a threat to humans or a burden to the vast majority of ranchers.
- Because natural recolonization is unlikely, reintroducing a small number of wolves to western Colorado is the only certain way to reestablish a viable population that can be managed in a manner respectful of the needs and concerns of Coloradans.

The RMWP is supported by a community of individuals and organizations—from wildlife biologists to landowners to conservationists—dedicated to returning the wolf to western Colorado. The organization is based on the belief that wolf restoration advanced through education encourages thoughtful public conversations with all stakeholders, including ranchers and sportsmen.

The work of the RMWP—especially if successful at reestablishing the wolf in western Colorado—could help fix a narrative that is vastly different from the one that has defined our activities since the first Homo sapiens huddled around fires and swapped stories hundreds of thousands of years ago. What would this new narrative be? A restorative and affirming relationship with nature rather than an exploitative and destructive one is possible.

From the Flat Tops Wilderness and surrounding parts of the White River and Routt National Forests in northwestern Colorado to Rocky Mountain National Park and adjacent Roosevelt National Forest on the east side, to the Weminuche Wilderness and surrounding parts of the San Juan National Forest in the southwestern part of the state, and everything in between—including the Grand Mesa, Uncompahgre, and Gunnison National Forests—the western half of Colorado is a mother lode of restoration opportunity for the wolf. If the US Fish and Wildlife Service or Colorado Parks and Wildlife ever set their mind to conducting reintroductions in western Colorado, restoration of a self-sustaining population of wolves would be as certain as water running off a duck's back.

Like few other species, the gray wolf elicits strong emotions and serves as an ideal lens for examining why humanity struggles with, dominates, and destroys wild places and wild things at an ever-increasing rate and at its own peril. Restoring wolves, the terrestrial carnivore most persecuted by humans, has a transcendent power to make clear that we can choose to have a beneficial and accommodating relationship with Mother Earth rather than a destructive and exploitative one.

With the sixth great extinction ripping creation apart at the seams, it is important to note that a Colorado wolf project would illustrate that restoration is an alternative to extinction. As this crisis tightens its grip on the planet, thus compromising all that is important, such an illustration is sorely needed and long overdue. Maybe, just maybe, a Colorado wolf restoration project would help to catalyze the foundational work to save creation.

If you are a person of faith, any work to save creation should be motivational. Loving the Creator should be synonymous with loving the creation. Or conversely, if you're a secular humanist who above all else believes in facts, logic, and empiricism, then the best science tells us that healthy, diverse landscapes that support more rather than less biological diversity are essential to humanity's well-being. Regardless of your moral compass, everyone should support efforts to arrest the extinction crisis. Wolf restoration is one such effort.

With sufficient time and engagement, a Colorado wolf project could help bring about a society that places a premium value on life. Such a society could give rise to a human nature that follows suit. Such a human nature is profoundly important since it would represent a bending of the sordid history of Homo sapiens with the rest of the natural world across the long sweep of time. Without such a bend, future prospects for most life remains bleak.

As reasoned by Durward Allen, an early pioneer in wildlife conservation and the founder of the seminal Isle Royale wolf-moose project: "Impartial sympathy toward all creatures, regardless of their diet, is an attitude of the cultivated mind. It is a measure of a man's civilization. If ever we are to achieve a reasonable concord with the earth on which we live, it will be by our willingness to recognize and tolerate . . . the biological forces and relationships . . . in the living things about us."[56]

The path for restoring the gray wolf to western Colorado is straightforward and quickly navigated. A wolf population there would serve as the last piece of a forty-year puzzle to reestablish the species from the High Arctic to Mexico. Nowhere else in the world does such an opportunity exist to restore an iconic, unfairly maligned animal across such an inspiring and continental landscape. For those who celebrate the importance of wild and self-willed nature, it is an opportunity that must be seized (figure 6.4). Once accomplished, a Colorado wolf restoration project would help to illuminate a new relationship with nature, one that is restorative and accommodating and advances peace, prosperity, and justice for all life.

NOTES

1. B. Lopez, *Of Wolves and Men* (New York: Scribner Classic, 1978), 180–81.

2. M. J. Robinson, *Predatory Bureaucracy: The Extermination of Wolves and the Transformation of the West* (Boulder: University Press of Colorado, 2005).

3. C.R.S.A. 33-2-102.

4. Endangered and Threatened Wildlife and Plants; Removing the Gray Wolf (*Canis lupus*) from the List of Endangered and Threatened Wildlife and Maintaining Protections for the Mexican Wolf (*Canis lupus baileyi*) by Listing It as Endangered, 78 Fed. Reg. 35664-719 (2013).

5. ESA of 1973, Sec. 3.

6. ESA of 1973, Sec. 2.

7. ESA of 1973, Sec. 3.

8. A. Leopold, *A Sand County Almanac* (New York: Random House, 1966), 458.

9. J. A. Leonard, C. Vila, and R. K. Wayne, "Legacy Lost: Genetic Variability and Population Size of Extirpated US Grey Wolves (*Canis lupus*)," *Molecular Ecology* 14 (2005): 9–17.

10. cpw.state.co.us/Documents/Hunting/BigGame/Statistics/Elk/ and cpw .state.co.us/Documents/Hunting/BigGame/Statistics/Deer/.

11. T. K. Fuller, *Population Dynamics of Wolves in North-Central Minnesota*, Wildlife Monographs No. 105 (Bethesda, MD: The Wildlife Society, 1989).

12. L. E. Bennett, *Colorado Gray Wolf Recovery: A Biological Feasibility Study*, Final Report (Laramie: US Fish and Wildlife Service and University of Wyoming Fish and Wildlife Cooperative Research Unit, 1994).

13. M. K. Phillips, N. Fascione, P. Miller, and O. Byers, *Wolves in the Southern Rockies: A Population and Habitat Viability Assessment* (Apple Valley, MN: IUCN Conservation Breeding Specialist Group, 2000); Southern Rockies Ecosystem Project, *Summary of the Base Data and Landscape Variables for Wolf Habitat Suitability on the Vermejo Park Ranch and Surrounding Areas* (Bozeman, MT: Turner Endangered Species Fund, 2000); C. M. Carroll, K. Phillips, N. H. Schumaker, and D. W. Smith, "Impacts of Landscape Change on Wolf Restoration Success: Planning a Reintroduction Program Based on Static and Dynamic Spatial Models," *Conservation Biology* 17 (2003): 536–48.

14. A. D. Bright and M. J. Manfredo. "A Conceptual Model of Attitudes toward Natural Resource Issues: A Case Study of Wolf Reintroduction," *Human Dimensions in Wildlife* 1 (1996): 1–21.

15. R. Meadow, R. P. Reading, M. Phillips, and M. Mehringer, "The Influence of Persuasive Arguments on Public Attitudes toward a Proposed Wolf Restoration in the Southern Rockies," *Wildlife Society Bulletin* 33 (2005): 154–63 and Turner Endangered Species Fund, unpublished data.

16. C. Carroll, M. K. Phillips, N. H. Schumaker, and D. W. Smith, "Impacts of Landscape Change on Wolf Restoration Success: Planning a Reintroduction Program Based on Static and Dynamic Spatial Models," *Conservation Biology* 17 (2003): 536–48.

17. L. D. Mech, personal communication with Mike Phillips.

18. M. K. Phillips, B. Miller, K. Kunkel, P. C. Paquet, W. W. Martin, and D. W. Smith, "Potential for and Implications of Wolf Restoration in the Southern Rockies," in *Awakening Spirits: Wolves in the Southern Rockies*, ed. R. P. Reading, B. Miller, A. L. Masching, R. Edward, and M. K. Phillips (Golden, CO: Fulcrum, 2010), 197–219.

19. M. E. McNay, *A Case History of Wolf-Human Encounters in Alaska and Canada*, Wildlife Technical Bulletin No. 13 (Anchorage: Alaska Department of Fish and Game, 2002).

20. Lem Butler, Bruce Dale, Kimberlee Beckmen, and Sean Farley, "Findings Related to the March 2010 Fatal Wolf Attack near Chignik Lake, Alaska," Wildlife Special Publication, ADF&G/DWC/WSP-2011-2 (Palmer, AK: Alaska Department of Fish and Game, Division of Wildlife Conservation, December 2011), 19.

21. McNay, *Case History*.

22. International Wolf Center, "Wolves and Humans," August 2017.

23. L. D. Mech, D. W. Smith, and D. R. MacNulty, *Wolves on the Hunt: The Behavior of Wolves Hunting Wild Prey* (Chicago: University of Chicago Press, 2015).

24. D. R. MacNulty, D. R. Stahler, and D. W. Smith. "Understanding the Limits to Wolf Hunting Ability," *Yellowstone Science* 24 (2016): 35.

25. P. S. Gipson, B. B. Ballard, R. M. Nowak, and L. D. Mech, "Accuracy and Precision of Estimating Age of Gray Wolves by Tooth Wear," *Journal of Wildlife Management* 64 (2000): 752–58.

26. X. Wang and R. H. Tedford, *Dogs: Their Fossil Relatives and Evolutionary History* (New York: Columbia University Press, 2008).

27. R. O. Peterson and P. Ciucci, "The Wolf as a Carnivore," in *Wolf: Behavior, Biology, and Conservation*, ed. L. D. Mech and L. Boitani, (Chicago: University of Chicago Press, 2003), 104–30.

28. National Research Council, *Wolves, Bears, and Their Prey in Alaska: Biological and Social Challenges in Wildlife Management* (Washington, DC: National Academy Press, 1997).

29. K. E. Kunkel and D. L. Pletscher, "Species-Specific Population Dynamics of Cervids in a Multipredator Ecosystem," *Journal of Wildlife Management* 63 (1999): 1082–93.

30. S. Hazen, "The Impact of Wolves on Elk Hunting in Montana" (master's thesis, Montana State University, Bozeman, 2012), 78.

31. K. A. Griffin, et al., "Neonatal Mortality of Elk Driven by Climate, Predator Phenology, and Predator Community Composition," *Journal of Animal Ecology* 80, no. 6 (November 2011): 1246–57.

32. L. D. Mech and R. O. Peterson, "Wolf-Prey Relations," in *Wolves: Ecology, Behavior, and Conservation*, ed. L. D. Mech and L. Boitani (Chicago: University of Chicago Press, 2003), 131–60.

33. M. A. Wild, N. T. Hobbs, M. S. Graham, and M. W. Miller, "The Role of Predation in Disease Control: A Comparison of Selective and Non-Selective Removal of Prion Diseases in Deer," *Journal of Wildlife Diseases* 47 (2011): 86.

34. Ibid., 78.

35. R. J. Monello, J. G. Powers, N. T. Hobbs, T. R. Spraker, K. I. O'Rourke, and M. A. Wild, "Efficacy of Antemortem Rectal Biopsies to Diagnose and Estimate Prevalence of Chronic Wasting Disease in Free-Ranging Cow Elk (*Cervus elaphus nelsoni*)," *Journal of Wildlife Diseases* 49 (2013): 270–78 and T. Hobbs and N. Thompson, *A Model Analysis of Effects of Wolf Predation on Prevalence of Chronic Wasting Disease in Elk Populations of Rocky Mountain National Park* (Estes Park, CO: National Park Service, 2006).

36. A. Leopold, A. K. Sowls, and D. L. Spencer, "A Survey of Over-Populated Deer Ranges in the United States," *Journal of Wildlife Management* 11 (1947): 162–83.

37. A. Leopold, "Thinking Like a Mountain," in *A Sand County Almanac* (New York: Random House, 1966), 131–32.

38. R. L. Beschta and W. J. Ripple, "Large Predators and Trophic Cascades in Terrestrial Ecosystems of the Western United States," *Biological Conservation* 142 (2009): 2401–14 and J. Terborgh and J. A. Estes, *Trophic Cascades: Predators, Prey, and Changing Dynamics of Nature* (Washington, DC: Island Press, 2010).

39. R. O. Peterson, J. A. Vucetich, J. M. Bump, and D. W. Smith, "Trophic Cascades in a Multicausal World: Isle Royale and Yellowstone," *Annual Review of Ecology, Evolution, and Systematics* 45 (2014): 339.

40. R. L. Beschta and W. J. Ripple, "Riparian Vegetation Recovery in Yellowstone: The First Two Decades after Wolf Reintroduction," *Biological Conservation* 198 (2016): 101.

41. L. D. Mech, "Is Science in Danger of Sanctifying the Wolf?," *Biological Conservation* 150 (2012): 147.

42. For Yellowstone and Isle Royale National Parks, see Beschta and Ripple, "Riparian Vegetation Recovery" and Peterson et al., "Trophic Cascades." For northern Wisconsin, see R. Callan, "Are Wolves in Wisconsin Affecting the Biodiversity of Understory Plant Communities via a Trophic Cascade?" (PhD diss., University of Georgia, 2010). For Banff, see M. Hebblewhite, C. A. White, C. G. Nietvelt, J. A. McKenzie, T. E. Hurd, J. M. Fryxell, S. E. Bayley, and P. C. Paquet, "Human Activity Mediates a Trophic Cascade Caused by Wolves," *Ecology* 86 (2005): 2135–44. And for Olympic National Park, see R. L. Beschta and W. J. Ripple, "Wolves, Trophic Cascades, and Rivers in Western Olympic National Park," *Ecohydrology* 1 (2008): 118–30.

43. M. Hebblewhite and D. W. Smith, "Wolf Community Ecology: Ecosystem Effects of Recovering Wolves in Banff and Yellowstone National Park," in *The World of Wolves: New Perspectives on Ecology, Behaviour, and Management*, ed. M. L. Musiani, L. Boitani, and P. Paquet (Calgary: University of Calgary Press, 2010), 69–120.

44. E. Kolbert, *The Sixth Extinction: An Unnatural History* (New York: Henry Holt, 2014) and M. E. Soule, J. A. Estes, J. Berger, and C. Martinez del Rios, "Ecological Effectiveness: Conservation Goals for Interactive Species," *Conservation Biology* 17 (2003): 1238–50.

45. Beschta and Ripple, "Riparian Vegetation Recovery," 101.

46. J. A. Estes, J. Terborgh, J. S. Brashares, M. E. Power, J. Berger, W. J. Bond, S. R. Carpenter, T. E. Essington, R. D. Holt, J.B.C. Jackson, R. J. Marquis, L. Oksanen, R. T. Paine, E. K. Pikitch, W. J. Ripple, S. A. Sandin, M. Scheffer, T. W. Schoener, J. B. Shurin, A.R.E. Sinclair, M. E. Soule, R. Virtanen, and D. A. Wardle, "Trophic Downgrading of Planet Earth," *Science* 333 (2011): 301–6 and W. J. Ripple, J. A. Estes, R. L. Beschta, C. C. Wilmers, E. G. Ritchie, M. Hebblewhite, J. Berger, B. Elmhagen, M. Letnic, M. P. Nelson, O. J. Schmitz, D. W. Smith, A. D. Wallach, and A. J. Wirsing, "Status and Ecological Effects of the World's Largest Carnivores," *Science* 343 (2014): 1–11.

47. US Fish and Wildlife Service (FWS), *Northern Rocky Mountain Wolf Recovery Program 2014 Interagency Annual Report* (Denver: US Fish and Wildlife Service, 2015).

48. Ibid.

49. National Agricultural Statistics Service, "Cattle Death Loss" (Washington, DC: Agricultural Statistics Board, US Department of Agriculture, 2011), usda.mannlib. cornell.edu/usda/current/CattDeath/CattDeath-05-12-2011.pdf.

50. FWS, *Interagency Annual Report.*

51. S. H. Fritts, *Wolf Depredation on Livestock in Minnesota*, Resource Publication No. 145 (Washington, DC: US Fish and Wildlife Service, 1982); E. E. Bangs, J. Fontaine, M. Jiminez, T. Meier, C. Niemeyer, D. W. Smith, K. Murphy, D. Gurnsey, L. Handegard, M. Collinge, R. Krischke, J. Shivik, C. Mack, I. Babcock, V. Asher, and D. Domenici, "Grey Wolf Restoration in the Northwestern United States," *Endangered Species Update* 18 (2001): 147–52; J. K. Oakleaf, C. Mack, and D. L. Murray, "Effects of Wolves on Livestock Calf Survival and Movements in Central Idaho," *Journal of Wildlife Management* 67 (2003): 299–306; E. H. Bradley and D. H. Pletscher, "Assessing Factors Related to Wolf Depredation of Cattle in Fenced Pastures in Montana and Idaho," *Wildlife Society Bulletin* 33 (2005): 1256–65; and T. B. Muhl and M. Musiani, "Livestock Depredation by Wolves and the Ranching Economy in the Northwestern US," *Ecological Economics* 68 (2009): 2439–50.

52. C. A. Sime, E. Bangs, E. Bradley, J. E. Steuber, K. Glazier, P. J. Hoover, V. Asher, K. Laudon, M. Ross, and J. Trapp, "Gray Wolves and Livestock in Montana: A Recent History of Damage Management," in *Proceedings of the Twelfth Wildlife Damage Management Conference*, ed. D. L. Nolte, W. M. Arjo, and D. H. Stalman (Corpus Christi, TX, 2007): 16–35.

53. J. P. Ramler, M. Hebblewhite, D. Kellenberg, and C. Sime, "Crying Wolf? A Spatial Analysis of Wolf Location and Depredations on Calf Weight." *American Journal of Agricultural Economics* 96 (2014): 631–56.

54. Ibid., 20.

55. A. Treves, M. Krofel, and J. McManus, "Predator Control Should Not Be a Shot in the Dark," *Frontiers in Ecology and the Environment* 14 (2016): 380–88 and R. B. Wielgus and K. A. Peebles, "Effects of Wolf Mortality on Livestock Depredations," *PLOS One* 9 (2014): e113505.

56. D. Allen, *Our Wildlife Legacy* (New York: Funk and Wagnalls, 1954), 256–57.

BIBLIOGRAPHY

Allen, D. *Our Wildlife Legacy*. New York: Funk and Wagnalls, 1954.

Bangs, E. E., J. Fontaine, M. Jiminez, T. Meier, C. Niemeyer, D. W. Smith, K. Murphy, D. Gurnsey, L. Handegard, M. Collinge, R. Krischke, J. Shivik, C. Mack, I. Babcock, V. Asher, and D. Domenici. "Grey Wolf Restoration in the Northwestern United States." *Endangered Species Update* 18 (2001): 147–52.

Bennett, L. E. *Colorado Gray Wolf Recovery: A Biological Feasibility Study*. Final Report. Laramie: US Fish and Wildlife Service and University of Wyoming Fish and Wildlife Cooperative Research Unit, 1994.

Beschta, R. L., and W. J. Ripple. "Wolves, Trophic Cascades, and Rivers in Western Olympic National Park." *Ecohydrology* 1 (2008): 118–30.

Beschta, R. L., and W. J. Ripple. "Large Predators and Trophic Cascades in Terrestrial Ecosystems of the Western United States." *Biological Conservation* 142 (2009): 2401–14.

Beschta, R. L., and W. J. Ripple. "Riparian Vegetation Recovery in Yellowstone: The First Two Decades after Wolf Reintroduction." *Biological Conservation* 198 (2016): 93–103.

Bradley, E. H., and D. H. Pletscher. "Assessing Factors Related to Wolf Depredation of Cattle in Fenced Pastures in Montana and Idaho." *Wildlife Society Bulletin* 33 (2005): 1256–65.

Bright, A. D., and M. J. Manfredo. "A Conceptual Model of Attitudes toward Natural Resource Issues: A Case Study of Wolf Reintroduction." *Human Dimensions in Wildlife* 1 (1996): 1–21.

Butler, Lem, Bruce Dale, Kimberlee Beckmen, and Sean Farley. "Findings Related to the March 2010 Fatal Wolf Attack near Chignik Lake, Alaska." Wildlife Special Publication, ADF&G/DWC/WSP-2011-2. Palmer, AK: Alaska Department of Fish and Game, Division of Wildlife Conservation, December 2011.

Callan, R. "Are Wolves in Wisconsin Affecting the Biodiversity of Understory Plant Communities via a Trophic Cascade?" PhD diss., University of Georgia, 2010.

Carroll, C., M. K. Phillips, N. H. Schumaker, and D. W. Smith. "Impacts of Landscape Change on Wolf Restoration Success: Planning a Reintroduction Program Based on Static and Dynamic Spatial Models." *Conservation Biology* 17 (2003): 536–48.

Estes, J. A., J. Terborgh, J. S. Brashares, M. E. Power, J. Berger, W. J. Bond, S. R. Carpenter, T. E. Essington, R. D. Holt, J.B.C. Jackson, R. J. Marquis, L. Oksanen, R. T. Paine, E. K. Pikitch, W. J. Ripple, S. A. Sandin, M. Scheffer, T. W. Schoener, J. B. Shurin, A.R.E. Sinclair, M. E. Soule, R. Virtanen, and D. A. Wardle. "Trophic Downgrading of Planet Earth." *Science* 333 (2011): 301–6.

Fritts, S. H. *Wolf Depredation on Livestock in Minnesota*. Resource Publication No. 145. Washington, DC: US Fish and Wildlife Service, 1982.

Fuller, T. K. *Population Dynamics of Wolves in North-Central Minnesota*. Wildlife Monographs No. 105. Bethesda, MD: The Wildlife Society, 1989.

Gipson, P. S., B. B. Ballard, R. M. Nowak, and L. D. Mech. "Accuracy and Precision of Estimating Age of Gray Wolves by Tooth Wear." *Journal of Wildlife Management* 64 (2000): 752–58.

Griffin, K. A., et al. "Neonatal Mortality of Elk Driven by Climate, Predator Phenology, and Predator Community Composition." *Journal of Animal Ecology* 80, no. 6 (November 2011): 1246–57.

Hazen, S. "The Impact of Wolves on Elk Hunting in Montana." Master's thesis, Montana State University, 2012.

Hebblewhite, M., and D. W. Smith. "Wolf Community Ecology: Ecosystem Effects of Recovering Wolves in Banff and Yellowstone National Park." In *The World of Wolves: New Perspectives on Ecology, Behaviour, and Management*, ed. M. L. Musiani, L. Boitani, and P. Paquet, 69–120. Calgary: University of Calgary Press, 2010.

Hebblewhite, M., C. A., White, C. G. Nietvelt, J. A. McKenzie, T. E. Hurd, J. M. Fryxell, S. E. Bayley, and P. C. Paquet. "Human Activity Mediates a Trophic Cascade Caused by Wolves." *Ecology* 86 (2005): 2135–44.

Hobbs, T., and N. Thompson. *A Model Analysis of Effects of Wolf Predation on Prevalence of Chronic Wasting Disease in Elk Populations of Rocky Mountain National Park*. Estes Park, CO: National Park Service, 2006.

Kolbert, E. *The Sixth Extinction: An Unnatural History*. New York: Henry Holt, 2014.

Kunkel, K. E., and D. L. Pletscher. "Species-Specific Population Dynamics of Cervids in a Multipredator Ecosystem." *Journal of Wildlife Management* 63 (1999): 1082–93.

Leonard, J. A., C. Vila, and R. K. Wayne. "Legacy Lost: Genetic Variability and Population Size of Extirpated US Grey Wolves (*Canis lupus*)." *Molecular Ecology* 14 (2005): 9–17.

Leopold, A., A. K. Sowls, and D. L. Spencer. "A Survey of Over-Populated Deer Ranges in the United States." *Journal of Wildlife Management* 11 (1947): 162–83.

Leopold, A. *A Sand County Almanac*. New York: Random House, 1966.

Leopold, A. "Thinking Like a Mountain." In *A Sand County Almanac*, 137–41. New York: Random House, 1966.

Lopez, B. *Of Wolves and Men*. New York: Scribner Classic, 1978.

McNay, M. E. *A Case History of Wolf-Human Encounters in Alaska and Canada*. Wildlife Technical Bulletin No. 13. Anchorage: Alaska Department of Fish and Game, 2002.

MacNulty, D. R., D. R. Stahler, and D. W. Smith. "Understanding the Limits to Wolf Hunting Ability." *Yellowstone Science* 24 (2016): 34–36.

Meadow, R., R. P. Reading, M. Phillips, M. Mehringer. "The Influence of Persuasive Arguments on Public Attitudes toward a Proposed Wolf Restoration in the Southern Rockies." *Wildlife Society Bulletin* 33 (2005): 154–63.

Mech, L. D. 2012. "Is Science in Danger of Sanctifying the Wolf?" *Biological Conservation* 150 (2012): 143–49.

Mech, L. D., and R. O. Peterson. "Wolf-Prey Relations." In *Wolves: Ecology, Behavior, and Conservation*, ed. L. D. Mech and L. Boitani, 131–60. Chicago: University of Chicago Press, 2003.

Mech, L. D., D. W. Smith, and D. R. MacNulty. *Wolves on the Hunt: The Behavior of Wolves Hunting Wild Prey*. Chicago: University of Chicago Press, 2015.

Monello, R. J., J. G. Powers, N. T. Hobbs, T. R. Spraker, K. I. O'Rourke, and M. A. Wild. "Efficacy of Antemortem Rectal Biopsies to Diagnose and Estimate

Prevalence of Chronic Wasting Disease in Free-Ranging Cow Elk (*Cervus elaphus nelsoni*)." *Journal of Wildlife Diseases* 49 (2013): 270–78.

Muhl, T. B., and M. Musiani. "Livestock Depredation by Wolves and the Ranching Economy in the Northwestern US." *Ecological Economics* 68 (2009): 2439–50.

National Agricultural Statistics Service. "Cattle Death Loss." Washington, DC: Agricultural Statistics Board, US Department of Agriculture, 2011. usda.mannlib .cornell.edu/usda/current/CattDeath/CattDeath-05-12-2011.pdf.

National Research Council. *Wolves, Bears, and Their Prey in Alaska: Biological and Social Challenges in Wildlife Management*. Washington, DC: National Academy Press, 1997.

Oakleaf, J. K., C. Mack, and D. L. Murray. "Effects of Wolves on Livestock Calf Survival and Movements in Central Idaho." *Journal of Wildlife Management* 67 (2003): 299–306.

Peterson, R. O., and P. Ciucci. "The Wolf as a Carnivore." In *Wolf: Behavior, Biology, and Conservation*, ed. L. D. Mech and L. Boitani, 104–30. Chicago: University of Chicago Press, 2003.

Peterson, R. O., J. A Vucetich, J. M. Bump, and D. W. Smith. "Trophic Cascades in a Multicausal World: Isle Royale and Yellowstone." *Annual Review of Ecology, Evolution, and Systematics* 45 (2014): 325–45.

Phillips, M. K., N. Fascione, P. Miller, and O. Byers. *Wolves in the Southern Rockies: A Population and Habitat Viability Assessment*. Apple Valley, MN: IUCN Conservation Breeding Specialist Group, 2000.

Phillips, M. K., B. Miller, K. Kunkel, P. C. Paquet, W. W. Martin, and D. W. Smith. "Potential for and Implications of Wolf Restoration in the Southern Rockies." In *Awakening Spirits: Wolves in the Southern Rockies*, ed. R. P. Reading, B. Miller, A. L. Masching, R. Edward, and M. K. Phillips, 197–219. Golden, CO: Fulcrum Publishing, 2010.

Ramler, J. P., M. Hebblewhite, D. Kellenberg, and C. Sime. "Crying Wolf? A Spatial Analysis of Wolf Location and Depredations on Calf Weights." *American Journal of Agricultural Economics* 96 (2014): 631–56.

Ripple, W. J., J. A. Estes, R. L. Beschta, C. C. Wilmers, E. G. Ritchie, M. Hebblewhite, J. Berger, B. Elmhagen, M. Letnic, M. P. Nelson, O. J. Schmitz, D. W. Smith, A. D. Wallach, and A. J. Wirsing. "Status and Ecological Effects of the World's Largest Carnivores." *Science* 343 (2014): 1–11.

Robinson, M. J. *Predatory Bureaucracy: The Extermination of Wolves and the Transformation of the West*. Boulder: University Press of Colorado, 2005.

Shinneman, D., R. McClellan, and R. Smith. *The State of the Southern Rockies Ecoregion*. Nederland, CO: Southern Rockies Ecosystem Project, 2000.

Sime, C. A., E. Bangs, E. Bradley, J. E. Steuber, K. Glazier, P. J. Hoover, V. Asher, K. Laudon, M. Ross, and J. Trapp. "Gray Wolves and Livestock in Montana: A Recent History of Damage Management." In *Proceedings of the Twelfth Wildlife*

Damage Management Conference, ed. D. L. Nolte, W. M. Arjo, and D. H. Stalman, 16–35. Corpus Christi, 2007.

Soule, M. E., J. A. Estes, J. Berger, and C. Martinez del Rios. "Ecological Effectiveness: Conservation Goals for Interactive Species." *Conservation Biology* 17 (2003): 1238–50.

Southern Rockies Ecosystem Project. *Summary of the Base Data and Landscape Variables for Wolf Habitat Suitability on the Vermejo Park Ranch and Surrounding Areas.* Bozeman, MT: Turner Endangered Species Fund, 2000.

Terborgh, J., and J. A. Estes. *Trophic Cascades: Predators, Prey, and Changing Dynamics of Nature.* Washington, DC: Island Press, 2010.

Treves, A., M. Krofel, and J. McManus. "Predator Control Should Not Be a Shot in the Dark." *Frontiers in Ecology and the Environment* 14 (2016): 380–88.

US Fish and Wildlife Service. *Northern Rocky Mountain Wolf Recovery Program 2014 Interagency Annual Report.* Denver: US Fish and Wildlife Service, 2015.

Wang, X., and R. H. Tedford. *Dogs: Their Fossil Relatives and Evolutionary History.* New York: Columbia University Press, 2008.

Wielgus, R. B., and K. A. Peebles. "Effects of Wolf Mortality on Livestock Depredations." *PLOS One* 9 (2014): e113505.

Wild, M. A., N. T. Hobbs, M. S. Graham, and M. W. Miller. "The Role of Predation in Disease Control: A Comparison of Selective and Non-Selective Removal of Prion Diseases in Deer." *Journal of Wildlife Diseases* 47 (2011): 78–93.

About the Contributors

NORMAN A. BISHOP ("NORM") took his graduate forest recreation and wildlife management courses (1958–1961) at Colorado State University. He was a national park ranger for thirty-six years, from Rocky Mountain NP (1960–1962) to Yellowstone NP (1980–1997). He was a reviewer and compiler of the 1990 and 1992 "Wolves for Yellowstone? A Report to the United States Congress" and the 1994 Final Environmental Impact Statement, "The Reintroduction of Gray Wolves to Yellowstone National Park and Central Idaho." He was the principal interpreter of wolf restoration at Yellowstone from 1985 to 1997, when he retired. Until 2005, Bishop led field courses on wolves for the Yellowstone Association Institute. For his wolf work, he received the National Parks and Conservation Association's 1988 Stephen T. Mather Award, the Greater Yellowstone Coalition's 1991 Stewardship Award, a US Department of the Interior Meritorious Service Award, the Wolf Education and Research Center's 1997 Alpha Award, and the International Wolf Center's 2015 Who Speaks for Wolf Award.

BONNIE BROWN is the executive director for the Colorado Wool Growers Association, the Colorado Sheep and Wool Authority, and the Colorado Lamb Council. She actively works with producers and feeders on regulatory and legislative issues and to promote Colorado lamb and wool. She has been working for the sheep industry since 2000. Brown was born in Grand Junction, Colorado, and was raised on a cattle ranch in southwest New Mexico. She attended New Mexico State University for three years, studying agricultural engineering and ag economics. She graduated from Mesa State College in

Grand Junction with a bachelor's degree in geology. Prior to working for wool growers, she worked in coalbed methane research and development. Brown is an accomplished horsewoman and has successfully competed in versatility ranch horse competitions and extreme cowboy races. She is currently training her two Friesian geldings for both driving and riding.

TOM COMPTON and his wife, Penni, with the assistance of their children and grandchildren, own and operate a beef cattle ranch in southwest Colorado. He is a past president of the Colorado Cattlemen's Association and has served on the Mexican wolf reintroduction team. Compton holds a PhD in zoology from the University of Wyoming, where he studied the comparative ecology of mule deer, elk, and domestic livestock on the Sierra Madre of southern Wyoming. He also holds an MS in biology from the University of Alaska. He has served as the chairman of the Colorado Oil & Gas Conservation Commission.

CHENEY GARDNER is the media coordinator for the Turner Endangered Species Fund (TESF) and the Rocky Mountain Wolf Project (rockymountainwolfproject.org), where she is responsible for engaging the media, managing the project's digital presence and serving as the Colorado liaison. She attended University of North Carolina at Chapel Hill, where she received a degree in journalism after being awarded the prestigious Morehead-Cain scholarship. As a Morehead-Cain Scholar, she explored the remoteness of the Yukon and northern British Columbia; tracked the world's largest bumblebee across Chilean Patagonia; and studied natural fiber and dyeing processes in the Cusco region of Peru.

ANDREW GULLIFORD is a professor of history and environmental studies at Fort Lewis College in Durango, Colorado. He holds a PhD in American history and culture. He is the author of *America's Country Schools*, *Sacred Objects and Sacred Places: Preserving Tribal Traditions*, and *Boomtown Blues: Colorado Oil Shale*. He edited *Preserving Western History*, voted one of the best books on the Southwest by the Tucson-Pima County Library, and *Outdoors in the Southwest: An Adventure Anthology*. Gulliford has twice won the Colorado Book Award and the New Mexico-Arizona Book Award. Dr. Gulliford has received the National Volunteer Award from the US Forest Service for wilderness education and a certificate of recognition from the secretary of agriculture for "outstanding contributions to America's natural and cultural resources." He has held an Aldo and Estella Leopold Residency in the bungalow on the Carson National Forest that Leopold built near Tres Piedras, New Mexico, in 1912.

MIKE PHILLIPS has served as the executive director of the Turner Endangered Species Fund and an advisor to the Turner Biodiversity Divisions since he cofounded both with Ted Turner in June 1997. Starting in 1981, he worked for the US Fish and

Wildlife Service and the National Park Service. During his employment with the federal government, Dr. Phillips led historic efforts to restore red wolves to the southeastern United States and gray wolves to Yellowstone National Park. Throughout his career as a conservation biologist he has focused on the recovery of imperiled species, the integration of private land in conservation efforts, and the sociopolitical aspects of natural resource use and management. In 2013 Dr. E. O. Wilson nominated Phillips for the prestigious 2014 Indianapolis Prize. He has authored hundreds of project reports and over sixty-five publications, including peer-reviewed technical articles, book chapters, conference proceedings, government reports, popular articles, and one book. Phillips has served in the Montana Legislature since 2007 and will hold a seat in the state senate through 2020.

TOM WOLF grew up in east Denver and used to cut Arthur Carhart's lawn. He is a graduate of Colorado College, the University of California at Berkeley (PhD), and Colorado State University (master of forestry). During the Vietnam War he was the first Roman Catholic conscientious objector from Colorado—detailed in his history of the 10th Mountain Division, *Ice Crusaders: A Memoir of Cold War and Cold Sport*. He is also the author of *Colorado's Sangre de Cristo Mountains, In Fire's Way: A Practical Guide to Life in the Wildfire Danger Zone, Arthur Carhart: Wilderness Prophet*, and *La Guadalupana*, a comic novel about the ordination of the first women as priests in the Roman Catholic Church. He has taught at Brandeis University and Colorado College. Dr. Wolf has worked for the National Park Service, the Wyoming Outdoor Council, and The Nature Conservancy. During a stint as a ranger at Mesa Verde National Park, Tom would quip, "I'm the only wolf left in the park."

Index